T0136728

HUMAN VALUES AND THE DESIGN OF COMPUTER TECHNOLOGY

CSLI
Lecture Notes
Number 72

HUMAN VALUES AND THE DESIGN OF COMPUTER TECHNOLOGY

EDITED BY

BATYA FRIEDMAN

CSLI Publications
Center for the Study of
Language and Information
Stanford, California

CAMBRIDGE
UNIVERSITY PRESS

Copyright © 1997
CSLI Publications
Center for the Study of Language and Information
Leland Stanford Junior University
and the Press Syndicate of the University of Cambridge
The Pitt Building, Trumpington Street, Cambridge CB2 1RP
40 West 20th Street, New York, NY 10011-4211, USA
10 Stamford Road, Oakleigh, Melbourne 3166 Australia
01 00 99 98 97   5 4 3 2 1

This book was set by CSLI Publications in Minion, a typeface designed by Robert
Slimbach. The book was printed and bound in the United States of America.

Library of Congress Cataloging-in-Publications Data

Human values and the design of computer technology / edited by Batya Friedman
p.   cm.   Includes bibliographical references.
ISBN: 1-57586-081-3 (hc : alk. paper).
ISBN: 1-57586-080-5 (pbk. : alk. paper)
1. Computers—Social aspects.   2. Technology—Social aspects
1. Friedman, Batya.
QA76.9.C66H837   1997
174'.90904—dc21   97–12953
CIP

∞ The acid-free paper used in this book meets the minimum requirements of the
American National Standard for Information Sciences – Permanence of Paper for
Printed Library Materials, ANSI Z39.48-1984.

CSLI was founded early in 1983 by researchers from Stanford University, SRI International, and Xerox PARC to further research and development of integrated theories of
language, information, and computation. CSLI headquarters and CSLI Publications
are located on the campus of Stanford University.

CSLI Publications reports new developments in the study of language, information,
and computation. In addition to lecture notes, our publications include monographs,
working papers, revised dissertations, and conference proceedings. Our aim is to make
new results, ideas, and approaches available as quickly as possible. Please visit our
website at
http://csli-www.stanford.edu/publications/
for comments on this and other titles, as well as for changes and corrections by the
author and publisher.

To my mother
Sybil Friedman
and to my brother
Matthew Lee Friedman

Contents

Acknowledgments

For close to a decade, Terry Winograd has encouraged my research on the social and ethical dimensions of computing. He also provided early but critical support for this volume. Ben Shneiderman has been an active supporter and welcome critic. Helen Nissenbaum has become a long-term collaborator and friend.

I thank the contributing authors, all of whom chart new directions. Thanks also to those who pointed me to interesting materials and authors, provided reviews of specific chapters, and reacted to this project at various stages: Sarah Kuhn, Jim Larson, Marta Laupa, Jim Moor, Randy Trigg, David Zeitlin, my students at Colby College, and several anonymous reviewers. The cover art for the paperback edition was inspired by the work of Alexander Calder. Dikran Karagueuzian has been my editor at the Center for the Study of Language and Information (CSLI), Stanford University. Alan Harvey has been my editor at Cambridge University Press. They have been a delight to work with. Thanks also to Maureen Burke and Tony Gee for copyediting, typesetting, and all of the other details of production.

This work was supported in part by funding from the Clare Boothe Luce Foundation and a grant from the Natural Science Division, Colby College. CSLI provided generous use of their facilities during summer 1996.

Batya Friedman
The Mina Institute, Covelo, California

Permission to reprint the following articles is gratefully acknowledged:

Chapter 1, Bias in Computer Systems, by Batya Friedman and Helen Nissenbaum. (Reprinted from *ACM Transactions on Information Systems* 14(3): 330–347, 1996. Note: Table in the above article reprinted from Williams, K.J., V.P. Werth, and J.A. Wolff. An Analysis of Resident Match. *New England Journal of Medicine*, 1981, 304(19), 1165–1166.)

Chapter 2, Accountability in a Computerized Society, by Helen Nissenbaum. (Reprinted from *Science and Engineering Ethics* 2: 25–42, 1996.)

Chapter 4, Do Categories Have Politics? The Language/Action Perspective Reconsidered, by Lucy Suchman. (Reprinted from *CSCW Journal* 2(3): 177–190, 1994.)

Chapter 5, Categories, Disciplines, and Social Coordination, by Terry Winograd. (Reprinted from *CSCW Journal* 2(3): 191–197, 1994.)

Chapter 6, Commentary on Suchman Article and Winograd Response, by Thomas W. Malone. (Reprinted from *CSCW Journal* 3: 37–38, 1994.)

Chapter 9, When the Interface Is a Face, by Lee Sproull, Mani Subramani, Sara Kiesler, Janet Walker, and Keith Waters. (Reprinted from *Human–Computer Interaction* 11: 97–124, 1996.)

Chapter 11, Reasoning about Computers as Moral Agents: A Research Note, by Batya Friedman and Lynette I. Millett. (Previously published as "It's the Computer's Fault – Reasoning about Computers as Moral Agents". *Conference Companion of the Conference on Human Factors in Computing Systems, CHI '95*, 1995, pp. 226–227. New York: Association for Computing Machinery.)

Chapter 12, Interface Agents: Metaphors with Character, by Brenda Laurel. (Reprinted from Brenda Laurel, ed., 1990, *The Art of Human–Computer Interface Design*, pp. 355–365, Addison-Wesley.)

Chapter 13, Human Agency and Responsible Computing: Implications for Computer System Design, by Batya Friedman and Peter H. Kahn, Jr. (Reprinted from the *Journal of Systems Software* 17: 7–14, 1992.)

Chapter 17, Social Choice about Privacy: Intelligent Vehicle-Highway Systems in the United States, by Philip E. Agre and Christine A. Mailloux. (Adapted from/reprinted from Philip E. Agre and Christine A. Harbs *Information Technology and People* 7(4): 63–90, 1994.)

Contributors

PHILIP E. AGRE is Assistant Professor of Communication at the University of California, San Diego. His current research concerns the social and political aspects of networking and computing.

B.J. FOGG graduated with a Ph.D. in Communication from Stanford University. His research investigates what makes interactive technologies likable and persuasive.

BATYA FRIEDMAN is Associate Professor of Computer Science at Colby College and codirector of The Mina Institute. Her areas of specialization include human–computer interaction and the human relationship to technology.

HARRY HOCHHEISER is an independent software development consultant. He is interested in the role that software professionals play in determination of development agendas, and how developers might build software that effectively accounts for human values.

PETER H. KAHN, JR. is on the faculty at Colby College and codirector (with Batya Friedman) of The Mina Institute – an organization which seeks to promote, from an ethical perspective, the human and humane relationship with nature and technology.

SARA KIESLER is Professor of Social and Decision Sciences at Carnegie Mellon University and a faculty member in the Human Computer Interaction Institute. Over the last fifteen years, she has studied how computing and computer networking changes group dynamics and communication in organizations.

EUN-YOUNG KIM is a Ph.D. candidate in Communication at Stanford University. Her area of specialization is human–computer interaction and natural responses to media using physiological measures.

BRENDA LAUREL is a member of the Research Staff at Interval Research Corporation in Palo Alto, California where she has led a three-year effort in researching gender differences among children in relation to technology. She is also a founder and Vice-President for Design of a new company, Purple Moon.

ELIZABETH MACKEN is Associate Director of the Center for the Study of Language and Information and the leader of the Archimedes Project. Her research interests focus on improving the accessibility of information for individuals with disabilities.

CHRISTINE A. MAILLOUX is a telecommunications and technology law attorney with Blumenfeld & Cohen in San Francisco. She specializes in telecommunication regulatory policy and privacy law.

THOMAS W. MALONE is the Patrick J. McGovern Professor of Information Systems at the MIT Sloan School of Management and the founder and director of the MIT Center for Coordination Science. His research focuses on how computer and communications technology can change the ways people work together in groups and organizations.

JANICE L. MCKINLEY has collaborated with the Archimedes Project since 1993 as part of her employment at the Western Blind Rehabilitation Center (WBRC), Department of Veteran Affairs Palo Alto Health Care System. Her current research interests reflect her concern about the impact of graphical user interfaces on blind computer users.

LYNETTE I. MILLETT is currently a Ph.D. student in Computer Science at Cornell University. Her research interests include transformation-based programming languages, programming language theory, gender issues in science and technology, and technology and public policy.

YOUNGME MOON is Assistant Professor in the Program in Writing and Humanistic Studies at M.I.T. She has written and presented numerous articles on social responses to computer technology. She is also a research consultant for Hewlett-Packard Labs.

JOHN MORKES, a science and technology writer and editor since 1990, is a Ph.D. candidate in Communication at Stanford University. His current research focuses on human–computer interaction, interface design, and communication theory.

CLIFFORD I. NASS is Associate Professor of Communication at Stanford University and is codirector of the Social Responses to Communication Technology project at the Center for the Study of Language and Information.

HELEN NISSENBAUM is Associate Director of the University Center for Human Values and the Program in Ethics & Public Affairs at Princeton University. She publishes in the area of social and ethical implications of science and technology.

JOHN PERRY is the Director of Center for the Study of Language and Information and the Henry Walgrave Stuart Professor of Philosophy and Symbolic Systems at Stanford University. In addition to problems of access to information for individuals with disabilities, his research interests have centered on the philosophy of mind, the philosophy of language, and semantics.

ANNE ROSE is a Faculty Research Assistant in the Human–Computer Interaction Laboratory at the University of Maryland at College Park. Her research interests include user interface design with an emphasis on information visualization and software engineering methods.

NEIL SCOTT is the Chief Engineer for the Archimedes Project at Stanford University's Center for the Study of Language and Information. He has been working with computers since 1968 and began developing special access systems for people with disabilities in 1977. His mission with the Archimedes Project is to make computers just as easy for disabled people to use as they are for everyone else.

BEN SHNEIDERMAN is Professor of Computer Science, Head of the Human–Computer Interaction Laboratory, and Member of the Institute for Systems Research, all at the University of Maryland at College Park. He is the originator of the Hyperties hypermedia system.

LEE SPROULL is Professor of Management at Boston University. For the past fifteen years she has investigated how electronic communication is changing groups, organizations, and social institutions. Her current work emphasizes large-scale electronic groups and group dynamics in video communication.

MANI SUBRAMANI is a Ph.D. candidate in Management Information Systems at Boston University. His research interests include the implications of information technologies for the design of work in organizations.

LUCY SUCHMAN has been a researcher at Xerox Palo Alto Research Center, where she is currently a Principal Scientist and heads the Work Practice and Technology area since 1979. Her research concerns the relation of everyday working practices to computer systems design.

JOHN C. TANG works in the Collaborative Computing group, an advanced development group within Sun Microsystems, Inc. He studies collaborative work activity in order to guide the design and development of multimedia collaborative systems.

JOHN C. THOMAS is Executive Director of Speech Systems and Network Assurance, for NYNEX Science and Technology, where he is responsible for Venture Funds, Network Testing Facilities in New York City and Framingham, Mass., Speech Technology, Applications, and Platforms, Human Computer Interaction, Advanced Software Development Environments, and Organizational Learning.

JANET WALKER is a psychologist interested in visual media. At the time the work reported in this chapter was conducted, she was a member of the research staff at Digital Equipment Corporation Cambridge Research lab.

KEITH WATERS is currently a member of the research staff at Digital Equipment Corporation Cambridge Research Lab. His interests include computer graphics, multimedia, and computer vision.

TERRY WINOGRAD is Professor of Computer Science at Stanford University where he directs the Project on People, Computers, and Design, and the teaching and research program on Human–Computer Interaction Design. He is one of the principal investigators in the Stanford Digital Libraries Initiative project.

Introduction

BATYA FRIEDMAN

Many of us when we design and implement computer technologies focus on making a machine work – reliably, efficiently, and correctly. Rarely do we focus on human values. Perhaps we believe in value-neutral technology. Perhaps we believe that issues of value belong only to social scientists, philosophers, or policy makers. Neither belief is correct. In their work, system designers necessarily impart social and moral values. Yet how? What values? Whose values? For if human values – such as freedom of speech, rights to property, accountability, privacy, and autonomy – are controversial, then on what basis do some values override others in the design of, say, hardware, algorithms, and databases? Moreover, how can designers working within a corporate structure and with a mandate to generate revenue bring value-sensitive design into the workplace?

This volume brings together leading researchers and system designers who take up these questions, and more. In this introduction, I situate these questions within a larger conceptual framework. I also motivate the need to embrace value-sensitive design as part of the culture of computer science. Then I offer an overview of each of the chapters. Roughly half of the chapters are new material, and the remainder are reprints of pivotal articles from recent years. For readers with specialized interests, Table 1 arranges the chapters by technical topic; Table 2 by core human value.

DOES TECHNOLOGY HAVE VALUES?

Does technology have values? Consider a few examples. In the early 1900s, missionaries introduced a technological innovation – steel ax heads – to the Yir Yoront of Australia, a native people. The missionaries did so without regard for traditional restrictions on ownership, and indiscriminately distributed the ax heads to men, women, old people, and young adults alike. In so doing, they altered relationships of dependence among family members and reshaped conceptions of property within the culture (Sharp, 1952/1980). Another example: About four decades ago, snowmobiles were introduced into the Inuit communities of the Arctic, and have now largely replaced travel by dog sleds. This technological innovation thereby altered not only patterns of transportation, but symbols of social status, and moved the Inuit toward a dependence on a money economy (Houston, 1995; Pelto, 1973). Or a computer example. Electronic mail rarely displays the sender's status. Is the sender a curious lay person, system analyst, full professor, journalist, assistant professor, entry level programmer, senior scientist, high school student? Who knows until the e-mail is read, and maybe not even then. This design feature (and associated conventions) has thereby played a significant role in allowing electronic communication to cross traditional hierarchical boundaries and to contribute to the restructuring of organizations (Sproull & Kiesler, 1991). The point is this: In various ways, technological innovations do not stand apart from human values. But, still, what would it mean to say that technology has values?

Endogenous and exogenous views have emerged in recent years. The endogenous view holds that through the process of designing and implementing technology, the very meaning and intentions that we designers and builders bring to our task literally become a part of the technology (cf. Appadurai, 1988; Cole, 1991). But this view seems false in the sense that it imputes mental states to things which do not have the capacity to have them. Is the claim, for example, that a gun itself intends to kill someone? That proposition seems incorrect. Although arguable, it similarly seems incorrect to impute mental states to computational systems. In chapter 13, Friedman and Kahn discuss this position in more detail. In contrast, the exogenous view holds that values reside with the users, not the technology. Proponents of this view are likely to say "guns don't kill people, people do"; or similarly, "hammers don't pound nails, people do" or "computer databases don't track workers, people do." But this view ignores our everyday experience that particular tools lend themselves to particular tasks in particular ways; otherwise, one tool would serve all purposes well and we know this is not the case. Try pounding a nail with a computer database.

A third view – which I think is correct – holds that the way people design tools makes the tools more suitable for some uses over others. Scheffler (1991) suggests, for example, that a hammer is well suited for driving nails, poorly suited as a soup ladle, and perhaps amenable as a doorstop, bookend, or paper weight. In other words, human activity is constrained and perhaps even prodded by features of the technology, but not determined by it.

In terms of computer system design, we are not so privileged as to determine rigidly the values that will emerge from the systems we design. But neither can we abdicate responsibility. For example, let us for the moment agree with Perry et al. in chapter 3 that disabled people in the workplace should be able to access technology, just as they should be able to access a public building. As system designers we can make the choice to try to construct a technological infrastructure which disabled people can access. If we do not make this choice, then we single-handedly undermine the principle of universal access. But if we do make this choice, and are successful, disabled people would still rely, for example, on employers to hire them. Suitability (as a feature of the technology) is necessary for, but does not assure equal access (a human value).

Users, of course, are not always powerless when faced with unwelcomed value-oriented features of a technology. For example, students in one of my classes conducted an informal ethnographic investigation of computer use in a local accounting firm. The previous year, this firm had acquired an off-the-shelf packaged software program for preparing tax returns that automatically reported the number of tax returns completed by each employee. But such overt comparisons among employees resulted in office discord. Employees did not believe that the numbers fairly portrayed their overall value to the firm, let alone the real income they generated. Note that this problem arose unsolicited because of the built-in features of the software. This firm operated within a cooperative family-style work culture. Thus, in this situation, the firm members agreed to destroy the comparative data when it was produced. However, it takes courage to turn away from quantitative data that tell us how things are going even if we rationally believe the numbers are misleading and incomplete.

HUMAN VALUES: A WORKING DEFINITION

In some sense, we can say that any human activity reflects human values. I drink tea instead of soda. I recently attended a Cezanne exhibit instead of a ball game. I have personal values. We all do. But these are not the type of human values which this volume takes up. Rather, this volume is principally concerned with values that deal with human welfare and justice.

This demarcation between personal and moral values follows from the psychological literature which has investigated empirically what have been referred to as three domains of social knowledge: the moral, conventional, and

personal (Nucci, 1996; Smetana, 1983; Turiel, 1983). The moral domain refers
to prescriptive judgments which people justify based on considerations of justice, fairness, rights, or human welfare. Conventional issues refer to behavioral uniformities designed to promote the smooth functioning of social interactions. Personal issues refer to those which lie under the jurisdiction of the self.
Over eighty-five empirical studies, in western and nonwestern countries, have
demonstrated that young children, adolescents, and adults differentiate these
three forms of knowledge (for reviews of the literature, see Smetana, 1995; Tisak, 1995; Turiel, 1983, in press; Turiel, Killen, & Helwig, 1987). In addition,
many of these studies have analyzed how social issues can often embody all
three aspects (Smetana, 1982; Turiel, Hildebrandt, & Wainryb, 1991). Abortion, for example, is a particularly controversial social issue not only because it
involves a controversial assumption about when life begins, but because personal values (that a woman has personal jurisdiction over her own body) can
conflict with moral values (that involve the potential welfare and rights of a fe-
tus). It is also the case that personal and conventional issues can become moral, in specific contexts. For example, most people in western countries believe
that if a man chooses to wear a bathrobe, that is his personal choice. But in
certain contexts there are also conventions about appropriate dress. Thus, if a
man wears his bathrobe to a dignitary's funeral, many people would judge the
act not only as a conventional violation, but a moral violation – as a sign of
disrespect.

   This form of analysis can bring clarity into understanding the social aspects
of computing. For example, a particular feature of a computer system (the positioning of the track ball on a laptop computer) may make a system easier to
use. But unless the difficulty of use systematically prevents certain groups of
individuals from using the technology, ease of use per se is not a moral value,
but a personal one. Or consider a voting booth for use in national elections. A
person may prefer to cast his or her vote by marking an old-fashioned "X"
next to a candidate's name instead of using an electronic voting system that requires punching out a dot on a voting card. But if the person can easily vote
with the latter system, then preferring one system over the other reflects a personal value. On the other hand, if the system requires a short voter to pull a le-
ver that is above his or her reach, as has actually happened (Roth, 1994), then
the system prevents fair participation in the voting process. Accordingly, the
human values at stake become moral, not simply personal.

   When designing computer systems, conflicts also often arise between conventional and moral considerations. Think of standardization. On the one
hand, standardization relies on conventional uniformities to enhance the

smooth functioning among different components of a system or among different users of a system. Imagine if communication protocols on the internet were not standardized. In this light, standardization is vital. On the other hand, standardization requires individuals to give up some degree of control over the technology. Think of the frustrations some workers encounter when companies require every worker to use the identical word processor. Indeed, the debate in this volume between Suchman (chapter 4) and Winograd (chapter 5) can be understood in these terms. Suchman objects to standardized communication on the grounds that individuals are coerced by the system. Winograd counters that through the social conventional coordination of communication, more successful and beneficial communication is supported (and individual welfare increases).

The human values addressed in this volume principally refer to moral values. But I prefer to use the broader term "human values" instead of simply moral values to highlight the complexity of social life, and to provide the basis for analyses wherein personal and conventional values can become morally implicated.

DISTINGUISHING VALUE-SENSITIVE DESIGN FROM USABILITY

Some system designers have a tendency to conflate value-sensitive design with usability. This problem arises with good reason. Namely, usability is itself a human value, although not always a moral one. But when it is, both can be addressed by the same design. For example, systems which can be modified by users to meet the needs of specific individuals or organizations enhance their usability (cf. Adler & Winograd, 1992). At the same time, such systems can help users to realize their goals and intentions through their use of the technology – a human value which Nissenbaum and I (Friedman, 1996) refer to as autonomy.

Sometimes, however, usability conflicts with value-sensitive design. Nielsen (1993), for example, asks us to imagine a computer system that checks for fraudulent applications of people who are applying for unemployment benefits by asking applicants numerous personal questions, and then checking for inconsistencies in their responses. Nielsen's point is that some people may not find the system socially acceptable (based on the value of privacy) even if the system receives high usability scores – that is, it is easy to learn, easy to use, error free, efficient, and so on. Indeed, in this volume, Tang (chapter 15) provides a case study of just such a conflict. Tang describes the issues which a design team faced in deciding how to power a microphone. The solution they settled upon was to power a microphone directly from the workstation. They thereby eliminated a separate hardware on/off switch on the microphone. From a usability perspective, Tang points to benefits from this design decision insofar as a separate battery could wear down, and thereby cause an inconvenience to the user. Moreover, to preserve the battery users would no longer need to remember to turn the microphone off when it was not in use. However, despite these usability advantages, Tang also shows that the design undermined the moral values which some users placed on privacy and security.

In short, our language and conceptualizations within the field currently provide solid means by which to pursue issues of usability (cf. Adler & Winograd, 1992; Norman, 1988; Norman & Draper, 1986; Nielsen, 1993). This work is important. At a minimum, usability represents social organizational values needed to make systems work in a functional sense. At times, usability can also support human values of moral import. But at times we need to give ground on usability to promote human values, and, conversely, at times we need to give ground on human values to promote usability. Such optimizations require judicious decisions, carefully weighing and coordinating the advantages of each.

ABOUT THIS BOOK

From a variety of perspectives, there has been increasing interest in the social implications of computer technology. Methods from anthropology, sociology and psychology, for example, have been used in understanding computing and human values from individual and organizational perspectives (Kling, 1980; 1996; Nass & Reeves, 1996; Sproull & Kiesler, 1991; Suchman, 1987; Zuboff, 1988). The literature on computer ethics has revealed the philosophical dimensions of computing (Ermann, Williams, & Gutierrez, 1990; Forester, 1989; Johnson, 1994; Johnson & Nissenbaum, 1995; Ladd, 1989; Moor, 1985). The computer-supported cooperative work (CSCW) and participatory design (PD) communities have enhanced collaboration and the democratic participation of individuals within organizations (Blomberg, Suchman, & Trigg, 1996; Bodker, 1991; Clement & Van den Besselaar, 1994; Ehn, 1988; Greenbaum & Kyng, 1991; Greif, 1988; Kuhn, 1996; Schular & Namioka, 1993). More broadly, the human–computer interaction (HCI) community has been increasingly aware of and concerned about the social dimensions of design (Baecker, Grudin, Buxton, & Greenberg, 1995; Brown & Duguid, 1994; Fernandes, 1995; Laurel, 1990; Shneiderman, 1992; Tognazzini, 1995; Winograd, 1996; Winograd & Flores, 1986). All of these perspectives have offered important if not crucial lines of inquiry. This volume adds to this growing body of literature by offering a principled and practical framework for promoting human values in system design, particularly values with moral import.

PART I: CONCEPTUALIZING HUMAN VALUES IN DESIGN

The papers in this first section examine computer technology in relation to the values of accountability, autonomy, freedom from bias, privacy, and universal access. Some of these papers illustrate how value-oriented problems can be closely tied to technical decisions. For example, Friedman and Nissenbaum (chapter 1) include an analysis of Corbató's multi-level scheduling algorithm which has been implemented in a variety of timesharing systems. They suggest that when systems are placed under heavy use, the algorithm may unfairly discriminate against users with long-running computations. Other value-oriented problems are more deeply embedded within a social context. For example, Nissenbaum (chapter 2) analyzes systems which are constructed out of modules or modified from previously existing code in order that no single individual understands the entire system. In such situations, it can be difficult to identify the locus of responsibility for computer-mediated action. Similarly, Perry et al. (chapter 3) show that in order to solve the problem of access for the disabled, designers may need to find the best (or a reasonable) balance between the responsibilities of the individual user and the responsibilities of the computer industry, if not the larger society.

Over forty years ago, Norbert Wiener said that in the coming years access to information would be relatively easy, and that the hard problem for computer science would be to provide access to useful information. Today, Wiener would find little disagreement. Just note some of the millions of users as they try (often unsuccessfully) to meaningfully access the billions of accessible words on the World Wide Web. Many of the emerging solutions to this problem currently depend on filters of some sort. Filters, in turn, depend on the activity of categorization: being able to identify items which are similar along one or more dimensions, and different along others. It is here that the three chapters on categorization by Suchman, Winograd, and Malone are of great importance.

Suchman (chapter 4) begins by offering strong words of caution: that whoever determines the categories – and how those categories can be used – imputes their own personal values into the system and has power over the user. As noted above, Winograd (chapter 5) responds to Suchman by pointing to the frequent need for socially coordinated activity in which groups of people seek to share information and technology. In such activity, Winograd argues that we need some degree of standardization wherein designers impose categories. That is their job. The key, according to Winograd, is to cultivate regularized activity without becoming oppressive: or, in a sense, to use power wisely. In turn, Malone (chapter 6) responds to Suchman by arguing that not only are categories often useful, but to some extent they are necessary given the structure of human cognition. At the same time, Malone suggests that no category system is complete, and therefore designs need to be adaptable, often by their users.

Consider this debate in terms of this present introduction. Recall that Table 1 categorizes the chapters by technical topic, and Table 2 categorizes the chapters by human value. Suchman would have us recognize that as the editor of this volume, I have imposed my own categories onto these chapters. For example, I categorized the chapters by Suchman, Winograd, and Malone as involving the human value of autonomy. But at least three other decisions were possible. First, I could have chosen one or more other categories: following Suchman, perhaps that of politics or power. Such a choice would lead in different, and interesting, directions. Second, I could have provided no categorization. But following Winograd and Malone, categories can serve as an effective way to quickly orient readers to the subset of chapters (aka the subset of information) that might be of greatest interest to them. Third, I could have asked the contributors to categorize their own chapters, either according to a predetermined set of categories or to a category of their choosing. While such delegation was certainly possible, it would have transformed my role from one of editor, seeking to shape and provide coherence to this volume, to one of coordinator seeking to reflect the perspectives of the contributors. Since multi-authored volumes often suffer from a lack of coherence, I decided that delegating control was on balance a poor choice. My point is that the tensions encountered in using and selecting categories to characterize the chapters in this volume illustrate the same issues we face with the use of categories in system design: that appropriate, if not good, resolutions depend on finding in context the right balance between competing values.

Shneiderman and Rose (chapter 7) move this discussion on value-sensitive design to the level of codification. Based on the idea of an environmental impact statement, they propose that designers be encouraged, if not required, to provide a "social impact statement" which assesses the social impact of their designs on direct and indirect users. A key toward developing one's social impact statement would be the early identification and involvement of stakeholders in the design. Shneiderman and Rose discuss this proposal in the context of their current design for the Maryland Department of Juvenile Justice. Agre and Mailloux (chapter 17) also recommend such stakeholder involvement in their discussion of intelligent vehicle highways.

PART II: COMPUTERS AS PERSONS? — IMPLICATIONS FOR DESIGN

Whether a designer chooses to present the technology to the user as an "agent," "person," "persona," or some other anthropomorphized form, might not appear to be a heavily laden value question. After all, we rarely think of the anthropomorphism of automobiles, sailing vessels, or stuffed animals as cause for alarm. The concern with computer technology arises, however, from the way in which people engage with computer technology as if it were a person to a greater extent than previously realized. Thus, as system designers, we need to understand how anthropomorphism occurs, and then decide whether or not to design features which promote it. This is the distinction I was making earlier between suitability (design features) and values (promoting computers as persons). Possibly for the first time in one place, this part brings together the growing body of work on this topic.

Typically, we think of social interaction as involving two or more people, even if people are physically distant from one another, as when talking on the telephone, reading electronic mail, or even having an internal dialogue with a friend. But can an interaction be social, or at least fully social, with computer technology? Nass et al. (chapter 8) lean toward an affirmative response. They begin by documenting that with minimal social cues (e.g., text-only), people will exhibit behavior with computers that in comparable situations parallels their behavior with other human beings (e.g., following politeness norms). Accordingly, they suggest that there may be a place to design, for example, "likable" computers which flatter their users and that adhere to human conventions of politeness. More boldly, following the title of their chapter, "Computers are Social Agents", they suggest that in system design interpersonal communication should become the metaphor and mechanism for human–computer interaction.

Sproull and Kiesler and their colleagues (chapter 9) provide evidence which support Nass et al.'s initial claim. In their study, subjects changed their personas and behavior in the presence of a simulated face (e.g., they presented themselves more positively to the simulated face than to a text interface) and attributed some personality traits to the simulated face. Other results reported by Kiesler and Sproull (chapter 10, which expands on their work in chapter 9) show that people will trust and behave cooperatively with a computer partner. Yet, in contrast to Nass and his colleagues, Kiesler and Sproull offer a more cautious interpretation of the data. It is one thing to say, as they do, that when the interface takes on a human persona through characteristics people typically associate with people – such as human speech and physiognomy – then it is likely to elicit what looks like social behavior in users. It is another thing to say, which they do not, that people think of machines as people.

Part of the difficulty in interpreting the above studies arises by trying to use data on human social behavior in interaction with computers to infer human cognition. Thus Friedman and Millett (chapter 11) offer a different methodology: social–cognitive interviews. Based on this method, they assessed individuals' reasoning about computer agency and computer capabilities, and their judgments of moral responsibility in two situations that involved delegation of decision making to a complex computer system. Results showed a complex pattern of results. On the one hand, most of the individuals attributed either decision making or intentions to computers, and over one-fifth of the individuals explicitly held computers morally responsible for error. On the other hand, most of the individuals judged computer decision making and computer intentions to be different from that of humans. Reasoning focused on rule-based systems (e.g., "[the computer] can decide in a sense that somebody has programmed rules, which it follows, and in that sense it chooses a course") and algorithmic processes (e.g., "[the computer] is deciding based on a very clear strict algorithm... it's a decision but not an open-ended one"). Based on these and other data, this study does not support the stronger claims by Nass et al. that people treat computers as social actors. It does suggest that in certain respects people attribute agency to computer technology, and that such attributions go well beyond superficial use of language.

Laurel (chapter 12) would probably be neither surprised nor bothered by a user's attribution of agency to a computer. In her chapter, written in 1990 before all of the other writings in this section, Laurel distinguishes between full-bodied and unidimensional characters. By characters she means something like portrayals of people, as in characters in a play. Full-bodied characters, like real people, are complex and at times engage in unpredictable behavior. Accordingly, Laurel suggests that as a metaphor for interface design full-bodied characters lead to ineffective designs. She proposes that the appropriate metaphor should be that of an unidimensional character (or caricature): simple and predictable. Laurel suggests that such an interface would facilitate usability by minimizing ambiguity. It would also build on a user's inclination to attribute agency to a computer.

Alternatively, Friedman and Kahn (chapter 13) are reluctant to build on such user inclinations. Their reasoning follows from the philosophical position that computers, as they are known today in material and structure, are not persons capable of moral agency. They also show how serious problems arise when human beings believe to the contrary and hold computers responsible for computer-mediated action. Similar arguments are made by Nissenbaum (chapter 2) in the broader context of her discussion on maintaining accountability in a computerized society. If this line of reasoning is correct, then it follows that the use of social cues in computer systems to elicit social behavior constitutes a form of deception. Of course, deceptions may not always be wrong. A social psychologist, for example, may initially deceive his or her subjects on the nature of an experiment in order to collect certain types of social-scientific data. Thus, even if one argued that encouraging a social interaction with a computer counts as a form of deception, a decision would still need to be made on whether such deception is warranted. Yet, in most cases, Friedman and her colleagues argue it is not. This does not mean that all agent technology need be abandoned. Rather, Friedman and her colleagues argue for system design that clarifies and makes salient to the user that the computer is an "it" and not a "who" – a machine and not a person – and that only people can be responsible for computer-mediated action.

PART III: PRACTICING VALUE-SENSITIVE DESIGN

Until now, a designer working within a corporate structure might say something like "nice theory, but so what?" How is it really possible to bring value-sensitive design into the workplace? The four chapters within Part III take up this question. The chapters report on diverse work environments, including hardware development in a medium-sized hardware company (SunSoft), research and development efforts in a communications corporation (NYNEX), in-house software development in a large urban hospital (the name is being kept anonymous), and policy analysis of intelligent vehicle highway systems at an academic institution (University of California, San Diego).

As a collection, these chapters call attention to three common questions that arise when designers explicitly address human values. First, how can one design proactively so as to minimize harm and injustice to human lives? Hochheiser (chapter 14) discusses his efforts to do so in the design of a database to aid instrument repair technicians in a large urban hospital. Part of Hochheiser's challenge was to anticipate abuses which had not yet occurred and to convince potential users and management that preventing such abuses are worthy of design time and resources. Second, is there an economic benefit to attending to human values in design? Tang (chapter 15) says that in most cases the answer is yes; and that it is the designer's responsibility to examine these benefits, and to speak the economic language of the corporate world. Toward estimating the economic benefits of value-sensitive design, Tang suggests that one can estimate lost revenue from potential buyers who would otherwise not purchase the product. In Tang's case, buyers with concerns for security, such as the federal government, might not purchase a workstation that lacked a hardware on/off switch on a microphone. Third, when in the design process is the right time to address human values? In what way? In all four chapters, the authors agree that the time to get involved is as early in the design process as possible and to continue that involvement throughout the project. Moreover, both Hochheiser (chapter 14) and Tang (chapter 15) show how important it is to address human values in the context of one's own design projects; Thomas (chapter 16) shows how to influence organizational practice and culture; and both Thomas (chapter 16) and Agre and Mailloux (chapter 17) show how to influence professional organizations, standards, and policy.

CONCLUSION

I have sought to convey some of the challenges and controversies which are arising in this emerging field of human values and system design. I have also suggested that as a community we need to embrace value-sensitive design as part of the culture of computer science. To do so moves us in important directions. It moves us toward the conceptualizations needed to identify shortcomings in current designs and to seek remedies which promote human well-being. It moves us toward the language needed to discuss the often immense social consequences of our work with the public at large. And it moves us toward holding out value-sensitive design as a criterion – along with the traditional criteria of reliability, efficiency, and correctness – by which systems may be judged poor and designers negligent. As with the traditional criteria, we need not require perfection, but commitment, which contributors to this volume demonstrate, with verve.

Table 1: Chapters Arranged by Technical Topic

Technical Topic	Chapter	Author(s)
Agents & Anthropomorphism	2 Accountability in…	Nissenbaum
	8 Computers are Social Actors…	Nass et al.
	9 When the Interface is a Face	Sproull et al.
	10 'Social' Human-Computer…	Kiesler & Sproull
	11 Reasoning about Computers…	Friedman & Millett
	12 Interface Agents…	Laurel
	13 Human Agency and…	Friedman & Kahn
Algorithms	1 Bias in Computer Systems	Friedman & Nissenbaum
Database	1 Bias in Computer Systems…	Friedman & Nissenbaum
	7 Social Impact Statements…	Shneiderman & Rose
	14 Workplace Database Systems…	Hochheiser
	17 Social Choice about Privacy…	Agre & Mailloux
Electronic Communication among People	4 Do Categories have Politics?…	Suchman
	5 Categories, disciplines…	Winograd
	6 Commentary on Suchman…	Malone
	15 Eliminating a Hardware Switch…	Tang
	16 Steps Toward Universal Access…	Thomas
Expert Systems	1 Bias in Computer Systems	Friedman & Nissenbaum
	11 Reasoning about Computers"…	Friedman & Millett
	13 Human Agency and…	Friedman & Kahn
Hardware	3 Disability, Inability and Cyberspace	Perry et al.
	15 Eliminating a Hardware Switch…	Tang
	17 Social Choice about Privacy…	Agre & Mailloux
Interface	1 Bias in Computer Systems	Friedman & Nissenbaum
	3 Disability, Inability and Cyberspace	Perry et al.
	8 Computers are Social Actors…	Nass et al.
	9 When the Interface is a Face	Sproull et al.
	10 'Social' Human–Computer…	Kiesler & Sproull
	11 Reasoning about Computers…	Friedman & Millett
	12 Interface Agents…	Laurel
	13 Human Agency and…	Friedman & Kahn
	16 Steps Toward Universal Access…	Thomas
Organizational Computing	1 Bias in Computer Systems	Friedman & Nissenbaum
	2 Accountability in…	Nissenbaum
	3 Disability, Inability, and Cyberspace	Perry et al.
	4 Do Categories Have Politics?…	Suchman
	5 Categories, Disciplines…	Winograd
	6 Commentary on Suchman…	Malone
	7 Social Impact Statements…	Shneiderman & Rose
	13 Human Agency and…	Friedman & Kahn
	14 Workplace Database Systems…	Hochheiser
	15 Eliminating a Hardware Switch…	Tang
	16 Steps Toward Universal Access…	Thomas
	17 Social Choice about Privacy…	Agre & Mailloux

Table 2: Chapters Arranged by Human Value

Human Value	Chapter	Author(s)
Accountability	2 Accountability in a Computerized...	Nissenbaum
	7 Social Impact Statements...	Shneiderman & Rose
	11 Reasoning about Computers...	Friedman & Millett
	13 Human Agency and...	Friedman & Kahn
	14 Workplace Database Systems...	Hochheiser
	17 Social Choice about Privacy...	Agre & Mailloux
Autonomy	4 Do Categories have Politics?...	Suchman
	5 Categories, Disciplines...	Winograd
	6 Commentary on Suchman...	Malone
	7 Social Impact Statements...	Shneiderman & Rose
	14 Workplace Database Systems...	Hochheiser
Freedom from Bias	1 Bias in Computer Systems	Friedman & Nissenbaum
	3 Disability, Inability and Cyberspace	Perry et al.
	7 Social Impact Statements...	Shneiderman & Rose
	16 Steps Toward Universal Access	Thomas
Privacy	7 Social Impact Statements...	Shneiderman & Rose
	14 Workplace Database Systems...	Hochheiser
	15 Eliminating a Hardware Switch...	Tang
	17 Social Choice about Privacy...	Agre & Mailloux
Universal Access	1 Bias in Computer Systems	Friedman & Nissenbaum
	3 Disability, Inability and Cyberspace	Perry et al.
	7 Social Impact Statements...	Shneiderman & Rose
	16 Steps Toward Universal Access...	Thomas

REFERENCES

Adler, P.S., and T. Winograd, eds. 1992. *Usability: Turning Technologies into Tools.* Oxford: Oxford University Press.

Appadurai, A., ed. 1988. *The Social Life of Things.* New York: Cambridge University Press.

Baecker, R., J. Grudin, W. Buxton, and S. Greenberg, eds. 1995. *Readings in Human-Computer Interaction: Toward the Year 2000* (2nd edition). San Francisco: Morgan Kaufmann.

Blomberg, J., L. Suchman, and R.H. Trigg. 1996. Reflections on a Work-Oriented Design Project. *Human-Computer Interaction,* 11(3):237–265.

Bodker, S. 1991. *Through the Interface: A Human Activity Approach to User Interface Design.* Hillsdale, NJ: Lawrence Erlbaum.

Brown, J.S., and J. Duguid. 1994. Borderline Issues: Social and Material Aspects of Design. *Human-Computer Interaction,* 9(1):3–36.

Clement, A., and P. Van den Besselaar. 1993. A Retrospective Look at PD Projects. *Communications of the ACM,* 36(4):29–37.

Cole, M. 1991 (April). Discussant to B. Friedman and P. H. Kahn, Jr. (Presenters). Who is Responsible for What? and Can What be Responsible? The Psychological Boundaries of Moral Responsibility. Paper session at the biennial meeting of the Society for Research in Child Development, Seattle.

Ehn, P. 1988. *Work-Oriented Design of Computer Artifacts.* Stockholm: Arbetslivscentrum. (Distributed by Lawrence Erlbaum, Hillsdale, NJ).

Ermann, M.D., M.B. Williams, and C. Gutierrez, eds. 1990. *Computers, Ethics, and Society.* Oxford: Oxford University Press.

Forester, T., ed. 1989. *Computers in the Human Context.* Cambridge, MA: The MIT Press.

Fernandes, T. 1995. *Global Interface Design.* Boston: AP Professional.

Friedman, B. 1996. Value-Sensitive Design. *Interactions,* III(6):17–23.

Greenbaum, J., and M. Kyng. 1991. *Design at Work.* Hillsdale, NJ: Lawrence Erlbaum.

Greif, I., ed. 1988. *Computer-Supported Cooperative Work: A Book of Readings.* San Mateo, CA: Morgan Kaufmann.

Houston, J. 1995. *Confessions of an Igloo Dweller.* New York: Houghton Mifflin.

Johnson, D.G. 1994. *Computer Ethics* (2nd edition). Englewood Cliffs, NJ: Prentice Hall.

Johnson, D.G., and H. Nissenbaum, eds. 1995. *Computers, Ethics and Social Values.* Englewood Cliffs, NJ: Prentice Hall.

Kling, R. 1980. Social Analyses of Computing: Theoretical Perspectives in Recent Empirical Research. *Computing Surveys,* 12(1):61–110.

Kling, R., ed. 1996. *Computerization and Controversy: Value Conflicts and Social Choices* (2nd edition). Boston: Academic Press.

Kuhn, S. 1996. Design for People at Work. In *Bringing Design to Software,* ed. T. Winograd, 273–289. Reading, MA: Addison-Wesley.

Ladd, J. 1989. Computers and Moral Responsibility: A Framework for Ethical Analysis. In *The Information Web: Ethical and Social Implications of Computer Networking,* ed. C. Gould, 207–227. Boulder, CO: Westview Press.

Laurel, B., ed. 1990. *The Art of Human-Computer Interaction.* Reading, MA: Addison-Wesley.

Moor, J.H. 1985. What is Computer Ethics? *Metaphilosophy*(16):266–275.

Nass, C., and B. Reeves. 1996. *The Media Equation: How People Treat Computers, Television and New Media Like Real People and Places.* Stanford, CA: CSLI Publications.

Nielsen, J. 1993. *Usability Engineering.* Boston: AP Professional.

Norman, D.A. 1988. *The Psychology of Everyday Things.* New York: Basic Books.

Norman, D.A., and S. W. Draper, eds. 1986. *User Centered System Design.* Hillsdale, NJ: Lawrence Erlbaum.

Nucci, L. 1996. Morality and the Personal Sphere of Actions. In *Values and Knowledge*, eds. E.S. Reed, E. Turiel, and T. Brown, 41–60. Mahwah, NJ: Lawrence Erlbaum.

Pelto, P.J. 1973. *The Snowmobile Revolution: Technology and Social Change in the Arctic.* Menlo Park, CA: Cummings Publishing Company.

Roth, S.K. 1994. The Unconsidered Ballot: How Design Affects Voting Behavior. *Visible Language*(28):48–67.

Scheffler, I. 1991. *In Praise of the Cognitive Emotions.* New York: Routledge.

Schuler, D., and A. Namioka, eds. 1993. *Participatory Design: Principles and Practices.* Hillsdale, NJ: Lawrence Erlbaum.

Sharp, L. 1980. Steel Axes for Stone-Age Australians. In *Conformity and Conflict*, eds. J. P. Spradley and D. W. McCurdy, 345–359. Boston: Little, Brown, & Company. (Reprinted from *Human Organization*, 1952(11) 17–22.)

Shneiderman, B. 1992. *Designing the User Interface: Strategies for Effective Human-Computer Interaction* (2nd edition). Reading, MA: Addison-Wesley.

Smetana, J.G. 1982. *Concepts of Self and Morality: Women's Reasoning about Abortion.* New York: Praeger.

Smetana, J.G. 1983. Social-Cognitive Development: Domain Distinctions and Coordinations. *Developmental Review*(3):131–147.

Smetana, J.G. 1995. Morality in Context: Abstractions, Ambiguities and Applications. In *Annals of Child Development* (Vol. 10), ed. R. Vasta, 83–130. London: Jessica Kingsley.

Sproull, L., and S. Kiesler. 1991. *Connections: New Ways of Working in the Networked Organization.* Cambridge, MA: The MIT Press.

Suchman, L. 1987. *Plans and Situated Actions.* Cambridge, UK: Cambridge University Press.

Tisak, M.S. 1995. Domains of Social Reasoning and Beyond. In *Annals of Child Development* (Vol. 11), ed. R. Vasta, 95–130. London: Jessica Kingsley.

Tognazzini, B. 1995. *Tog on Software Design.* Reading, MA: Addison-Wesley.

Turiel, E. 1983. *The Development of Social Knowledge.* Cambridge, UK: Cambridge University Press.

Turiel, E. In press. The Development of Morality. To appear in *Handbook of Child Psychology,* 5th Ed., Vol. 3, ed. W. Damon : ed. N. Eisenberg, *Social, Emotional, and Personality Development.* New York: Wiley.

Turiel, E., M. Killen, and C.C. Helwig. 1987. Morality: Its Structure, Functions and Vagaries. In *The Emergence of Morality in Young Children,* eds. J. Kagan and S. Lamb, 155–244. Chicago: University of Chicago Press.

Turiel, E., C. Hildebrandt, and C. Wainryb. 1991. Judging Social Issues: Difficulties, Inconsistencies, and Consistencies. *Monographs of the Society for Research in Child Development* 56(2, Serial No. 224).

Winograd, T., ed. 1996. *Bringing Design to Software.* Reading, MA: Addison-Wesley.

Winograd, T., and F. Flores. 1987. Understanding Computers and Cognition: A New Foundation for Design. Reading, MA: Addison-Wesley. (First issued by Ablex, 1986.)

Zuboff, S. 1988. *In the Age of the Smart Machine.* New York: Basic Books.

PART I

Conceptualizing Human Values in Design

Bias in Computer Systems

BATYA FRIEDMAN AND HELEN NISSENBAUM

Abstract: From an analysis of actual cases, three categories of bias in computer systems have been developed: preexisting, technical, and emergent. Preexisting bias has its roots in social institutions, practices, and attitudes. Technical bias arises from technical constraints or considerations. Emergent bias arises in a context of use. Although others have pointed to bias in particular computer systems and have noted the general problem, we know of no comparable work that examines this phenomenon comprehensively and which offers a framework for understanding and remedying it. We conclude by suggesting that freedom from bias should be counted among the select set of criteria – including reliability, accuracy, and efficiency – according to which the quality of systems in use in society should be judged.

To introduce what bias in computer systems might look like, consider the case of computerized airline reservation systems, which are used widely by travel agents to identify and reserve airline flights for their customers. These reservation systems seem straightforward. When a travel agent types in a customer's travel requirements, the reservation system searches a database of flights and retrieves all reasonable flight options that meet or come close to the customer's requirements. These options then are ranked according to various criteria, giving priority to nonstop flights, more direct routes, and minimal total travel time. The ranked flight options are displayed for the travel agent. In the 1980s, however, most of the airlines brought before the Antitrust Division of the United States Justice Department allegations of anti-competitive practices by American and United Airlines whose reservation systems – Sabre and Apollo, respectively – dominated the field. It was claimed, among other things, that the two reservations systems are biased (Shrifin, 1985).

One source of this alleged bias lies in Sabre's and Apollo's algorithms for controlling search and display functions. In the algorithms, preference is given

This research was funded in part by the Clare Boothe Luce Foundation. Earlier aspects of this work were presented at the 4S/EASST Conference, Goteborg, Sweden, August 1992, and at Inter-CHI '93, Amsterdam, April 1993. An earlier version of this article appeared as Tech. Rep. CSLI-94-188, CSLI, Stanford University.

We thank our research assistant Mark Muir for help with aspects of this analysis. We thank F. J. Corbató, John Ellis, Deborah Johnson, James Moor, John Mulvey, Peter Neumann, and Alvin Roth for discussions concerning bias; and we thank Rob Kling and anonymous reviewers for their comments on this article. We extend our appreciation to CSLI, Stanford University, for use of their facilities during December 1993.

to "on-line" flights, that is, flights with all segments on a single carrier. Imagine, then, a traveler who originates in Phoenix and flies the first segment of a round trip overseas journey to London on American Airlines, changing planes in New York. All other things being equal, the British Airlines' flight from New York to London would be ranked lower than the American Airlines' flight from New York to London even though in both cases a traveler is similarly inconvenienced by changing planes and checking through customs. Thus, the computer systems systematically downgrade and, hence, are biased against international carriers who fly few, if any, internal U.S. flights, and against internal carriers who do not fly international flights (Fotos, 1988; Ott, 1988).

Critics also have been concerned with two other problems. One is that the interface design compounds the bias in the reservation systems. Lists of ranked flight options are displayed screen by screen. Each screen displays only two to five options. The advantage to a carrier of having its flights shown on the first screen is enormous since ninety percent of the tickets booked by travel agents are booked by the first screen display (Taib, 1990). Even if the biased algorithm and interface can give only a small percent advantage overall to one airline, it can make the difference to its competitors between survival and bankruptcy. A second problem arises from the travelers' perspective. When travelers contract with an independent third party – a travel agent – to determine travel plans, travelers have good reason to assume they are being informed accurately of their travel options; in many situations, that does not happen.

As Sabre and Apollo illustrate, biases in computer systems can be difficult to identify let alone remedy because of the way the technology engages and extenuates them. Computer systems, for instance, are comparatively inexpensive to disseminate, and thus, once developed, a biased system has the potential for widespread impact. If the system becomes a standard in the field, the bias becomes pervasive. If the system is complex, and most are, biases can remain hidden in the code, difficult to pinpoint or explicate, and not necessarily disclosed to users or their clients. Furthermore, unlike in our dealings with biased individuals with whom a potential victim can negotiate, biased systems offer no equivalent means for appeal.

Although others have pointed to bias in particular computer systems and have noted the general problem (Johnson & Mulvey, 1983; Moor, 1985), we know of no comparable work that focuses exclusively on this phenomenon and examines it comprehensively.

In this chapter, we provide a framework for understanding bias in computer systems. From an analysis of actual computer systems, we have developed three categories: preexisting bias, technical bias, and emergent bias. Preexisting bias has its roots in social institutions, practices, and attitudes. Technical bias arises from technical constraints or considerations. Emergent bias arises in a context of use. We begin by defining bias and explicating each category, and then move to case studies. We conclude with remarks about how bias in computer systems can be remedied.

WHAT IS A BIASED COMPUTER SYSTEM?

In its most general sense, the term bias means simply "slant." Given this undifferentiated usage, at times the term is applied with relatively neutral content. A grocery shopper, for example, can be "biased" by not buying damaged fruit. At other times, the term bias is applied with significant moral meaning. An employer, for example, can be "biased" by refusing to hire minorities. In this chapter we focus on instances of the latter, for if one wants to develop criteria for judging the quality of systems in use – which we do – then criteria must be delineated in ways that speak robustly yet precisely to relevant social matters. Focusing on bias of moral import does just that.

Accordingly, we use the term bias to refer to computer systems that *systematically* and *unfairly discriminate* against certain individuals or groups of individuals in favor of others. A system discriminates unfairly if it denies an opportunity or a good or if it assigns an undesirable outcome to an individual or group of individuals on grounds that are unreasonable or inappropriate. Consider, for example, an automated credit advisor that assists in the decision of whether or not to extend credit to a particular applicant. If the advisor denies credit to individuals with consistently poor payment records we do not judge the system to be biased because it is reasonable and appropriate for a credit company to want to avoid extending credit privileges to people who consistently do not pay their bills. In contrast, a credit advisor that systematically assigns poor credit ratings to individuals with ethnic surnames discriminates on grounds that are not relevant to credit assessments and, hence, discriminates unfairly.

Two points follow. First, unfair discrimination alone does not give rise to bias unless it occurs systematically. Consider again the automated credit advisor. Imagine a random glitch in the system which changes in an isolated case information in a copy of the credit record for an applicant who happens to have an ethnic surname. The change in information causes a downgrading of this applicant's rating. While this applicant experiences unfair discrimination resulting from this random glitch, the applicant could have been anybody. In a repeat incident, the same applicant or others with similar ethnicity would not be in a special position to be singled out. Thus, while the system is prone to random error, it is not biased.

Second, systematic discrimination does not establish bias unless it is joined with an unfair outcome. A case in point is the Persian Gulf War, where United States Patriot missiles were used to detect and intercept Iraqi SCUD missiles. At least one software error identified during the war contributed to systematically poor performance by the Patriots (U.S. GAO, 1992). Calculations used to predict the location of a SCUD depended in complex ways on the Patriots' internal clock. The longer the Patriot's continuous running time, the greater the imprecision in the calculation. The deaths of at least twenty-eight Americans in Dhahran can be traced to this software error, which systematically degraded the accuracy of Patriot missiles. While we are not minimizing the serious consequence of this systematic computer error, it falls outside of our analysis because it does not involve unfairness.

FRAMEWORK FOR ANALYZING BIAS IN COMPUTER SYSTEMS

We derived our framework by examining actual computer systems for bias. Instances of bias were identified and characterized according to their source, and then the characterizations were generalized to more abstract categories. These categories were further refined by their application to other instances of bias in the same or additional computer systems. In most cases, our knowledge of particular systems came from the published literature. In total, we examined seventeen computer systems from diverse fields including banking, commerce, computer science, education, medicine, and law.

The framework that emerged from this methodology is comprised of three overarching categories – preexisting bias, technical bias, and emergent bias. Table 1 contains a detailed description of each category. In more general terms, they can be described as follows.

Preexisting Bias

Preexisting bias has its roots in social institutions, practices, and attitudes. When computer systems embody biases that exist independently, and usually prior to the creation of the system, then we say that the system embodies preexisting bias. Preexisting biases may originate in society at large, in subcultures, and in formal or informal, private or public organizations and institutions. They can also reflect the personal biases of individuals who have significant input into the design of the system, such as the client or system designer. This type of bias can enter a system either through the explicit and conscious efforts of individuals or institutions, or implicitly and unconsciously, even in spite of the best of intentions. For example, imagine an expert system that advises on loan applications. In determining an applicant's credit risk, the automated loan advisor negatively weights applicants who live in "undesirable" locations, such as low-income or high-crime neighborhoods, as indicated by their home addresses (a practice referred to as "red-lining"). To the extent the program embeds the biases of clients or designers who seek to avoid certain applicants on the basis of group stereotypes, the automated loan advisor's bias is preexisting.

Technical Bias

In contrast to preexisting bias, technical bias arises from the resolution of issues in the technical design. Sources of technical bias can be found in several aspects of the design process, including limitations of computer tools such as hardware, software, and peripherals; the process of ascribing social meaning to algorithms developed out of context; imperfections in pseudo-random number generation; and the attempt to make human constructs amenable to computers, when we quantify the qualitative, discretize the continuous, or formalize the nonformal. As an illustration, consider again the case of Sabre and Apollo described above. A technical constraint imposed by the size of the monitor screen forces a piecemeal presentation of flight options and, thus, makes the algorithm chosen to rank flight options critically important. Whatever ranking algorithm is used, if it systematically places certain airlines' flights on initial screens and other airlines' flights on later screens, the system will exhibit technical bias.

Emergent Bias

While it is almost always possible to identify preexisting bias and technical bias in a system design at the time of creation or implementation, emergent bias arises only in a context of use. This bias typically emerges some time after a design is completed, as a result of changing societal knowledge, population, or cultural values. Using the example of an automated airline reservation

Table 1: Categories of Bias in Computer System Design

These categories describe ways in which bias can arise in the design of computer systems. The illustrative examples portray plausible cases of bias.

1. Preexisting Bias

Preexisting bias has its roots in social institutions, practices, and attitudes. When computer systems embody biases that exist independently, and usually prior to the creation of the system, then the system exemplifies preexisting bias. Preexisting bias can enter a system either through the explicit and conscious efforts of individuals or institutions, or implicitly and unconsciously, even in spite of the best of intentions.

1.1 Individual

Bias that originates from individuals who have significant input into the design of the system, such as the client commissioning the design or the system designer. (E.g., a client embeds personal racial biases into the specifications for loan approval software.)

1.2 Societal

Bias that originates from society at large, such as from organizations (e.g., industry), institutions (e.g., legal systems), or culture at large. (E.g., gender biases present in the larger society that lead to the development of educational software that overall appeals more to boys than girls.)

2. Technical Bias

Technical bias arises from technical constraints or technical considerations.

2.1 Computer Tools

Bias that originates from a limitation of the computer technology including hardware, software, and peripherals. (E.g., in a database for matching organ donors with potential transplant recipients certain individuals retrieved and displayed on initial screens are favored systematically for a match over individuals displayed on later screens.)

2.2 Decontextualized Algorithms

Bias that originates from the use of an algorithm that fails to treat all groups fairly under all significant conditions. (E.g., a scheduling algorithm that schedules airplanes for take-off relies on the alphabetic listing of the airlines to rank order flights ready within a given period of time.)

2.3 Random-Number Generation

Bias that originates from imperfections in pseudo-random number generation or in the misuse of pseudo-random numbers. (E.g., an imperfection in a random-number generator used to select recipients for a scarce drug leads systematically to favoring individuals toward the end of the database.)

2.4 Formalization of Human Constructs

Bias that originates from attempts to make human constructs such as discourse, judgments, or intuitions amenable to computers: when we quantify the qualitative, discretize the continuous, or formalize the non-formal. (E.g., a legal expert system advises defendants on whether or not to plea bargain by assuming that law can be spelled out in an unambiguous manner that is not subject to human and humane interpretations in context.)

3. Emergent Bias

Emergent bias arises in a context of use with real users. This bias typically emerges some time after a design is completed, as a result of changing societal knowledge, population, or cultural values. User interfaces are likely to be particularly prone to emergent bias because interfaces by design seek to reflect the capacities, character, and habits of prospective users. Thus, a shift in context of use may well create difficulties for a new set of users.

3.1 New Societal Knowledge

Bias that originates from the emergence of new knowledge in society that cannot be or is not incorporated into the system design. (E.g., a medical expert system for AIDS patients has no mechanism for incorporating cutting edge medical discoveries that affect how individuals with certain symptoms should be treated.)

3.2 Mismatch Between Users and System Design

Bias that originates when the population using the system differs on some significant dimension from the population assumed as users in the design.

3.2.1 Different Expertise

Bias that originates when the system is used by a population with a different knowledge base from that assumed in the design. (E.g., an ATM with an interface that makes extensive use of written instructions – "place the card, magnetic tape side down, in the slot to your left" – is installed in a neighborhood with primarily a non-literate population.)

3.2.2 Different Values

Bias that originates when the system is used by a population with different values than those assumed in the design. (E.g., educational software to teach mathematics concepts is embedded in a game situation that rewards individualistic and competitive strategies but is used by students with a cultural background that largely eschews competition and instead promotes cooperative endeavors.)

system, envision a hypothetical system designed for a group of airlines all of whom serve national routes. Consider what might occur if that system was extended to include international airlines. A flight ranking algorithm that favors on-line flights when applied in the original context with national airlines leads to no systematic unfairness. However, in the new context with international airlines, the automated system would place these airlines at a disadvantage and, thus, comprise a case of emergent bias. User interfaces are likely to be particularly prone to emergent bias because interfaces by design seek to reflect the capacities, character, and habits of prospective users. Thus, a shift in context of use may well create difficulties for a new set of users.

APPLICATIONS OF THE FRAMEWORK

We now analyze actual computer systems in terms of the framework introduced above. It should be understood that the systems we analyze are by and large good ones, and our intention is not to undermine their integrity. Rather, our intention is to develop the framework, show how it can identify and clarify our understanding of bias in computer systems, and establish its robustness through real-world cases.

The National Resident Match Program (NRMP)

The NRMP implements a centralized method for assigning medical school graduates their first employment following graduation. The centralized method of assigning medical students to hospital programs arose in the 1950s in response to the chaotic job placement process and ongoing failure of hospitals and students to arrive at optimal placements. During this early period the matching was carried out by a mechanical card-sorting process, but in 1974 electronic data processing was introduced to handle the entire matching process. (For a history of the NRMP, see Graettinger & Peranson (1981a).) After reviewing applications and interviewing students, hospital programs submit to the centralized program their ranked list of students. Students do the same for hospital programs. Hospitals and students are not permitted to make other arrangements with one another or to attempt to directly influence each others' rankings prior to the match. With the inputs from hospitals and students, the NRMP applies its "Admissions Algorithm" to produce a match.

Table 2: The Simplest Case of Rank-Order Lists which the Desires of Students and Programs are in Conflict

Rank Order	Student I	Student II	Program A	Program B
1	Program A	Program B	Student II	Student I
2	Program B	Program A	Student I	Student II

Note: Each program in this example has a quota of one position.[1]

Over the years, the NRMP has been the subject of various criticisms. One charges that the Admissions Algorithm systematically favors hospital programs over medical students in cases of conflict (Graettinger & Peranson, 1981b; Roth, 1984; Sudarshan & Zisook, 1981; Williams et al., 1981). Consider the example developed by Williams, et al., which we reproduce:

> To generate a match from Table 2, the NRMP algorithm first attempts a so-called 1:1 run, in which concordances between the first choice of students and programs are matched (this table was constructed so that there would be none). The algorithm then moves to a 2:1 run, in which the students' second choices are tentatively run against the programs' first choices. Both students are matched with their second-choice programs. This tentative run becomes final, since no students or program is left unmatched. Matching is completed; both programs receive their first choices, and both students their second choices.
>
> The result of switching the positions of the students and programs in the algorithm should be obvious. After the 1:1 run fails, the 2:1 run under a switch would tentatively run the programs' second choices against the students' first choices, thus matching both programs with their second-choice students. Matching is again completed, but on this run, both students receive their first choices, and the programs...receive their second choices (Williams et al., 1981, p. 1165).

Does such preference for hospital programs reflect bias? We are inclined to answer yes because in cases of conflict there does not appear to be a good rationale for favoring hospital programs at the expense of students. Moreover, Graettinger and Peranson provide grounds for assessing the type of bias. They write, "The constraint inherent in the NRMP algorithm, in which preference is given to hospital choices when conflicts in rankings occur, duplicates what happens in an actual admissions process without a computerized matching program" (Graettinger & Peranson, 1981b, p. 526). Elsewhere, they write:

> Changing the (Admissions) algorithm would imply changing the NRMP's role from one of passive facilitator to one in which the NRMP would be intervening in the ad-

---

[1] This table is reprinted with permission from *The New England Journal of Medicine.*

missions process by imposing a different result than would be obtained without the matching program. This is not the role for which the NRMP was intended (p.526).

Thus, if the algorithm systematically and unfairly favors hospital over student preferences, it does so because of design specifications and organizational practices that predate the computer implementation. As such, the NRMP embodies a preexisting bias.

Earlier versions of the NRMP have also been charged with bias against married couples in cases where both the husband and wife were medical students. When the NRMP was originally designed, few such couples participated in the medical match process. Beginning, however, in the late 1970s and early 1980s more women entered medical schools, and not surprisingly, more married couples sought medical appointments through the NRMP. At this point, it was discovered that the original Admissions Algorithm placed married couples at a disadvantage in achieving an optimal placement as compared with their single peers (Roth, 1984; 1990). Roth describes the problem as follows:

> Prior to the mid-1980s, couples participating in the match were required to specify one of their members as the "leading member," and to submit a rank ordering of positions for each member of the couple; that is, a couple submitted two preference lists. The leading member was matched to a position in the usual way, the preference list of the other member of the couple was edited to remove distant positions, and the second member was then matched if possible to a position in the same vicinity as the leading member. It is easy to see how instabilities (non-optimum matches) would often result. Consider a couple whose first choice is to have two particular jobs in Boston and whose second choice is to have two particular jobs in New York. Under the couple's algorithm, the leading member might be matched to his or her first choice job in Boston, whereas the other member might be matched to some undesirable job in Boston. If their preferred New York jobs ranked this couple higher than students matched to those jobs, an instability would now exist (Roth,1990, p. 1528).

In this example, once the leading member of the couple is assigned a match in Boston no other geographic locations for the couple are considered. Thus, a better overall match with a hospital in New York is missed. The point here is that the bias – in this case emergent bias – against couples primarily emerged when a shift occurred in the social conditions, namely, when husband and wife medical students increasingly participated in the match process.

Compare the above two charges of bias with a third one, which accuses the NRMP of bias against hospitals in rural areas because of a consistent placement pattern over the years in which urban hospitals are far more successful in filling their positions than rural ones (Roth, 1984; Sudarshan & Zisook,

1981). The Admissions Algorithm does not take into account geographic distribution when determining a match, considering only the ranked preferences of hospitals and students. Because the best teaching hospitals tend to be in urban areas, the urban areas tend to fill their positions far more effectively, and with better students, than rural hospitals. Observing this uneven distribution some have concluded that the NRMP is biased against rural hospitals in favor of urban ones. Is this so?

While we are committed to a stance against injustice, we do not think the distinction between a rationally based discrimination and bias is always easy to draw. In some cases, reasonable people might differ in their judgments. In this case, we ourselves would shy away from viewing this as a bias in the system because we think this discrimination can be defended as having a reasonable basis. Namely, the discrimination reflects the preferences of match participants, and it is reasonable in our view for employment decisions to be determined largely by the choices of employers and employees.

Bias in the NRMP is particularly troubling because of the system's centralized status. Most major hospitals agree to fill their positions with the NRMP assignments. Thus, for an individual or couple to elect not to participate in the NRMP is tantamount to forgoing the possibility of placement in most hospital programs. In this manner, centralized computing systems with widespread use can hold users hostage to whatever biases are embedded within the system.

A Multi-Level Scheduling Algorithm (MLSA)

In timeshare computer systems many individuals make use of a single computer. These systems face a common problem of how to schedule the processing demands of the many individuals who make use of the processor at the same time. When posed with how to share equitably a limited resource, accepted social practice often points toward a first-come, first-served basis. But the practical shortcomings of this approach are readily apparent. Imagine a person who uses the computer for interactive editing. Such work entails many small jobs that take very little time to process. Should another user with a large job requiring several minutes or hours of computation come along, the first user would experience a noticeable delay between execution of editing commands. Likely enough, frustrations would run high and users would be dissatisfied. Thus, a balance must be struck between providing a reasonable response time and relatively efficient computation speed of large and long-running programs.

Proposed by F. J. Corbató in the 1960s, the MLSA represents one algorithm to address this balance (Corbató, et al., 1962). This algorithm was implemented in the CTSS timesharing system and in Multics. In brief, the MLSA works as follows. When a new command is received, it is executed for up to a quantum of time. If the process is not completed in that quantum of time, then the process is placed in a queue for "longer-running processes." Other new commands, if present, then are processed. Only when there are no new commands does the processor return to the process left in the queue for longer-running processes. Execution of this process is continued for a larger quantum of time. If the process is not completed in this larger quantum of time, then it is placed in yet another queue of "even longer-running processes." And again, the processor returns to execute any new commands and, after that, any processes in the queue for longer-running processes. Only when there are no new commands and the queue for longer-running processes is empty will the processor look to the queue of even longer-running processes for unfinished processes. In this manner the MLSA gives processing attention to all processes as quickly as possible that are beginning a new command. Thus, assuming the system is not saturated with too many users, short-running processes are speedily processed to completion. At the same time, however, in principle a long-running process could wait all day to finish.

Does the balance between response time and computation speed of long-running programs achieved by the MLSA systematically disadvantage some users? To help answer this question, consider a situation in which many people use a timeshare system at the same time on a regular basis. Of these individuals, most use relatively small programs on relatively short tasks, such as the interactive editing mentioned above. However, one or two individuals consistently use the system to execute long-running programs. According to the MLSA, the long-running programs of these individuals will necessarily end up with a lower priority than the short-running tasks of the other users. Thus, in terms of overall service from the processor, these individuals with long-running programs are systematically disadvantaged. According to Corbató (electronic communication, December 17, 1993), in response to this situation, some users with long-running programs uncovered the MLSA's strategy and developed a counterstrategy: By using a manual button to stop execution of a long-running process and a moment later restarting the process from where it left off, users effectively ran their long-running tasks in small chunks. Each small chunk, of course, was placed by MLSA into the top priority queue and executed speedily.

Having established systematic discrimination in the MLSA, we next ask whether this systematic discrimination is unfair. Consider that in other sorts of mundane queuing situations, such as movies or banks, we generally perceive that the "first-come first-served" strategy is fairest. It is also true that we can appreciate alternative strategies if they can complement and replace the strategy. In supermarkets, for example, we can appreciate express checkouts. But we likely would perceive as unfair a checkout system in which customers with fewer than, say, ten items in their baskets could push ahead of anyone else in the line with more than ten items. Similarly, it seems to us that by systematically favoring short jobs, the MLSA violates the fairness preserved in the "first-come first-served" strategy.

While a human context gave rise to the need for the scheduling algorithm, it is important to understand that there was no prior bias against individuals with longer-running jobs. That is, the algorithm's bias did not arise from social factors, say, to dissuade users from large computational projects or to encourage interactive editing and debugging. Had this been the case, the bias would be preexisting. Rather the bias is technical, for the algorithm arose in the attempt to satisfy a difficult technical requirement to allocate a scarce resource. It does so by giving processing attention to all processes as quickly as possible.

Another algorithm might have eluded the MLSA's form of technical bias by balancing response time and long-running computations in a manner that did not lead to systematic disadvantage for individuals with long-running programs. However, we also recognize that in the attempt to strike a balance between two apparently conflicting claims on a processor, it may not be possible to achieve a solution that is completely fair to all of those using the system. In cases like the MLSA, an awareness may be needed that one group is disadvantaged by the system, and an attempt made to minimize that disadvantage from within the system or to address it by some other means.

The British Nationality Act Program (BNAP)

Before discussing bias in the BNAP, a bit of history. In 1981 the Thatcher government passed the British Nationality Act as a means to redefine British citizenship. The act defined three new categories: British citizenship, citizenship of the British Dependent Territories, and British overseas citizenship. Only full British citizens in the first category would have the right to live in Britain. While the Thatcher Government and some British citizens defended the act, others raised objections. For example, within Britain, according to *The Lon-*

don Times, "The Labour Shadow Cabinet ... decided to oppose the Bill on the grounds that it contains elements of racial and sexual discrimination" (Berlins & Hodges, 1981). Similarly, in India, the *Hindustan Times* reported (quoted by Fishlock (1981)):

> Racial discrimination, by whatever name or device, is still discrimination of the most reprehensible kind. The Bill formalizes and legitimates racism toward people of a different hue which reflects the xenophobic paranoia that afflicts a section of British society today. The proposed three tiers of citizenship are a fine sieve which will allow into Britain only those of the desired racial stock.

Beginning in 1983, M. J. Sergot and his colleagues at the Imperial College, University of London undertook to translate the British Nationality Act into a computer program so that "consequences of the act can be determined mechanistically" (Sergot et al., 1986).[2] Critics have charged BNAP of gender bias. Consider the following. One of the most compelling grounds for establishing British citizenship is to have at least one parent who is a British citizen. As specified in Section 50-(9) of the British Nationality Act itself and implemented in BNAP, "a man is the 'father' of only his legitimate children, whereas a woman is the 'mother' of all her children, legitimate or not" (Sergot, et al., 1986). Consider then the instance of an unmarried man and woman who live together with the children they have jointly conceived. If the mother is a British citizen, and the father is not, then the children have one parent who is considered a British citizen. But if the situation is reversed (that is, if the father is a British citizen, and the mother is not), then the children have no parents who are considered British citizens. Thus the British Nationality Act is biased against the illegitimate descendants of British men. Accordingly, to the extent the BNAP accurately represents the British Nationality Act, the program embodies preexisting bias.

Two further concerns with the BNAP can be understood in terms of emergent bias. First, the system was designed in a research environment, among people with sophisticated knowledge of immigration law. Its users, however, are likely to be at best paralegal or immigration counselors in Britain, if not lay persons in foreign countries with only limited access to British legal expertise.

---

[2]Although the program authors (Sergot et al., 1986) state "It was never our intention to develop the implementation of the act into a fully functional program" (p. 371), it is difficult to take their disclaimer entirely seriously. For in the same text the authors also state (as noted above) that their goal is to translate the British Nationality Act so that "the consequences of the act can be determined mechanistically" (p. 370), and they place their work in the context of other legal expert systems designed for use with real users.

A problem thus arises for nonexpert users. Some of the program's queries, for example, require expert knowledge to answer. More generally, nonexperts advising British citizen hopefuls are not alerted to alternative legal frameworks that complement the British Nationality Act. Thus nonexperts – particularly in developing countries – would be inclined to accept decisively the BNAP's response to their client's situation. In such ways, the BNAP comes to act as an instrument of bias against the nonexperts and their clients. Because this bias arises from a shift in the population using the system from the one apparently held in mind by the system's creators (from expert to nonexpert users) we identify this bias as emergent.

Another source for emergent bias can arise in the following way. At the time of the BNAP's initial implementation (1983) no mechanism was built into the program to incorporate relevant case law as it came into being (Sergot et al., 1986). Should the accumulation of case law lead to changes in the way the Act is interpreted – say, by granting new subgroups British citizenship – BNAP would systematically misinform members of this subgroup regarding their status as British citizens (Leith, 1986). Again, we identify this bias as emergent because it depends on a shift in the social context, in this instance one concerning knowledge within the legal community. Emergent bias poses a potential problem for any legal expert system, especially in a society where legal systems depend on evolving case law. Indeed, to varying degrees, any expert system (independent of content area) that does not possess a reasonable mechanism for integrating new knowledge may be vulnerable to a similar form of emergent bias.

CONSIDERATIONS FOR MINIMIZING BIAS IN COMPUTER SYSTEM DESIGN

As our framework helps delineate the problems of bias in computer systems, so does it offer ways to remedy them. But, before saying more along these lines, it is important to address two potential concerns that the reader may have about the framework itself.

First, as we have noted earlier, computer systems sometimes help implement social policies on which reasonable people can disagree regarding whether the policies are fair or unfair. Does the NRMP, for example, embody a bias against rural hospitals? Other examples might include affirmative-action hiring programs, tax laws, and some federal funding programs. According to our framework, would computer systems that help implement such discriminative policies embody bias? The answer follows the initial (controversial) question – namely, "Is the policy under consideration fair or unfair?" Does affirmative action, for example, help redress past unfairness or not? The answer to most of these questions is beyond the scope of this article. But we do say that if unfairness can be established in the system's systematic discrimination, then the charge of bias follows.

Second, although we have talked about bias in computer systems, the presence of bias is not so much a feature inherent in the system independent of the context of use, but an aspect of a system in use. This distinction can be seen clearly in an example of emergent bias. Consider the case of an intelligent tutoring system on AIDS whose intended users are to be college students. Here, a high degree of literacy can be assumed without incurring bias. In contrast, the same level of literacy cannot be assumed without introducing bias in designing a system to provide AIDS education in a public space such as a shopping mall or metro station. For in such public spaces less educated people would be at an unfair disadvantage in using the system. Or consider again the case of technical bias with the MLSA (which favors users with short jobs over long jobs). While technical bias is embedded in the program, the bias is a phenomenon of the system in use, in a context wherein users with short and long jobs outpace the system's capacity.

Remedying bias from a practical perspective involves at least two types of activities. First, we need to be able to identify or "diagnose" bias in any given system. Second, we need to develop methods of avoiding bias in systems and correcting it when it is identified. We offer below some initial directions this work could take.

Toward minimizing preexisting bias, designers must not only scrutinize the design specifications, but must couple this scrutiny with a good understanding of relevant biases out in the world. The time to begin thinking about bias is in the earliest stages of the design process, when negotiating the system's specifications with the client. Common biases might occur to populations based on cultural identity, class, gender, literacy (literate/less literate), handedness (right-handed/left-handed), and physical disabilities (e.g., being blind, colorblind, or deaf). As the computing community develops an understanding of these biases, we can correspondingly develop techniques to avoid or minimize them. Some current computer systems, for instance, address the problem of handedness by allowing the user to toggle between a right- or left-handed configuration for user input and screen display. Similarly, systems could minimize bias due to colorblindness by encoding information not only in hue, but in its intensity, or in some other way encoding the same information in a format un-related to color. In addition, it can prove useful to identify potential user popu-lations which might otherwise be overlooked and include representative indi-viduals in the field test groups. Rapid prototyping, formative evaluation, and field testing with such well-conceived populations of users can be an effective means to detect unintentional biases throughout the design process.

Technical bias also places the demand on a designer to look beyond the fea-tures internal to a system and envision it in a context of use. Toward prevent-ing technical bias, a designer must envision the design, the algorithms, and the interfaces in use so that technical decisions do not run at odds with moral val-ues. Consider even the largely straightforward problem of whether to display a list with random entries or sorted alphabetically. In determining a solution, a designer might need to weigh considerations of ease of access enhanced by a sorted list against equity of access supported by a random list.

Minimizing emergent bias asks designers to envision not only a system's in-tended situations of use, but to account for increasingly diverse social contexts of use. From a practical standpoint, however, such a proposal cannot be pur-sued in an unbounded manner. Thus, how much diversity in social context is enough, and what sort of diversity? While the question merits a lengthy dis-cussion, we offer here but three suggestions. First, designers should reason-ably anticipate probable contexts of use and design for these. Second, where it is not possible to design for extended contexts of use, designers should at-tempt to articulate constraints on the appropriate contexts of a system's use. As with other media, we may need to develop conventions for communicating the perspectives and audience assumed in the design. Thus, if a particular ex-pert system because of its content matter, goals, and design requires expert us-ers to be used effectively, this constraint should be stated clearly in a salient place and manner, say, on one of the initial screens. Third, system designers and administrators can take responsible action if bias emerges with changes in context. The NRMP offers a good example. Although the original design of the Admissions Algorithm did not deal well with the changing social condi-tions (when significant numbers of dual-career couples participated in the match), those responsible for maintaining the system responded conscien-tiously to this societal change and modified the system's algorithm to place couples more fairly (Roth, 1990).

That said, even if a designer successfully detects bias in a proposed design, and has ideas on how to eradicate or minimize it, a client may be reluctant to remedy the bias for a variety of reasons. For example, airline executives whose companies serve national and international routes may knowingly support the bias in an automated reservation system that favors on-line flights. Situations such as these put designers in a difficult spot. What ought they to do if a client actually wants a bias to be present? Is it the designer's responsibility to speak out against a client, or is it simply to toe the line and produce a system, bias and all?

Readers who have followed discussions of professional ethics will be familiar with similar dilemmas. A quick answer is not possible, but one thing is clear. In order for designers to take an effective stand against a client regarding biased systems, it will be important for designers to find support for such action from their professional community. The criteria of reliability and safety offer a perspective on this point. Through extensive discussion and solid technical work, the computing community over the recent years has recognized that good systems must be judged on criteria that include reliability and safety. Such consensus provides individual system designers with substantial backing if and when they are required to make their cases to skeptical clients or employers. Something similar is needed for bias. The more the computing community explicitly recognizes bias as a feature of computer systems that is worth addressing and minimizing, the more individual designers will have clout in shaping the practice of computing in the work place and elsewhere.

While we advocate serious attention to bias in system design, we also recognize there are limits to what system designers can accomplish. Some biases extend beyond computing to larger societal problems. An empirical result from work by Huff and Cooper (1987) on gender bias in the design of educational software provides a helpful illustration. In their study, subjects were asked to propose designs for software to teach seventh graders the correct use of commas. One group of subjects was asked to design the software for seventh-grade boys, the second group to design for seventh-grade girls, and the third group to design for seventh-graders, gender unspecified. Huff and Cooper report that along a number of dimensions the designs proposed by subjects in the gender-unspecified group closely resembled the designs proposed by subjects who designed for boys and were significantly different from the designs proposed by subjects who designed for girls. This study illustrates how preexisting biases, in the form of expectations about what software will appeal to each gender, coupled with the implicit assumption that the generic "user" of software is likely to be male, can influence design and give rise to bias in software. Huff and Cooper report, furthermore, that many of their subjects were aware of and had expressed open concern about how computers were frequently perceived to be in the male domain. We thus infer that in this case the biased designs were unintended and, instead, reflected gender-biases deeply rooted in the culture at large. While creating nongender-biased educational software contributes to addressing the larger social problems tied to gender bias and computing, resolving problems like gender bias goes beyond system design. More broadly, where biases in the larger society flourish, bias-free system design forms but one part of a movement to a more equitable society.

CONCLUSION

Because biased computer systems are instruments of injustice – though admittedly, their degree of seriousness can vary considerably – we believe that freedom from bias should be counted among the select set of criteria according to which the quality of systems in use in society should be judged. The methods delineated here can be used to assess and minimize bias in the design of systems. Concern with bias in system design and experience with these methods can be integrated with other software engineering methods as part of the standard for a computer science curriculum.

As with other criteria for good computer systems, such as reliability, accuracy, and efficiency, freedom from bias should be held out as an ideal. As with these other criteria, this ideal might be difficult if not impossible to achieve. Nonetheless, in practice we must approach actively the task of minimizing bias in our designs. Furthermore, as a community we must hold our designs accountable to a reasonable degree of freedom from bias against which negligence can be judged.

REFERENCES

Berlins, M., and L. Hodges. 1981. Nationality Bill Sets Out Three New Citizenship Categories. *The London Times* (January 15) 1: 15.

Corbató, F.J., M. Merwin-Daggett, and R.C. Daley. 1962. An Experimental Time-sharing System. In *Proceedings of the Spring Joint Computer Conference*, 335–344. Spartan Books.

Fishlock, T. 1981. Delhi Press Detect Racism in Nationality Bill. *The London Times* (January 20).

Fotos, C.P. 1988. British Airways Assails U.S. Decision to Void CRS Agreement with American. *Aviation Week & Space Technology* (October 24): 78.

Graettinger, J.S., and E. Peranson. 1981a. The Matching Program. *New England Journal of Medicine* 304:1163–1165.

Graettinger, J.S., and E. Peranson. 1981b. National Resident Matching Program (Letter to the Editor). *The New England Journal of Medicine* 305:526.

Huff, C., and J. Cooper. 1987. Sex Bias in Educational Software: The Effect of Designers' Stereotypes on the Software They Design. *Journal of Applied Social Psychology* 17:519-532.

Johnson, D. G., and J. M. Mulvey. 1993. *Computer Decisions: Ethical Issues of Responsibility and Bias* (SOR-93-11). Statistics and Operations Research Series, Dept. of Civil Engineering and Operations Research, Princeton University, Princeton, NJ.

Leith, P. 1986. Fundamental Errors in Legal Logic Programming. *The Computer Journal* 29:225–232.

Moor, J. 1985. What is Computer Ethics? *Metaphilosophy* 16:266–275.

Ott, J. 1988. American Airlines Settles CRS Dispute with British Airways. *Aviation Week & Space Technology* (July 18).

Roth, A.E. 1984. The Evolution of the Labor Market for Medical Interns and Residents: A Case Study in Game Theory. *Journal of Political Economy* 92(6):991–1016.

Roth, A.E. 1990. New Physicians: A Natural Experiment in Market Organization. *Science* 250 (December 14):1524–1528.

Sergot, M.J., F. Sadri, R.A. Kowalski, F. Kriwaczek, P. Hammond, and H.T. Cory. 1986. The British Nationality Act as a Logic Program. *Communications of the ACM* 29: 370–386.

Shifrin, C.A. 1985. Justice Will Weigh Suit Challenging Airlines' Computer Reservations. *Aviation Week & Space Technology* (March 25):105–111.

Sudarshan, A., and S. Zisook. 1981. National Resident Matching Program (Letter to the editor). *New England Journal of Medicine* 305:525–526.

Taib, I.M. 1990. Loophole Allows Bias in Displays on Computer Reservations Systems. *Aviation Week & Space Technology* (February):137.

U.S. General Accounting Office. 1992. *Patriot Missile Defense: Software Problem Led to System Failure at Dhahran, Saudi Arabia* (GAO/IMTEC-92-26). Washington, D.C.

Williams, K.J., V.P. Werth, and J.A. Wolff. An Analysis of the Resident Match. *New England Journal of Medicine* 304(19):1165–1166.

2

Accountability in a Computerized Society
HELEN NISSENBAUM

Abstract: This essay warns of eroding accountability in computerized societies. It argues that assumptions about computing and features of situations in which computers are produced create barriers to accountability. Drawing on philosophical analyses of moral blame and responsibility, four barriers are identified: (1) the problem of many hands, (2) the problem of bugs, (3) blaming the computer, and (4) software ownership without liability. The paper concludes with ideas on how to reverse this trend.

> *If a builder has built a house for a man and has not made his work sound, and the house which he has built has fallen down and so caused the death of the householder, that builder shall be put to death.*
>
> *If it destroys property, he shall replace anything that it has destroyed; and, because he has not made sound the house which he has built and it has fallen down, he shall rebuild the house which has fallen down from his own property.*
>
> *If a builder has built a house for a man and does not make his work perfect and a wall bulges, that builder shall put that wall into sound condition at his own cost.*
>
> —*Laws of Hammu-rabi [229, 232, 233]*[1]*, circa 2027 B.C.*

Computing is an ongoing source of change in the way we conduct our lives. For the most part we judge these changes to be beneficial, but we also recognize that imperfections in the technology can, in significant measure, expose us to unexpected outcomes as well as to harms and risks. Because the use of computing technology is so widespread these impacts are worrisome not only because harms can be severe, but because they pervade and threaten almost every sphere of public and private life. Lives and well-being are increasingly

Several people have contributed generously to this work. Michael Davis, Deborah G. Johnson, Arthur Kuflik, Pamela Samuelson, Debra Satz, Richard De George, Larry May, and Dennis Thompson read drafts and made invaluable suggestions. Reviewers for *Science and Engineering Ethics* offered thorough and challenging commentary. An earlier version of this work was presented at The American Philosophical Association, Eastern Division Meeting, December 1993, where audience comments and questions led to clarification of several key issues.

[1]G.R. Driver and John C. Miles (Editors and Translators), *The Babylonian Laws,* Volume II, Clarendon Press, Oxford, 1955.

dependent on computerized life-critical systems that control aircraft (fly-by-wire), spacecraft, motor cars, military equipment, communications devices and more. Quality of life is also at stake in the enormous array of information systems, communications networks, bureaucratic infrastructures of governments, corporations, and high finance, as well as everyday conveniences such as personal computers, telephones, microwaves and toys that are controlled and supported by computers.

The extensive presence of computing in these many spheres of life suggests two related concerns. The one is a concern with achieving a suitable degree of reliability and safety for these systems so as to minimize risks and harms; the other is a concern with entrenching and maintaining in those sectors of society that produce and purvey computing technologies a robust culture of accountability, or answerability, for their impacts. The first of these two has, in recent years, achieved increasing recognition among prominent members of the computer community.[2] They question whether many of the systems in use are sufficiently sound for the uses to which they are put. Citing cases of failure and poor programming practices, they appeal to the computer community,[3] corporate producers, and government regulators, to pay more heed to system safety and reliability in order to reduce harms and risks (Borning, 1987; Leveson, 1986; Leveson & Turner, 1993; Littlewood & Strigini, 1992; Neumann; Parnas, Schouwen, & Kwan, 1990) arguing that lives, well-being, and quality-of-life, are vulnerable to poor system design and the all too likely occurrence of failure.

But it is upon the second of these concerns, the concern for accountability, that this paper will focus. In the same way that experts within the computer community have exposed the critical need to improve standards of reliability for computer systems, this paper urges attention to the neglected status of accountability for the impacts of computing, specifically for the harms and risks of faulty and malfunctioning systems. Thus, while our vulnerability to system failure and risk argues for greater attention to system safety, reliability, and sound design, and calls for the development of technical strategies to achieve them, it also underscores the need for a robust tradition of *accountability* for failures, risks, and harm that do occur. A culture of accountability is particu-

---

[2]For example, Joseph Weizenbaum, and more recently Nancy Leveson, Peter Neumann, David Parnas, and others.

[3]The community of people who dedicate a significant proportion of their time and energy to building computer and computerized systems, and to those engaged in the science, engineering, design, and documentation of computing.

larly important for a technology still struggling with standards of reliability because it means that even in cases where things go awry, we are assured of answerability. However, just the opposite is occurring. This paper argues that conditions under which computer systems are commonly developed and deployed, coupled with popular conceptions about the nature, capacities, and limitations of computing, contribute in significant measure to an *obscuring* of lines of accountability. Unless we address these conditions and conceptions, we will see a disturbing correlation – increased computerization, on the one hand, with a decline in accountability, on the other.

A strong culture of accountability is worth pursuing for a number of reasons. For some, a developed sense of responsibility is a good in its own right, a virtue to be encouraged. Our social policies should reflect this value appropriately by expecting people to be accountable for their actions. For others, accountability is valued because of its consequences for social welfare. Firstly, holding people accountable for the harms or risks they bring about provides strong motivation for trying to prevent or minimize them. Accountability can therefore be a powerful tool for motivating better practices, and consequently more reliable and trustworthy systems. A general culture of accountability should encourage answerability not only for the life-critical systems that cause or risk grave injuries, damage infrastructure, and cause large monetary losses, but even for the malfunctions that cause individual losses of time, convenience, and contentment. Secondly, maintaining clear lines of accountability means that in the event of harm through failure, we have a reasonable starting point for assigning just punishment as well as, where necessary, compensation for victims.

For the remainder of the paper I explain more fully the conditions in which computer systems are commonly produced and describe common assumptions about the capabilities and limitations of computing, showing how both contribute toward an erosion and obscuring of accountability. Four of these, which I henceforth call "the four barriers to accountability," will be the focus of most of the discussion. In identifying the barriers I hope at the same time to convince readers that as long as we fail to recognize and do something about these barriers to accountability, assigning responsibility for the impacts of computing will continue to be problematic in the many spheres of life that fall under its control. And unless we pursue means for reversing this erosion of accountability, there will be significant numbers of harms and risks for which no one is answerable and about which nothing is done. This will mean that computers may be "out of control"[4] in an important and disturbing way. I conclude the paper with brief remarks on how we might overcome the barriers and restore accountability.

ACCOUNTABILITY, BLAME, RESPONSIBILITY — CONCEPTUAL FRAMEWORK

The central thesis of this paper, that increasing computerization may come at the cost of accountability, rests on an intuitive understanding of accountability closely akin to "answerability." The following story captures its core in a setting that, I predict, will have a ring of familiarity to most readers.

> Imagine a teacher standing before her sixth-grade class demanding to know who shot a spit-ball in her ear. She threatens punishment for the whole class if someone does not step forward. Fidgety students avoid her stern gaze, as a boy in the back row slowly raises his hand.

This raising of his hand wherein the boy answers for his action signifies accountability. From the story alone, we do not know whether he shot at the teacher intentionally or merely missed his true target, whether he acted alone or under goading from classmates, or even whether the spit-ball was in protest for an unreasonable action taken by the teacher. While these factors may be relevant to determining a just response to the boy's action, we can say that the boy, in responding to the teacher's demand for an answer to who shot the spit-ball, has taken an important first step toward fulfilling the valuable social obligation of accountability. In this story, the boy in the back row has answered for, been accountable for, his action; in real life there can be conditions that obscure accountability.

For a deeper understanding of the barriers to accountability in a computerized society and the conditions that foster them, it is necessary to move beyond an intuitive grasp and to draw on ideas from philosophical and legal inquiry into moral responsibility and the cluster of interrelated concepts of liability, blame and accountability. Over the many years that these concepts have been discussed and analyzed, both by those whose interest is theoretical in nature and those whose interest is more practical (Hammu-rabi's four-thousand year old legal code is an early example), many analyses have been put forth, and many shadings of meaning have been discovered and described.

---

[4]Thanks to Deborah Johnson for suggesting this phrase.

Emerging from this tradition, contemporary work by Joel Feinberg on moral blame provides a framework for this paper's inquiry (Feinberg, 1985). Feinberg proposes a set of conditions under which an individual is morally blameworthy for a given harm.[5] Fault and causation are key conditions. Accordingly, a person is morally blameworthy for a harm if: (1) his or her actions caused the harm, or constituted a significant causal factor in bringing about the harm; and (2) his or her actions were "faulty."[6] Feinberg develops the idea of faulty actions to cover actions that are guided by faulty decisions or intentions. This includes actions performed with an intention to hurt someone and actions for which someone fails to reckon adequately with harmful consequences. Included in the second group are reckless and negligent actions. We judge an action reckless if a person engages in it even though he foresees harm as its likely consequence but does nothing to prevent it; we judge it negligent, if he carelessly does not consider probable harmful consequences.

Applying Feinberg's framework to some examples, consider the case of a person who has intentionally installed a virus on someone's computer which causes extensive damage to files. This person is blameworthy because her intentional actions were causally responsible for the damage. In another case, one that actually occurred, Robert Morris, then a graduate student in computer science at Cornell University, whose Internet Worm caused major upheaval on the internet and infiltrated thousands of connected computers, was held blameworthy, even though the extensive damage was the consequence of a bug in his code and not directly intended. Critics judged him reckless because they contended that someone with Morris's degree of expertise ought to have foreseen this possibility.[7]

Although moral blame is not identical to accountability, an important correspondence between the two makes the analysis of the former relevant to the study of the latter. An important set of cases in which one may reasonably expect accountability for a harm is that in which an analysis points to an individual (or group of individuals) who are morally blameworthy for it.[8] In these

---

[5]Of course there are many situations in which harm and injury occur but are no one's fault; that is, no one is to blame for them.

[6]Feinberg's analysis is more complex, involving several additional conditions and refinements. Since these are not directly relevant to our discussion, for the sake of simplicity I have omitted them here.

[7]Readers interested in this case may refer to Denning, P. (1990) *Computers Under Attack.* New York: ACM Press.

[8]The overlap, though significant, is only partial. Take for example, circumstances in which a per-

cases at least, moral blameworthiness provides a reasonable standard for answerability and, accordingly, Feinberg's conditions can be used to identify cases in which one would reasonably expect, or judge, that there ought to be accountability. The four barriers, explained in the sections below, are systematic features of situations in which we would reasonably expect accountability but for which accountability is obscured. For many situations of these types (though not all) the simplified version of Feinberg's analysis has helped bring into focus the source of breakdown.

THE PROBLEM OF MANY HANDS[9]

Most computer systems in use today are the products not of single programmers working in isolation but of groups or organizations, typically corporations. These groups, which frequently bring together teams of individuals with a diverse range of skills and varying degrees of expertise, might include designers, engineers, programmers, writers, psychologists, graphic artists, managers, and salespeople. Consequently, when a system malfunctions and gives rise to harm, the task of assigning responsibility – the problem of identifying who is accountable – is exacerbated and obscured. Responsibility, characteristically understood and traditionally analyzed in terms of a single individual, does not easily generalize to collective action. In other words, while the simplest quest for accountability would direct us in search of "the one" who must step forward (for example, the boy in the back row answering for the spit-ball), collective action presents a challenge. The analysis of blame, in terms of cause and fault, can help to clarify how in cases of collective action accountability can be lost, or at least, obscured.

Where a mishap is the work of "many hands," it may not be obvious who is to blame because frequently its most salient and immediate causal antecedents do not converge with its locus of decision making. The conditions for blame, therefore, are not clearly satisfied in a way normally satisfied when a single individual is held blameworthy for a harm. Indeed, some cynics argue that institutional structures are designed in this way precisely to avoid ac-

---

son – frequently an office-holder – is by convention, or by prior agreement, held answerable. In such cases one would expect accountability even though blame is not appropriate.

[9]This phrase was first coined by Dennis Thompson in his book-chapter "The Moral Responsibility of Many Hands" (Thompson, 1987) which discusses the moral responsibilities of political office holders and public officials working within large government bureaucracies.

countability. Furthermore, with the collective actions characteristic of corporate and government hierarchies, decisions and causes themselves are fractured. Team action, the endeavor of many individuals working together, creates a product which in turn causally interacts with the life and well-being of an end user. Boards of directors, task forces, or committees issue joint decisions, and on the occasions where these decisions are not universally approved by all their members but are the result of majority vote, we are left with the further puzzle of how to attribute responsibility. When high-level decisions work their way down from boards of directors to managers, from mangers to employees, ultimately translating into actions and consequences, the lines that bind a problem to its source may be convoluted and faint. And as a consequence the connection between an outcome and the one who is accountable for it is obscured. This obscuring of accountability can come about in different ways. In some cases, it may be the result of intentional planning, a conscious means applied by the leaders of an organization to avoid responsibility for negative outcomes, or it may be an unintended consequence of a hierarchical management in which individuals with the greatest decision-making powers are only distantly related to the causal outcome of their decisions. Whatever the reason, the upshot is that victims and those who represent them, are left without knowing at whom to point a finger. It may not be clear even to the members of the collective itself who is accountable. The problem of many hands is not unique to computing but plagues other technologies, big business, government, and the military (De George, 1991; Feinberg, 1970; Ladd, 1989; Thompson, 1987; Velasquez, 1991).

Computing is particularly vulnerable to the obstacles of many hands. First, as noted earlier, most software systems in use are produced in institutional settings, including small and middle-sized software development companies, large corporations, government agencies and contractors, and educational institutions. Second, computer systems themselves, usually not monolithic, are constructed out of segments or modules. Each module itself may be the work of a team of individuals. Some systems may also include code from earlier versions, while others borrow code from different systems entirely, even some that were created by other producers. When systems grow in this way, sometimes reaching huge and complex proportions, there may be no single individual who grasps the whole system or keeps track of all the individuals who have contributed to its various components (Johnson & Mulvey, 1993; Weizenbaum, 1972). Third, many systems being developed and already in use operate on top of other systems (such as intermediate level and special function programs and operating systems). Not only may these systems be unreliable, but there may merely be unforeseen incompatibilities between them.[10] Fourth, performance in a wide array of mundane and specialized computer-controlled machines – from rocket ships to refrigerators – depends on the symbiotic relationship of machine with computer system. When things go wrong, as shown below, it may be unclear whether the fault lies with the machine or with the computer system.

The case of the Therac-25, a computer-controlled radiation treatment machine, that massively overdosed patients in six known incidents[11] provides a striking example of the way many hands can obscure accountability. In the two-year period from 1985 to 1987, overdoses administered by the Therac-25 caused severe radiation burns, which in turn, caused death in three cases and irreversible injuries (one minor, two very serious) in the other three. Built by Atomic Energy of Canada Limited (AECL), Therac-25 was the further development in a line of medical linear accelerators which destroy cancerous tumors by irradiating them with accelerated electrons and X-ray photons. Computer controls were far more prominent in the Therac-25 both because the machine had been designed from the ground up with computer controls in mind and also because the safety of the system as a whole was largely left to software. Whereas earlier models included hardware safety mechanisms and interlocks, designers of the Therac-25 did not duplicate software safety mechanisms with hardware equivalents.

After many months of study and trial-and-error testing, the origin of the malfunction was traced not to a single source, but to numerous faults, which included at least two significant software coding errors ("bugs") and a faulty microswitch.[12] The impact of these faults was exacerbated by the absence of hardware interlocks, obscure error messages, inadequate testing and quality assurance, exaggerated claims about the reliability of the system in AECL's safety analysis, and in at least two cases, negligence on the parts of the hospitals where treatment was administered. Aside from the important lessons in safety engineering that the Therac-25 case provides, it offers a lesson in accountability – or rather, the breakdown of accountability due to "many hands."

---

[10]Most users of personal computers will have experienced occasions when their computers freeze. Neither the manufacturer of the operating system nor of the applications assume responsibility for this, preferring to blame the problem on "incompatibilities."

[11]The primary sources for my discussion are Leveson and Turner's excellent and detailed account (1993) and an earlier paper by Jacky (1989).

[12]Much credit is due to Fritz Hager, the hospital physicist in Tyler, Texas, who took upon himself the task of uncovering the problem and helped uncover software flaws.

In cases like Therac-25, instead of identifying a single individual whose faulty actions caused the injuries, we find we must systematically unravel a messy web of interrelated causes and decisions. Even when we may safely rule out intentional wrongdoing it is not easy to pinpoint causal agents who were, at the same time, negligent or reckless. As a result, we might be forced to conclude that the mishaps were merely accidental in the sense that no one can reasonably be held responsible, or to blame, for them. While a full understanding of the Therac-25 case would demand a more thorough study of the details than I can manage here, the sketch that follows is intended to show that though the conditions of many hands might indeed obscure accountability, they do not imply that answerability can be foregone.

Consider the many whose actions constituted causal antecedents of the Therac-25 injuries and in some cases contributed significantly to the existence and character of the machine. From AECL, we have designers, software and safety engineers, programmers, machinists, and corporate executives; from the clinics, we have administrators, physicians, physicists, and machine technicians. Take for example, those most proximately connected to the harm, the machine technicians who activated the Therac-25 by entering doses and pushing buttons. In one of the most chilling anecdotes associated with the Therac-25 incident, a machine technician is supposed to have responded to the agonized cries of a patient by flatly denying that it was possible that he had been burned. Should the blame be laid at her feet?

Except for specific incidents like the one involving the technician who denied a patient's screams of agony, accountability for the Therac-25 does not rest with the machine technicians because by and large they were not at fault in any way relevant to the harms and because the control they exercised over the machine's function was restricted to a highly limited spectrum of possibilities. By contrast, according to Leveson and Turner's discussion, there is clear evidence of inadequate software engineering, testing and risk assessment. For example, the safety analysis was faulty in that it systematically overestimated the system's reliability and evidently did not consider the role software failure could play in derailing the system as a whole. Moreover, computer code from earlier Therac models, used in the Therac-25 system, was assumed unproblematic because no similar malfunction had surfaced in these models. However, further investigation showed that while the problem *had* been present in those systems, it had simply not surfaced because earlier models had included mechanical interlocks which would override software commands leading to fatal levels of radiation. The Therac-25 did not include these mechanical interlocks.

There is also evidence of a failure in the extent of corporate response to the signs of a serious problem. Early response to reports of problems were particularly lackluster. AECL was slow to react to requests to check the machine, understand the problem, or to remediate (for example by installing an independent hardware safety system). Even after a patient filed a lawsuit in 1985 citing hospital, manufacturer, and service organization as responsible for her injuries, AECL's follow up was negligible. For example, no special effort was made to inform other clinics operating Therac-25 machines about the mishaps. Because the lawsuit was settled out of court, we do not learn how the law would have attributed liability.

Even Leveson and Turner, whose detailed analysis of the Therac-25 mishaps sheds light on both the technical as well as the procedural aspects of the case, hold back on the question of accountability. They refer to the malfunctions and injuries as "accidents" and remark that they do not wish "to criticize the manufacturer of the equipment or anyone else" (Leveson & Turner, 1993). I mention this not as a strong critique of their work, because after all their central concern is unraveling the technical and design flaws in the Therac-25, but to raise the following point. Although a complex network of causes and decisions, typical of situations in which many hands operate, may obscure accountability, we ought not conclude therefore that the harms were mere accidents. I have suggested that a number of individuals ought to have been answerable (though not in equal measure), from the machine operator who denied the possibility of burning to the software engineers to quality assurance personnel and to corporate executives. Determining their degree of responsibility would require that we investigate more fully their *degree* of causal responsibility, control, and fault. By preferring to view the incidents as accidents,[13] however, we may effectively be accepting them as agentless mishaps, yielding to the smoke-screen of collective action and to a further erosion of accountability.

The general lesson to be drawn from the case of the Therac-25 is that many hands obscured accountability by diminishing in key individuals a sense of responsibility for the mishaps. By contrast, a suitably placed individual (or several) ought to have stepped forward and assumed responsibility for the malfunction and harms. Instead, for two years, the problem bounced back and forth between clinics, manufacturer and various government oversight agen-

---

[13]Michael Davis, in commenting on this paper, points out that in certain contexts, for example automobile accidents, our manner of speaking allows for "accidents" for which we may yet blame someone.

cies before concrete and decisive steps were taken. In collective action of this type, the plurality of causal antecedents and decision makers helps to define a typical set of excuses for those low down in the hierarchy who are "only following orders," as well as for those of higher rank who are more distantly related to the outcomes. However, we should not mistakenly conclude from the observation that accountability is *obscured* due to collective action that no one is, or ought to have been, accountable. The worry that this paper addresses is that if computer technology is increasingly produced by "many hands," and if, as seems to be endemic to many hands situations, we lose touch with who is accountable (such as occurred with the Therac-25), then we are apt to discover a disconcerting array of computers in use for which no one is answerable.

BUGS

The source of a second barrier to accountability in computing is omnipresent bugs and the way many in the field routinely have come to view them. To say that bugs in software make software unreliable and cause systems to fail is to state the obvious. However, not quite as obvious is how the way we *think* about bugs affects considerations of accountability. (I use the term "bug" to cover a variety of types of software errors including modeling, design and coding errors.) The inevitability of bugs escapes very few computer users and programmers and their pervasiveness is stressed by most software, and especially safety, engineers. The dictum, "There is always another software bug," (Leveson & Turner, 1993) especially in the long and complex systems controlling life-critical and quality-of-life-critical technologies, captures the way in which many individuals in the business of designing, building and analyzing computer systems perceive this fact of programming life. Errors in complex functional computer systems are an inevitable presence in ambitious systems (Corbató, 1991). David Parnas has made a convincing case that "errors are more common, more pervasive, and more troublesome, in software than in other technologies," and that even skilled program reviewers are apt to miss flaws in programs (Parnas et al., 1990).[14] Even when we factor out sheer incompetence, bugs in significant number are endemic to programming. They are the natural hazards of any substantial system.

---

[14]See also Smith (1985) for an explanation of why software is particularly prone to errors.

Although this way of thinking about bugs is helpful because it underscores the vulnerability of complex systems, it also creates a problematic mind-set for accountability. On the one hand, the standard conception of responsibility directs us to the person who either intentionally or by not taking reasonable care causes harm. On the other, the view of bugs as inevitable hazards of programming implies that while harms and inconveniences caused by bugs are regrettable, they cannot – except in cases of obvious sloppiness – be helped. In turn, this suggests that it is unreasonable to hold programmers, systems engineers, and designers, to blame for imperfections in their systems.

Parallels from other areas of technology can perhaps clarify the contrast that I am trying to draw between cases of failures for which one holds someone accountable, and frequently blameworthy, and cases where – despite the failures – one tends to hold no one accountable. As an example of the former, consider the case of the space-shuttle *Challenger*. Following an inquiry into the *Challenger's* explosion, critics found fault with NASA and Morton-Thiokol because several engineers, aware of the limitations of the O-Rings, had conveyed to management the strong possibility of failure under cold-weather-launch conditions. We hold NASA executives accountable, and judge their actions reckless, because despite this knowledge and the presence of cold-weather conditions, they went ahead with the space-shuttle launch.

In contrast, consider an experience that was common during construction of several of the great suspension bridges of the late 19th century, such as the St. Louis and Brooklyn Bridges. During construction, hundreds of bridge workers succumbed to a mysterious disease then referred to as "the bends," or "caisson disease."[15] Although the working conditions and inadequate response from medical staff were responsible for the disease, we cannot assign blame for the harms suffered by the workers or find any individual or distinct group, such as the bridge companies, their chief engineers, or even their medical staff, accountable because causes and treatments of the disease were beyond the scope of medical science of the day.

For the great suspension bridges, it was necessary to sink caissons deep underground in order to set firm foundations – preferably in bedrock – for their enormous towers. Upon emerging from the caissons, workers would erratically develop an array of symptoms which might include dizziness, double vision, severe pain in torso and limbs, profuse perspiration, internal bleeding, convulsions, repeated vomiting and swollen and painful joints. For some, the

---

[15]This case is drawn from David McCullough's book about the building of the Brooklyn Bridge (McCullough, 1972).

symptoms would pass after a matter of hours or days, while for others symptoms persisted and they were left permanently paraplegic. Others died. While bridge doctors understood that these symptoms were related to workers' exposure to highly pressured air, they could not accurately pinpoint what caused "the bends." They offered a variety of explanations, including newness to the job, poor nutrition, and overindulgence in alcohol. They tried assigning caisson work only to those they judged to be in "prime" physical shape, reducing the time spent in the caissons, and even outfitting workers with bands of zinc and silver about their wrists, arms, and ankles. All to no avail.

We have since learned that "decompression sickness" is a condition brought on by moving too rapidly from an atmosphere of compressed air to normal atmospheric conditions. It is easily prevented by greatly slowing the rate of decompression. Ironically, a steam elevator that had been installed in both the Brooklyn Bridge and St. Louis Bridge caissons, as a means of alleviating discomfort for bridge workers so they would not have to make the long and arduous climb up a spiral staircase, made things all the more dangerous. Nowadays, for a project the scope of the Brooklyn Bridge, a decompression chamber would be provided as a means of controlling the rate of decompression. Bridge companies not following the recommended procedures would certainly be held blameworthy for harms and risks.

What is the relation of these two examples to the way we conceive of bugs? When we conceive of bugs as an inevitable byproduct of programming we are likely to judge bug-related failures in the way we judged early handling of the bends: inevitable, albeit unfortunate, consequence of a glorious new technology for which we hold no one accountable. The problem with this conception of bugs, is that it is a barrier to identifying cases of bug-related failure that more closely parallel the case of the *Challenger*. In these types of cases we see wrongdoing and expect someone to "step forward" and be answerable. The bends case shows, too, that our standard of judgment need not remain fixed. As knowledge and understanding grows, so the standard changes. Today, bridge building companies are accountable for preventing cases of decompression sickness. An explicitly more discerning approach to bugs that indicates a range of acceptable error would better enable discrimination of the "natural hazards," the ones that are present despite great efforts and adherence to the highest standards of contemporary practice, from those that with effort and good practice, could have been avoided.

Finally, if experts in the field deny that such a distinction can be drawn, in view of the inevitability of bugs and their potential hazard, it is reasonable to think that the field of computing is not yet ready for the various uses to which it is being put.

THE COMPUTER AS SCAPEGOAT

Most of us can recall a time when someone (perhaps ourselves) offered the excuse that it was the computer's fault – the bank clerk explaining an error, the ticket agent excusing lost bookings, the student justifying a late paper. Although the practice of blaming a computer, on the face of it, appears reasonable and even felicitous, it is a barrier to accountability because, having found one explanation for an error or injury, the further role and responsibility of human agents tend to be underestimated – even sometimes ignored. As a result, no one is called upon to answer for an error or injury.

Consider why blaming a computer *appears* plausible by applying Feinberg's analysis of blame. First, the causal condition: Computer systems frequently mediate the interactions between machines and humans, and between one human and another. This means that human actions are distanced from their causal impacts (which in some cases could be harms and injuries) and, at the same time, that the computer's action is a more direct causal antecedent. In such cases the computer satisfies the first condition for blameworthiness. Of course, causal proximity is not a sufficient condition. We do not, for example, excuse a murderer on grounds that it was the bullet entering a victim's head, and not he, who was directly responsible for the victim's death. The fault condition must be satisfied too.

Here, computers present a curious challenge and temptation. As distinct from many other inanimate objects, computers perform tasks previously performed by humans in positions of responsibility. They calculate, decide, control, and remember. For this reason, and perhaps even more deeply rooted psychological reasons (Turkle, 1984), people attribute to computers and not to other inanimate objects (like bullets) the array of mental properties, such as intentions, desires, thoughts, preferences, that lead us to judge human action faulty and make humans responsible for their actions.[16] Were a loan adviser to approve a loan to an applicant who subsequently defaulted on the loan, or a

---

[16]Apparently this phenomenon is firmly rooted. In a study by Friedman and Millett, interviews with male undergraduate computer science majors found that a majority attributed aspects of agency to computers and significant numbers held computers morally responsible for errors (Friedman & Millett, 1997).

doctor to prescribe the wrong antibiotic for a patient who died, or an intensive care attendant incorrectly to assess the prognosis for an accident victim and deny the patient a respirator, we would hold accountable the loan adviser, the doctor, and the attendant. When these human agents are replaced with computerized counterparts (the computerized loan adviser, and expert systems MYCIN, that suggests the appropriate antibiotics for a given conditions, and APACHE, a system that predicts a patient's chance of survival [Fitzgerald, 1992]), it may seem reasonable to hold the systems answerable for harms. That is, there is a *prima facie* case in favor of associating blame with the *functions* even though they are now performed by computer systems and not humans.

Not all cases in which people blame computers rest on this tendency to attribute to computers the special characteristics that mark humans as responsible agents. In at least some cases, by blaming a computer, a person is simply shirking responsibility. In others, typically cases of collective action, a person cites a computer because she is genuinely baffled about who *is* responsible. When an airline reservation system malfunctions, for example, lines of accountability are so obscure that to the ticket agent the computer indeed is the most salient causal antecedent of the problem. Here, the computer serves as a stopgap for something elusive, the one who is, or should be, accountable. Finally, there are the perplexing cases, discussed earlier, where computers perform functions previously performed by humans in positions of responsibility leading to the illusion of computers as moral agents capable of assuming responsibility. (For interesting discussions of the viability of holding computers morally responsible for harms see Ladd, 1989 and Snapper, 1985.) In the case of an expert system, working out new lines of accountability may point to designers of the system, the human experts who served as sources, or the organization that chooses to put the system to use.[17] Unless alternate lines of accountability are worked out, accountability for these important functions will be lost.

OWNERSHIP WITHOUT LIABILITY

The issue of property rights over computer software has sparked active and

---

[17]B. Friedman and P. Kahn in this volume argue that systems designers play an important role in preventing the illusion of the computer as a moral agent. They argue that certain prevalent design features, such as anthropomorphizing a system, delegating decision making to it, and delegating instruction to it diminish a user's sense of agency and responsibility (Friedman & Kahn, 1997).

vociferous public debate. Should program code, algorithms, user-interface ("look-and-feel"), or any other aspects of software be privately ownable? If yes, what is the appropriate form and degree of ownership – trade secrets, patents, copyright, or a new *(sui generis)* form of ownership devised specifically for software? Should software be held in private ownership at all? Some have clamored for software patents, arguing that protecting a strong right of ownership in software, permitting owners and authors to "reap rewards," is the most just course. Others urge social policies that would place software in the public domain, while still others have sought explicitly to balance owners' rights with broader and longer-term social interests and the advancement of computer science (Nissenbaum, 1995; Stallman, 1987). Significantly, and disappointingly, absent in these debates is any reference to owners' responsibilities.[18]

While ownership implies a bundle of rights, it also implies responsibilities. In other domains, it is recognized that along with the privileges and profits of ownership comes responsibility. If a tree branch on private property falls and injures a person under it, if a pet Doberman escapes and bites a passerby, the owners are accountable. Holding owners responsible makes sense from a perspective of social welfare because owners are typically in the best position to control their property directly. Likewise in the case of software, its owners (usually the producers) are in the best position to affect the quality of the software they release to the public. Yet the trend in the software industry is to demand maximal property protection while denying, to the extent possible, accountability. This trend creates a vacuum in accountability as compared with other contexts in which a comparable vacuum would be filled by property owners.

This denial of accountability can be seen, for example, in the written license agreements that accompany almost all mass-produced consumer software which usually includes one section detailing the producers' rights, and another negating accountability. According to most versions of the license agreement, the consumer merely licenses a copy of the software application and is subject to various limitations on use and access, while the producer retains ownership over the program itself as well as the copies on floppy-disk. The disclaimers of liability are equally explicit. Consider, for example, phrases taken from the *Macintosh Reference Manual* (1990): "Apple makes no warranty or representation, either expressed or implied with respect to software, its quali-

---

[18]For an exception see Samuelson's recent discussion of liability for defective information (Samuelson, 1993).

ty, performance, merchantability, or fitness for a particular purpose. As a result, this software is sold 'as is,' and you, the purchaser are assuming the entire
risk as to its quality and performance." The Apple disclaimer goes on to say,
"In no event will Apple be liable for direct, indirect, special, incidental, or con-
sequential damages resulting from any defect in the software or its documentation, even if advised of the possibility of such damages." The Apple disclaimer is by no means unique to Apple, but in some form or another accompanies
virtually all consumer software.

The result is that software is released in society, for which users bear the
risks, while those who are in the best position to take responsibility for potential harms and risks appear unwilling to do so. Although several decades ago
software developers might reasonably have argued that their industry was not
sufficiently well developed to be able to absorb the potentially high cost of the
risks of malfunction, the evidence of present conditions suggests that a reevaluation is well warranted. The industry has matured, is well entrenched,
reaches virtually all sectors of the economy, and quite clearly offers the possibility of stable and sizable profit. It is therefore appropriate that the industry
be urged to acknowledge accountability for the burden of its impacts.

RESTORING ACCOUNTABILITY

The systematic erosion of accountability is neither a necessary nor inevitable
consequence of computerization; rather it is a consequence of co-existing factors discussed above: many hands, bugs, computers-as-scapegoat, and ownership without liability, which act together to obscure accountability.[19] Barriers
to accountability are not unique to computing. Many hands create barriers to
responsible action in a wide range of settings, including technologies other
than computing; failures can beset other technologies even if not to the degree,
and in quite the same way, as bugs in computer systems. The question of who
should bear the risks of production – owners or users – is not unique to computing. Among the four, citing the computer as scapegoat may be one that is
more characteristic of computing than of other technologies. The coincidence
of the four barriers, perhaps unique to computing, makes accountability in a
computerized society a problem of significant proportion. I conclude with the
suggestion of three possible strategies for restoring accountability.

---

[19]Here and elsewhere I should not be understood as suggesting that the four barriers give a complete explanation of failures in accountability.

An Explicit Standard of Care

A growing literature discusses guidelines for safer and more reliable computer systems (for example, Leveson, 1986 and Parnas et al., 1990). Among these guidelines is a call for simpler design, a modular approach to system building, meaningful quality assurance, independent auditing, built-in redundancy, and excellent documentation. Some authors argue that better and safer systems would result if these guidelines were expressed as an explicit standard of care taken seriously by the computing profession, promulgated through educational institutions, urged by professional organizations, and even enforced through licensing or accreditation.[20] Naturally, this would not be a fixed standard but one that evolved along with the field. What interests me here, however, is another potential payoff of an explicit standard of care; namely, a nonarbitrary means of determining accountability. A standard of care offers a way to distinguish between malfunctions (bugs) that are the result of inadequate practices, and the failures that occur in spite of a programmer's or designer's best efforts, for distinguishing analogs of the failure to alleviate the bends in 19th-century bridge workers, from analogs of the *Challenger* space-shuttle. Had the guidelines discussed by Leveson and Turner (1993), for example, been accepted as a standard of care at the time the Therac-25 was created, we would have had the means to establish that corporate developers of the system were accountable for the injuries. As measured against these guidelines they were negligent and blameworthy.

By providing an explicit measure of excellence that functions independently of pressures imposed by an organizational hierarchy within which some computer systems engineers in corporations and other large organizations are employed, a standard of care could also function to back up professional judgment. It serves to bolster an engineer's concern for safety where this concern conflicts with, for example, institutional frugality. A standard of care may also be a useful vehicle for assessing the integrity of the field of computing more broadly. In a point raised earlier, I suggested that it is important to have a good sense of whether or when the "best efforts" as recognized by a field – especially one as widely applied as computing – are good enough for the many uses to which they are put.

Distinguishing Accountability from Liability

For many situations in which issues of responsibility arise, accountability and

---

[20]The issue of licensing software producers remains controversial.

liability are strongly linked. In spite of their frequent connection, however, their conceptual underpinnings are sufficiently distinct so as to make a difference in a number of important contexts. One key difference is that appraisals of liability are grounded in the plight of a victim, whereas appraisals of accountability are grounded in the relationship of an agent to an outcome.[21] The starting point for assessing liability is the victim's condition; liability is assessed backward from there. The extent of liability, frequently calculated in terms of sums of money, is determined by the degree of injury and damage sustained by any victims. The starting point for assessing accountability is the nature of an action and the relationship of the agent (or several agents) to the action's outcome. (In many instances, accountability is mediated through conditions of blameworthiness, where the so-called "causal" and "fault" conditions would be fulfilled.) Although those people who are accountable for a harm are very frequently the same as those who are liable, merging the notions of liability with accountability, or accepting the former as a substitute for the latter, can obscure accountability in many of the contexts targeted in earlier sections of this paper. Consider, for example, the problem of many hands and how it is affected by this.

The problem of many hands is profound and seems unlikely to yield easily to a general, or slick, solution. For the present, a careful case-by-case analysis of a given situation in order to identify relevant causal factors and fault holds the most promise. Such analysis is rarely easy or obvious for the much studied, widely publicized catastrophes such as the Therac-25, or the *Challenger,* and perhaps even more so for the preponderant smaller scale situations in which accountability is nevertheless crucial. Our grasp of accountability can be obscured, however, if we fail to distinguish between accountability and liability. Consider why. In cases of collective (as opposed to individual) action, if all we care about is liability, it makes sense to share the burden of compensation among the collective in order to lighten the burden of each individual. Moreover, because compensation is victim-centered, targeting one satisfactory source of compensation (the so-called "deep pocket"), can and often does let others "off the hook." In contrast, where we care about accountability, many hands do not offer a means of lessening or escaping its burden. No matter how many agents there are, each may be held equally and fully answerable for a giv-

---

[21]Dennis Thompson points out that common usage of the two terms may not track this distincin-ton as precisely as I suggest. For purposes of this discussion I hope to hold the issue of terminlogoy at bay and focus on the underlying ideas and their relevant distinctiveness.

en harm.[22] There is no straightforward analog with the deep-pocket phenomenon.

Although a good system of liability offers a *partial* solution because at least the needs of victims are addressed, it can deflect attention away from accountability. Decision makers may focus exclusively on liability and fail to grasp the extent of their answerability for actions and projects they plan. The Ford Pinto case provides an example. Although the case as a whole is too complex to be summarized in a few sentences one aspect bears directly on this issue. According to a number of reports, when Ford executives considered various options for the design of the Pinto, they focused on liability and predicted that losses due to injury-liability lawsuits for the cheaper design would be offset by the expected savings.[23] Ford corporation could spread the anticipated losses so as not to be significantly affected by them. By spreading the liability thin enough and covering it by the savings from the cheaper design, no individual or part of the company would face a cost too heavy to bear.

If Ford executives had been thinking as carefully about answerability (which cannot be spread, thinned and offset) as they were about liability, their decision might well have been different. I do not hereby impugn the general method of cost-benefit analysis for business decisions of this sort. Rather, I suggest that in reckoning only with liability, the spectrum of values the executives considered was too narrow and pushed them in the wrong direction. A professional culture where accountability prevails, where the possibility exists for each to be called to answer for his or her decisions, would not as readily yield to decisions like the one made by Ford executives. Many hands need not make, metaphorically speaking, the burden lighter.

Strict Liability and Producer Responsibility

In the previous section I suggested that liability should not be understood as a substitute for accountability. Acknowledging, or for that matter denying, one's liability for an outcome does not take care of one's answerability for it. Nevertheless, establishing adequate policies governing liability for impacts of computerization is a powerful means of expressing societal expectations and at least partially explicates lines of accountability. Well-articulated policies on

---

[22]Compare this to the judge's finding in the "Red Hook Murder" (Fried, 1993). Even though it was almost certainly known which one of the three accused pulled the trigger, the court viewed all three defendants to be equal and "deadly conspirators" in the death of the victim Patrick Daley.

[23]This prediction turned out, in fact, to be inaccurate, but this is not relevant to our central concern.

liability would serve the practical purpose of protecting public interests against some of the risks of computer system failure which are further amplified by a reluctance on the part of producers and owners of systems-in-use to be accountable for them. I propose that serious consideration be given to a policy of strict liability for computer system failure, in particular for those sold as consumer products in mass markets.

To be strictly liable for a harm is to be liable to compensate for it even though one did not bring it about through faulty action. (In other words, one "pays for" the harm if the causal condition is satisfied even though the fault condition is not.) This form of liability, which is found in the legal codes of most countries, is applied, typically, to the producers of mass-produced consumer goods, potentially harmful goods, and to the owners of "ultra-hazardous" property. For example, milk producers are strictly liable for illness caused by spoiled milk, even if they have taken a normal degree of care; owners of dangerous animals (for example, tigers in a circus) are strictly liable for injuries caused by escaped animals even if they have taken reasonable precautions to restrain them.

Supporters of strict liability argue that it is justified, in general, because it benefits society by placing the burden of risk where it best belongs. Its service to the public interest is threefold. First, it protects society from the risks of potentially harmful or hazardous goods and property by providing an incentive to sellers of consumer products and owners of potentially hazardous property to take *extra*ordinary care. Second, it seeks compensation for victims from those best able to afford it, and to guard against the harm. And third, it reduces the cost of litigation by eliminating the onerous task of proving fault. Critics, on the other hand, argue that not only is strict liability unjust, because people are made to pay for harms that were not their fault, but it might indeed work *against* the public interest by discouraging innovative products. Because of the prohibitive cost of bearing the full risk of malfunction and injury, many an innovation might not be pursued for fear of ruin. In the case of new and promising, but not yet well-established technologies, this argument may hold even more sway.

Whether or not strict liability is a good general strategy is an issue best reserved for another forum. However, themes from the general debate can cast light on its merits or weaknesses as a response to computer system failure, especially since our present system of liability does include strict liability as a viable answer. In early days of computer development, recognition of both the fragility and the promise of the field might have argued for an extra degree of protection for producers by allowing risk to be shifted to consumers and other users of computing. In other words, those involved in the innovative and promising developments were spared the burden of liability. Over the course of several decades we have witnessed a maturing of the field, which now shows clear evidence of strength and vitality. The argument for special protection is therefore less compelling. Furthermore, computing covers a vast array of applications, many resembling mass-produced consumer goods, and a number that are life-critical. This argues for viewing producers of computer software in a similar light to other producers of mass-produced consumer goods and potentially harm-inducing products.

By shifting the burden-of-accountability to the producers of defective software, strict liability would also address a peculiar anomaly. One of the virtues of strict liability is that it offers a means of protecting the public against the potential harms of risky artifacts and property. Yet in the case of computing and its applications, we appear to live with a strange paradox. On the one hand, the prevailing lore portrays computer software as prone to error in a degree surpassing most other technologies, and portrays bugs as an inevitable by-product of computing itself. Yet on the other hand, most producers of software explicitly deny accountability for the harmful impacts of their products, even when they malfunction. Quite the contrary should be the case. Because of the always-lurking possibility of bugs, software seems to be precisely the type of artifact for which strict liability is appropriate; it would assure compensation for victims, and send an emphatic message to producers of software to take *extra*ordinary care to produce safe and reliable systems.

REFERENCES

Borning, A. 1987. Computer System Reliability and Nuclear War. *Communications of the ACM* 30(2):112–131.

Corbató, F.J. 1991. On Building Systems That Will Fail. *Communications of the ACM* 34(9):73–81.

De George, R. 1991. Ethical Responsibilities of Engineers in Large Organizations: The Pinto Case. In *Collective Responsibility*, eds. L. May and S. Hoffman, 151–166. Lanham, MD: Rowman and Littlefield.

Feinberg, J. 1970. Collective Responsibility. In *Doing and Deserving*, ed. J. Feinberg. Princeton, NJ: Princeton University Press.

Feinberg, J. 1985. Sua Culpa. In *Ethical Issues in the Use of Computers*, eds. D.G. Johnson and J. Snapper. Belmont, CA: Wadsworth.

Fitzgerald, S. 1992. Hospital Computer Predicts Patients' Chance of Survival. *The Miami Herald.* July 19, 1992.

Fried, J.P. 1993. Maximum Terms for Two Youths in Red Hook Murder. *New York Times*, July 7, 1993.

Friedman, B., and P.H. Kahn, Jr. 1997. Human Agency and Responsible Computing: Implications for Computer System Design. In *Human Values and the Design of Computer Technology*, ed. Batya Friedman. Stanford, CA: CSLI Publications.

Friedman, B., and L.I. Millett. 1997. Reasoning about Computers as Moral Agents: A Research Note. In *Human Values and the Design of Computer Technology*, ed. Batya Friedman. Stanford, CA: CSLI Publications.

Jacky, J. 1989. *Safety-Critical Computing: Hazards, Practices, Standards and Regulations.* University of Washington. Unpublished Manuscript.

Johnson, D.G., and J.M. Mulvey. 1993. *Computer Decisions: Ethical Issues of Responsibility and Bias.* Statistics and Operations Research Series, Princeton University, SOR-93-11.

Ladd J. 1989. Computers and Moral Responsibility: A Framework for an Ethical Analysis. In *The Information Web: Ethical and Social Implications of Computer Networking*, ed. C. Gould. Boulder, CO: Westview Press.

Leveson, N. 1986. Software Safety: Why, What, and How. *Computing Surveys* 18(2): 125–163.

Leveson, N., and C. Turner. 1993. An Investigation of the Therac-25 Accidents. *Computer* 26(7): 18–41.

Littlewood, B., and L. Strigini. 1992. The Risks of Software. *Scientific American,* November: 62–75.

McCullough, D. 1972. *The Great Bridge.* New York: Simon & Schuster.

Neumann, P. G. (monthly column) Inside Risks. *Communications of the ACM.*

Nissenbaum, H. 1995. Should I Copy My Neighbor's Software? In *Computers, Ethics, and Social Values*, ed. D.G. Johnson and H. Nissenbaum. Englewood: Prentice-Hall.

Parnas, D., J. Schouwen, and S.P. Kwan. 1990. Evaluation of Safety-Critical Software. *Communications of the ACM* 33(6): 636–648.

Samuelson, P. 1992. *Adapting Intellectual Property Law to New Technologies: A Case Study on Computer Programs.* National Research Council Report.

Samuelson, P. 1993. Liability for Defective Information. *Communications of the ACM* 36(1): 21–26.

Smith, B.C. 1985. *The Limits of Correctness.* CSLI-85-35. Stanford, CA: CSLI Publications .

Snapper, J.W. 1985. Responsibility for Computer-Based Errors. *Metaphilosophy* 16: 289–295.

Stallman, R.M. 1987. The GNU Manifesto. *GNU Emacs Manual* 175–84. Cambridge, MA: Free Software Foundation.

Thompson, D. 1987. *Political Ethics and Public Office.* Cambridge, MA: Harvard University Press.

Thompson, D. 1987. The Moral Responsibility of Many Hands. In *Political Ethics and Public Office,* ed. D. Thompson, 46–60. Cambridge, MA: Harvard University Press.

Turkle, S. 1984. *The Second Self.* New York: Simon & Schuster.

Velasquez, M. 1991. Why Corporations Are Not Morally Responsible for Anything They Do. In *Collective Responsibility,* eds. L. May and S. Hoffman, 111–131. Rowman and Littlefield.

Weizenbaum, J. 1972. On the Impact of the Computer on Society. *Science* 176(12): 609–614.

3

Disability, Inability and Cyberspace

JOHN PERRY, ELIZABETH MACKEN, NEIL SCOTT, AND
JANICE L. MCKINLEY

Abstract: The cyberspace revolution has the potential to "level the playing field" for individuals with disabilities with respect to many kinds of jobs and other activities. Individuals with disabilities may need nonstandard input and output devices, but once these devices are provided, their disabilities are irrelevant to their performance. In practice, however, nonstandard input and output needs often create huge pr0oblems. To level the playing field, these problems need to be understood and confronted. In this chapter we provide a framework that we hope will lead to better designs for all individuals. We use concepts from the philosophy of action and information to contrast two concepts of disability and handicap that we call the "intrinsic" and "circumstantial." We discuss an architecture for accessibility, the Total Access System, that solves some of the inherent problems in efforts to provide access for everyone to all computers while at the same time keeping computers affordable and compact and not impeding other sorts of technological advancements. Finally, we suggest some guidelines for providing equal access to information via computer technology that follow the spirit of recent Americans with Disabilities Act (ADA) decisions and are in accordance with the circumstantial conception of disability.

Computers, the internet, and the larger communications network of which it is a part, provide an informational structure within which many of us spend a large part of our working day and a significant part of our leisure. During those periods we are "infonauts in cyberspace," using the internet to obtain information from places near and remote, and acting in various ways via the internet to have an effect on computers and people in those places. This cyberspace revolution is changing the human condition in fundamental ways.

These changes have the potential to reduce differences between disabled and nondisabled individuals. As infonauts, none of us receives the information we need directly from our senses, nor do we produce the effects we intend directly by use of our limbs. We all depend on technology to aid our senses and magnify and transform the effects of our movements. Neither the blind person nor the quadriplegic nor the sighted mobile employee can access the latest government regulations or send instructions to colleagues in distant places without the help of the internet. The difference between individuals with disabilities and those without becomes simply a matter of the particular input and output devices that they need to access the computer network. The first

We are thankful to Batya Friedman, James Moor and Mark Breimhorst for helpful comments on earlier drafts of this essay.

person needs voice or Braille output, the second needs voice input, and the sighted employee is used to using a monitor and a keyboard.

From a theoretical perspective, the differences in input and output needs seem minor in comparison to the shared dependence on technological infrastructure. As a practical matter these differences can be immense. Increased computing power is complicating the lives of disabled people because more and more applications are becoming available with inaccessible user interfaces. Complex sound, ever faster and more brilliant graphics, and real-time video all create problems for some individuals with disabilities.[1]

Part of the problem is economic. Because the financial resources of mainstream computer companies are linked to applications, access issues take a back seat. But part of the problem is lack of imagination. Too often the designer focuses on the standard mix of sensory and motor abilities, with at most some vague plan to later retrofit solutions for individuals with disabilities.

We believe that decisions and innovations that create difficulties for individuals with disabilities are often more a result of confused thinking than ill will. In this chapter we will try to provide a framework for thinking about design that we hope will lead to better designs for all individuals.

In the next section we distinguish between an impairment, a disability, an inability, and a handicap , and we use these to distinguish two perspectives on the connection between disability and handicap, which we call the intrinsic and the circumstantial perspectives.

In the third section, we discuss achievement space, distinguish tools from infrastructure, and define cyberspace according to these concepts. We note that individuals who cannot access cyberspace have an inability; this inability

---

[1]A potentially tragic case is the graphical user interface (GUI) problem for blind computer users. Fifteen years ago computers standardly output information on a screen with 24 rows and 80 columns, each cell filled with an ascii character. Such text could be automatically converted to speech by screen-reader programs. Blind computer users usually can adapt to a reading speed of two to three times normal talking speed. Blind computer users could work as efficiently as their sighted co-workers, using the same hardware and software, augmented only by the screen-reader.

The rise of the graphical user interface, of the sort introduced by Macintosh and made ubiquitous by Microsoft Windows, with its icons and multiple windows, has been a disaster for blind computer users. Text-based screen-readers cannot handle the graphic displays. Considerable ingenuity is now being invested in providing an interface to the graphical user interface for blind users. But these efforts are taking time. Access programs for MS Windows 3.1 became available at about the same time as the program was superseded by Windows 95. Much remains to be done before blind users have anything approaching parity with sighted users. In the meantime, many blind workers cannot be as productive as they once were, and some have even lost their jobs. This problem is discussed more extensively in the Appendix.

is a serious handicap in today's information age regardless of whether or not the reason for the inability is a disability. In the fourth section, we discuss some dilemmas connected with potential access solutions. In the fifth section, we present an architecture for accessible design, the "Total Access System." We show how it is based on the circumstantial conception of disability and how it minimizes the difficulties of designing for access, and discuss some implementations. In the last section, we relate the circumstantial model and the Total Access System to the Americans with Disabilities Act (the ADA) and argue that from the point of view of the circumstantial conception of disability and handicap, the requirements legislated by the ADA are simply the application of the same approach to inability that society takes toward others, to individuals with disabilities .

TWO CONCEPTS OF DISABILITY AND HANDICAP

In order for individuals with disabilities to become full partners in the cyberspace era, their situation must be considered early in the design process of products and work environments. We believe that the key to good preliminary design is an elimination of a confusion that is all too common concerning the connection between disabilities and handicaps.

In untangling the confusion we use the following glosses on "impairment," "disability" and "handicap" that basically follow the World Health Organization (WHO); we add the term "inability" to fill an important logical gap (WHO, 1980.)

- An inability is anything a person cannot do.
- An impairment is a physiological disorder or injury.
- A disability is an inability to execute some class of movements, or pick up sensory information of some sort, or perform some cognitive function, that typical unimpaired humans are able to execute or pick up or perform.
- A handicap is an inability to accomplish something one might want to do, that most others around one are able to accomplish.[2]

A disability may be *directly* or *circumstantially* linked to an inability or handicap. The link is direct if having the disability leads, independently of cir-

---

[2]In the formulation of these definitions we were assisted by comments by James H. Moor, Professor of Philosophy at Dartmouth College (personal communication) and an essay by R. Amundson (see footnote 3).

cumstances, to having the inability: there is simply no way a person with the disability can accomplish the task in question. The link is circumstantial if, although in some circumstances there is no way for a person with the disability to accomplish the task, in other circumstances, where the right tools and structures to support them are available, there are ways.

Paraplegia, a disability, is directly linked to the inability to walk. But it is only circumstantially linked to the inability to move around under one's own power. This inability can be removed with a wheelchair. Blindness is directly linked to the inability to see text on computer monitor, but it is only circumstantially linked to an inability to gather the information presented there. The inability to get information from displayed or printed text can be removed through the use of Braille displays and speech-output screen readers. This example brings up an important distinction that must be made between information (the content of the textual message) and the form of information (displayed text, printed text, Braille text, audio text, etc.); we will discuss this concept again in the last section.

The term "handicap" is sometimes now avoided, but we think it can be put to good use, in the way WHO does. A handicap is an inability that leaves one at a comparative disadvantage. So conceived, a handicap is a special case of an inability. The connection between handicap and disability is much looser. We can be handicapped, even when we are not disabled. Americans who do not speak Japanese will be handicapped when they visit Tokyo, because while most people will be able to gather important information by reading signs on buildings, they will not. In addition, one can be disabled, without being handicapped relative to many tasks, if the proper tools and supporting structures are provided.

The concepts we now want to introduce are the "intrinsic conception of disability, inability, and handicap" and the "circumstantial conception of disability, inability, and handicap." For short we will refer to them in an abbreviated form: the *intrinsic conception* of disability and the *circumstantial conception* of disability.

The intrinsic conception of disability goes like this:

> A disabled individual is one who cannot make some movement that the majority of the population can make, or lacks some sensory capacity that the majority of the population has. As a result, disabled individuals are handicapped in many ways; they cannot realistically expect to accomplish many goals that others can accomplish. A disabled individual must either regain the motor or sensory abilities, or abandon the goals.

In contrast, the circumstantial conception goes like this:

A disabled individual is one who cannot make some movement that the majority of the population can make, or lacks some sensory capacity that the majority of the population has. As a result, an individual with a disability may need to use different means than nondisabled individuals standardly use to accomplish certain goals. Handicaps are created when the tools and infrastructure to support these alternative methods are not available.

Ron Amundson puts the point this way, in his excellent article "Disability, Handicap, and the Environment"(Amundson, 1992).

…a disability such as paraplegia becomes a handicap only to the extent that the para-plegic person's environment isolates him from some need or goal. A wheelchair user has virtually no mobility handicap in a building with accessible doorways, elevators, and work areas. But he is greatly handicapped when his goals are located up or down a flight of stairs. This is the *environmental concept of handicap* … A handicap results from the interaction between a disability and an environment; it does not flow natu-rally from the disability alone. We humans frequently construct our environments in handicap-producing ways. The reason is obvious. We design and construct our envi-ronments with a certain range of biologically typical humans in mind (110).[3]

The life of Franklin Roosevelt, President of the United States from 1933–1945, illustrates the difference between the two conceptions. Roosevelt was disabled as a result of polio; the muscles in his legs were wasted.[4] For a long time he tried to learn to walk again, to overcome the effect polio had had on his legs through exercise, grit and hard work. He was in the grip of the first conception of disability. He was not successful in walking again.

At a certain point he decided to put his time and energy into politics rather than into the struggle to walk again. He used a wheelchair to move about his homes and offices. He had ramps and other structures built to accommodate his wheelchair.

---

[3]In his essay, Amundson is concerned to point out that disabilities simply do not fit many of the medical categories under which they are subsumed. Disabilities are not diseases (although they are often the results of diseases); being disabled is not a form of being unhealthy or frail or chron-ically ill. Amundson defines disability as "lack of species typical functioning at the basic personal level." Although sympathetic to the civil-rights approach to issues of access, Admundson aruges that the exact justification and scope of the right to access needs fuller examination by philoso-phers, who have been handicapped by inadequate conceptions of disability and handicap.

[4]Information about Roosevelt is from Hugh Gallagher's *FDR's Splendid Deception* (Gallagher, 1985). We take this opportunity to thank Paul Longmore, Professor of History at San Francisco State University for his class on Disabilities and Society which introduced us to this book. Many of the ideas espoused here had their roots in discussions in this class and in papers Paul has present-ed, for example, Longmore (1993).

Roosevelt had an impairment, atrophied leg muscles, which left him with a disability, he could not walk. Because of the disability, he was handicapped; he could not move around under his own power. He tried two methods for getting rid of the handicap. First he tried to get rid of the disability. Then he gave up on that, and simply adopted a different method for moving about under his own power.

After Roosevelt died, the ramps were removed from Hyde Park, his home. As a result, for a long time some of the visitors to Hyde Park were handicapped (relative to the goal of moving about quickly and efficiently), in a way that Roosevelt himself had not been.

From the point of view of the circumstantial conception of disability, using a wheelchair was a reasonable decision on Roosevelt's part. It is similar in structure to the decision a commuter makes to buy a car, rather than getting in shape to run to work – or learning to fly. Or the decision a teacher might make to use a microphone, rather than learn to shout. Or the decision an executive might make, to buy a Rolodex rather than enroll in a memory course. It was simply a matter of using technology to get rid of an inability – something each one of us does all the time. The only difference in the case of Roosevelt was that the inability to move around resulted from a disability.

Roosevelt felt that it would be political suicide to reveal to the American public that he used a wheelchair. It's not that Americans wanted to see their President walk everywhere. It was acceptable to the public for him to get from place to place by car – for there he was employing a bit of technology that non-disabled individuals also use. It was not acceptable, however, for him to use a wheelchair. Roosevelt knew that the American public was in the grip of the intrinsic conception of disability. At meetings in the White House, he would always be seated where he wanted to be, in a regular chair, when guests entered, and remain there when they left. He used heavy iron supports on his legs, that clamped into a position that kept his leg rigid, when he had to give a speech standing up. In certain situations, Roosevelt had to appear to walk to a podium to deliver a speech. In these situations his sons or associates would move him forward in such a way that his legs would swing forward as if he were walking with a little help. In fact he could not supply locomotion at all.

The illusion was thus created that Roosevelt had learned to walk again, but just couldn't do it very well. Being a poor walker was acceptable to the American public. The truth, that Roosevelt had become an adept and efficient wheelchair user, was not acceptable. Most Americans who were alive when Roosevelt was President were unaware that he used a wheelchair. This fact became common knowledge only years after he died.

This attitude towards the President was pretty silly. As Roosevelt's career demonstrates, it simply was not essential that he be able to walk in order to perform the tasks required of a President. Applicants for the Presidency of the United States, like applicants for any job, should be judged on their ability to accomplish the tasks that the job requires, not on whether they perform them in the standard way.

CYBERSPACE AND ACCOMPLISHMENT SPACE

It is especially important to appreciate the circumstantial concept of disability in the cyberspace era. Cyberspace offers an opportunity to level the playing field for individuals with disabilities for several reasons. First, the number of tasks that can be accomplished via cyberspace is increasing daily and will continue to multiply at rapid rates for the foreseeable future. Second, disabilities are invisible in cyberspace. Third, no stigma attaches to using the tools of cyberspace. Individuals who find it crucial to use cyberspace because of a disability will not be perceived as different from individuals who find it convenient for any other reason. Finally, cyberspace, depending as it does on digital convergence, can, in principle at least, facilitate the need for different forms of input and output. All of these points gain in importance, in the context of the Americans with Disabilities Act; cyberspace provides a structure that can be used to help make many "reasonable accommodations" to the needs of individuals with disabilities.

To argue these points we want to demonstrate that cyberspace is a giant step in the extension of what we call *accomplishment space*.[5]

We will say a goal is in a person's accomplishment space if it is something he or she can intentionally accomplish. That is, (a) there is some sequence of movements the person can execute, which in the person's circumstances, will be a way of bringing about the goal, and (b) the person has, or has a way of obtaining the required information about the circumstances in order to accomplish the goal.

What we'll call *primitive accomplishment space* includes only accomplishments that are made without the help of *tools* or the intervention of other people – accomplishments like reaching out, picking up an apple and eating it. These acts will involve effects on our immediate environment, guided by the

---

[5]See (Israel et al., 1991) and (Israel et al., 1993) for a development of the framework for action implicit in this discussion.

information we can pick up From our senses. At one time human agents lived and worked mainly in primitive accomplishment space. Perhaps at that time the intrinsic concept of disability would have been appropriate. But today, we all live in *extended accomplishment space*. One way to extend our accomplishment space is through *communication*. Mary sits in the living room, and asks her husband in the kitchen if there is an apple in the bowl there. She is able to find out relevant facts about the space beyond her senses. If he says "Yes," she may ask him to wash it and bring it to her. She has an effect on things she cannot reach.

Another way of extending accomplishment space is through tools. If Mary had a long pole, she might be able to shake loose apples high on a tree. Tools magnify or transform the effects of a human movement, giving a movement a quite different effect than it would have otherwise, and changing the shape of accomplishment space. Without the pole, Mary's movement would not be a way of getting an apple, but only a way of looking silly, as if she were gesturing to the apple tree. With the pole, executing this movement is a way of getting the apple to fall.

A third way is through *infrastructure*. Suppose that steps have been nailed to the tree. Mary has to move her limbs in a certain "climbing" way to use this bit of infrastructure. Moving her legs in that fashion wouldn't be a way of doing much of anything without the steps, but with them, it is a way of climbing high into the tree.

Although we find the distinction between tools and infrastructure useful, it is hardly clear and precise. We think of tools as closely related to certain effectors (moving parts) and types of movements of them. The tool-user learns that certain movements with the tool in position have new effects. These become, if not additional basic movements, very low-level actions, that the agent can perform at will in a wide variety of circumstances, with many different ends-in-view. And we think of tools as paradigmatically portable and often personal, traveling with an agent, and staying with the same agent. Thus a wheelchair is a tool that provides a way of moving in various directions by moving one's arms in certain ways.[6]

Infrastructure is paradigmatically associated with a structure, and accessible to many agents. A bit of infrastructure changes the effects of movements made by agents that use it, but not in ways that are closely tied to particular effectors and kinds of movements. A ramp is a part of the infrastructure of a

---

[6]Or some other bodily part, such as one's head or fingers, if the wheelchair is powered.

building. Everyone can use it. Some walk up and down it, some roll up and down it.

In between paradigmatic tools and paradigmatic bits of infrastructure there are many intermediate cases. If Mary carries a rope ladder with her, it will have some of the features of tools and some of the features of infrastructure.[7]

The internet is creating large changes in accomplishment space for those who have access to it. Assume Mary lives and works in California. Mary wants to order a book from a publisher in Europe. She finds the fax number on the internet, and then faxes an order for the book, providing her Visa number so that her account can be charged. As a result of her actions in California, various things happen in Europe. Someone pulls the book off the shelf, wraps it, and sends it to her. Mary made these things happen; the movements of the person in Europe are the intentional, planned result of the movements of Mary's fingers in California.

In terms of the movements that are executed, Mary's acts in this case are not much more complicated than eating an apple. But they are much more complicated in the structure on which they depend. The success of Mary's actions depends on the telephone cable and microwave connections that made it possible for her to pick up information on the web and send an order via fax. They also depend on the cultural institutions and commercial mechanisms that make communication via language possible, and the commercial mechanisms that make credit cards possible. When she is operating in cyberspace, using internet, telephone and fax, Mary can obtain information from places she cannot perceive, and affect events that are thousands of miles beyond her reach. Her accomplishment space is immense.

Note that the basic structure of action is the same in this case as in eating the apple. Mary has a goal: bringing it about that someone in Europe send her a certain book. She has a way of bringing that about: faxing the order with the Visa number entered. She has a way of obtaining the necessary information, so that the order will be faxed to the right person: look up the number on the World Wide Web. She also has the capacity suit her action to the facts – to dial the correct number that will send the fax to the right person.

Cyberspace is thus the accomplishment space created by a huge infrastructure that accommodates communication – communication among people and communication among people and all of the information nodes (web

---

[7]As Batya Friedman has pointed out (personal communication), our conception of a tool is also incomplete; it doesn't account for tools that enhance our mental capabilities as with an abacus to enhance mental calculations or knots in a string to enhance memory.

pages, airline schedules, commodities vendors, libraries, etc.) that are stored on the network of computers. Cyberspace is the latest stage in a long process of extending accomplishment space beyond the limitations of our natural senses and abilities.

In general, the more our accomplishment space is extended by communication, tools and infrastructure, the less appropriate the intrinsic conception of disability becomes. It should have been obsolete by the 1930s, when Roosevelt felt obligated to cover up his use of a wheelchair. It deserves to be a dimly remembered fossil in the era of cyberspace.

DILEMMAS OF ACCESS

Unfortunately, the circumstantial concept does not solve all problems by itself. A well-intentioned designer or employer with a good understanding of the circumstantial concept of disability can be presented with many dilemmas when it comes to providing access.

In most cases, the main problem is not the lack of an access strategy that is technologically feasible. Increased computing power makes it possible to implement superb access technologies. Advanced input strategies that are now viable include: special keyboards, document scanning, high performance speech recognition, head-tracking, eye-tracking, monitoring of facial expressions and interpretation of biological electrical signals. Viable output strategies include: alternative screen technologies such as direct laser stimulation of the retina, high quality speech synthesis, multi-dimensional sound, tactile devices that stimulate the sense of touch, haptic devices that use force feedback, and robotic devices. Advanced access tools such as these have the potential to make almost any disabled individual more independent and highly competitive in the workplace.

However, the fact that a technology has been, or could be, developed, does not mean that it is commercially available, much less at a reasonable price. The high cost and unavailability of access technology can pose almost insurmountable problems. These problems are compounded by the fact that users now often use many computers. Not so long ago, it was unusual for an individual to have access to more than one computer. Now it is commonplace for a person to use several computers each day. Even when it is feasible to modify a single computer to make it accessible to an individual, modifying every computer he or she uses may not be.

Not only do individuals use multiple computers, many computers have multiple users. It is quite likely that several of the computers a person uses on a daily basis belong to some institution, such as a bank or school, and will be used by a number of people throughout the day. Devices, such as ATMs and information kiosks are really computers in disguise and pose the same problems.

Computers with multiple users present more dilemmas. Whose responsibility is it to make publicly available computers accessible? Which disabilities should be accommodated on a publicly accessible computer? How is a system made accessible without exposing it to intentional or unintentional vandalism?

The most perplexing problem is how to accommodate all of the necessary disabilities without making the computer so complex that no one can figure out how to use it. Consider information kiosks, for example. A typical information kiosk is designed with a certain "standard" individual in mind. This person can stand close to the kiosk and can use arms and fingers to operate keys or a touch screen. She can see the information displayed on a screen, can pick up paper output and read it, and can hear voice output. The inclusive designer cannot make these assumptions. A person who uses a wheelchair may not be able to reach the relevant buttons or see the screen easily. A blind person may be not be able to choose which buttons to push for various purposes, or see the output on the monitor or in print. A deaf person may be unable to hear the tones or spoken output, or be aware that it is occurring. For each of these problems there is a solution, but is there a solution for all of them at once? Lowering the kiosk for the paraplegic may mean that others have to stoop uncomfortably to use it. Making all the output in speech may solve some of the blind person's problems, while exacerbating those of the person who is deaf. Perhaps a kiosk could be designed that offered every kind of input and output, with monitors and buttons at various heights, comfortable for all, and every needed input and output option built in – but what would it cost?

The Archimedes Project is developing a system that we feel poses solutions to some of these dilemmas. We call this the "Total Access System."

AN ARCHITECTURE FOR ACCESSIBILITY: THE TOTAL ACCESS SYSTEM

Individuals with disabilities have problems accessing computers because of keyboards, mice and monitors. But these devices only come into play when computers communicate with people. When computers communicate with each other, keyboards, mice and monitors aren't involved. This suggests a way of separating the problem of access into two. First we provide an individual who has a disability with complete access to one computer. Then we provide them with access to any computer, by letting the one computer to which they have access take over the job of communicating with the rest. The Total Access System is based on a this separation.

The Total Access System was initially conceived by Neil Scott,[8] and key pieces of the system have been designed and implemented by him and others at the Archimedes Project at Stanford University (see box).

> The Archimedes Project is a project at Stanford whose mission is to provide individuals with disabilities to computers and access to people through computer technology. The Project is based on the philosophy espoused in this paper which it embodies in the following six principles:
>
> • Everyone requires help in gaining and effectively using information, not only those individuals who have disabilities.
>
> • In itself, information is neither accessible nor inaccessible; the form in which it is presented makes it so.
>
> • To be disabled is not necessarily to be handicapped. Handicaps can often be removed where disabilites cannot.
>
> • Handicaps often arise from decisions to design tools exclusively for individuals with the standard mix of perceptual and motor abilities.
>
> • Designed access is preferable to retrofitted access.
>
> • Solutions that provide general access can benefit everyone.

---

[8]In 1988 Neil Scott proposed a "Universal Access System" (now called the Total Access System (TAS)) that would make it much simpler for disabled individuals to access any computer or computer-based device. This was in response to inquiries about compliance with the 1973 Rehabilitation Act as amended in 1986 by passage of Section 508 of Public Law 99-506. At that time Scott was a disability access engineer at California State University, Northridge. The Total Access System split the access problem into three separate and much simpler components; an "accessor" to handle the specific access requirements of the disabled individual, a Total Access Port (TAP) to provide a standardized interface to any computer or computer-based device, and a communications protocol to enable any accessor to communicate with any TAP. The Universal Access System project moved to Stanford in 1993 when Scott became one of the founding members of the Archimedes Project. Ongoing research is improving the performance of the system and broadening the range of devices that can be controlled.

This separation is embodied in the Total Access System in its two main components, the *Personal Accessor* and the Total Access Port or *TAP.* Personal Accessors vary from person to person according to the user's abilities and preferences. TAPs link the Personal Accessor to any host computers that the user wants to work on.[9] The Personal Accessor and the TAP communicate with each other in a high-level functional language we call the Archimedes Protocol.

A Personal Accessor is the conceptual solution to the first set of issues: providing an individual with access to one computer. A Personal Accessor is a personal computer with built-in hardware and software for the accessibility devices that a particular person needs. A quadriplegic, for example, would have speech and head-pointing or eye-tracking built into his or her accessor. A person with advanced amyotrophic lateral sclerosis (ALS) would have eye-tracking, but not speech or head-pointing (since he cannot use these). A blind individual's accessor might include a speech synthesizer or a tactile display.

An accessor can be made small and portable and can travel with the user in the same way that many people now carry palmtops and laptops. It can be exactly tailored to the individual's needs and preferences, containing what is needed and not using memory or physical space for things that are not needed. Its only function is to provide access, thus it does not become obsolete when host operating systems or applications are changed. Because it is modular, it can be easily upgraded as access tools improve. It separates input and output functions from applications in order to provide a consistent interface across devices and applications. It allows access to any host and computer-driven technology outfitted with TAPs including kiosks and microwave ovens.

A TAP is the conceptual solution to the second set of issues: access to *any* computer. A TAP attaches to a host computer through the keyboard and mouse ports. The connection between Accessors and TAPs is through a (wire or wireless) link that uses a specially developed serial communications protocol that is independent of both the accessor and the host. Standardization of the protocol allows any accessor to operate with any host device. From the perspective of the host, an accessor is indistinguishable from standard I/O devices. Input from the accessor through the TAP emulates a keyboard and mouse; output from the host computer through the TAP is displayed by the accessor in a manner appropriate to the user.

---

[9]The Accessor can also serve as a communication aid for face-to-face conversation by transferring the user's inputs to an output device such as a speech synthesizer or connecting directly with another accessor used by a conversational participant.

Because the TAP fools the host into thinking that it is getting its own keyboard and mouse input, Personal Accessors work on all applications and interfaces. Some alternative input strategy is used to "press" the key and "move and click" the mouse. It might be voice, Morse code, or single switch scanning. No matter what is used, it is all the same to the host computer; it is interpreted as keyboard and mouse input.

In this sense, accessors work equally well for all applications. Accessors can be made to work more efficiently for a given application by means of user-defined macros that are specific to the task and user preference.

The TAP keeps the adaptive work outside of the host and therefore doesn't interfere with the functionality or speed of any of the applications running on the host. It is small (slightly larger than a computer mouse), relatively low cost, and simple to install, all of which encourage widespread access adaptation.

Future TAPs will also collect control signals, raw text, raw video, and raw sound from the host and transfer this information back to the Accessor for processing into a form that is accessible to the user. This is a crucial piece of the solution to the Graphical User Interface problem for blind computer users. [10]

Consider Jorge, a quadriplegic who uses his voice to control his computer. While at work Jorge's accessor is usually connected to a Macintosh desk top computer. Jorge speaks into a microphone. His words are recognized by a voice recognition program running on his accessor. The intensive memory and CPU demands of the voice recognition program do not affect Jorge's Macintosh. Jorge's accessor contains a software shell that allows Jorge to use intuitive macros suited to different applications, for example, he might say "begin fax," "read mail," "replace word," "spell checker," "print file," etc. The data from the accessor bypasses the keyboard and mouse of Jorge's Macintosh. The Macintosh-TAP converts the data to virtual keystrokes and mouse movements – Jorge's Macintosh is unaware that it is being controlled by voice rather than by fingers.

Later in the day, Jorge needs to use a Sun workstation. The accessor and the macros remain the same. The Sun TAP converts the data from the accessor to signals that supply virtual keystrokes and mouse movements to a Sun.

Jorge takes his accessor with him when he goes home. There he could in principle use it not only to operate his home computer, but also to operate his television, stereo, VCR, microwave, and so forth. The TAS design concept

---

[10]For further information on the Scott/Archimedes implementation of the Total Access System see (Scott, n.d.) and (Scott and Britell, 1993.)

would apply equally well to kiosks and ATMs. Kiosks and ATMs outfitted with TAP s would be accessible to everyone with an accessor.[11]

Design Advantages

The TAS strategy is contrasted with the traditional "in-host" strategy: locating the assistive hardware and software in the host computer the individual with a disability uses. The basic advantage that the TAS offers over the in-host strategy can be seen as roughly the difference between addition and multiplication. On the TAS strategy, one has to develop an accessor that outputs the Archimedes protocol for each input device and develop a TAP that inputs the Archimedes protocol, for each type of computer. To compute the number of technological problems, we add the number of assistive devices to the number of types of machines. With the in-host strategy, each combination of input device and type of host constitutes a separate problem. To compute the number of technological problems, one needs to multiply the number of input devices times the number of hosts. There are further advantages, too. First, and foremost, TAS isolates the user from the whims of hardware and software designers. The accessor interfaces to host computers through a TAP which emulates the electrical operation of the physical keyboard and mouse. Keyboard and mouse functions are fundamental to computing and manufacturers get little advantage from changing them in anything but purely cosmetic ways. The IBM PS/2 keyboard and mouse, for example, is becoming a de facto standard throughout much of the computer industry, even among competing products. The ubiquity of the keyboard and mouse makes them a point of stability in an otherwise constantly changing world. They have become part of the infrastructure.Variations to the mouse, such as trackballs, finger pointers, touchpads, and the like, all use the same electrical protocols as a basic mouse. TAS currently supports TAP interfaces to IBM PC, SGI, Macintosh, and Sun computers. Any computer based device or appliance can be made accessible by connecting a suitable TAP. The TAP becomes part of the infrastructure.

---

[11]The Archimedes Project has commercialized TAPs for Macs, Suns, IBM PCs, and Silicon Graphics Machines. TAPs are presently licensed through Stanford University and are being distributed through Synapse Corporation in San Rafael, California. These can be used with a variety of available speech accessors. Other accessors mentioned in this section, namely, combined speech and head-pointing, specialized keyboards, input expansion routines, and eye-tracking are in use in the lab as prototypes. Other ongoing work includes the development of additional input devices, improved expansion routines for use in communication aids, and smaller and more portable accessors. A prototype accessible information kiosk is also under development.

Another significant advantage of TAS is that it allows a disabled person to use a single accessor to operate any computer or device that has been equipped with a TAP. A properly chosen and configured accessor provides a disabled user with a very high level of independence and will last a very long time. It therefore makes good economic sense to invest whatever it takes to match an accessor to the needs of a disabled individual.

Research at the Archimedes Project has shown yet another real advantage of using the TAS design. Many different technologies are potentially useful for disabled individuals. Developing the necessary hardware and software interfaces to real-world tasks, however, is usually a far from trivial exercise and many good ideas languish due to the effort required to evaluate them in a real application. The TAS provides an ideal vehicle for evaluating and incorporating new technologies because it automatically connects new access devices directly to the existing infrastructure. An eye-tracker, for example, follows the movement of a user's eye and generates a stream of data showing where the user is looking. With suitable software, the eye-tracker can be used to emulate a keyboard or mouse. The question is, which keyboard and mouse should it emulate? This question is moot if we configure the eye-tracker as an accessor. The researcher need not be concerned with what the eye-tracker is to be connected to since anything that can be controlled by a keyboard or mouse can be controlled by the eye-tracker.

The TAS allows several different accessors be used simultaneously on the same host system. This leads to several interesting possibilities. For example, more than one person can have equal access to a single host device and can therefore work cooperatively on a single project. Similarly, a single user can operate several different accessors at the same time and can therefore mix and match different input strategies to suit the tasks being performed. One very effective example of this is the combination of speech recognition and head-tracking. The speech accessor handles all text input, program commands, and pressing or clicking of the mouse buttons while the head-tracker handles all of the pointing functions. The combination of speech recognition and head-tracking is significantly more effective than either technology used by itself.

It is a small step to see that the TAS concept has advantages for nondisabled individuals whose experiences, preferences, or work conditions may dictate or encourage one type of access over another. For many professors, executives, physicians, and lawyers, for example, talking is easier and faster than typing. Individuals who drive and use cellular phones will need to speak rather than type to their computers. Car radios would be safer if we could operate them with our voices instead of with our eyes and hands. Employees of the telemarketing industry would be more productive if the spoken words used to confirm addresses and orders could simultaneously enter the data into the computer database. ATMs that could be operated by voice from within one's car would be popular with everyone. As John Thomas puts it in an article in this volume, accessible issues "force designers to think out of the box." He goes on to make the important point that when the communication system is made accessible to individuals with disabilities, everyone gains access to those individuals. He says, "Providing access for people with special needs is not just for them – it's for everyone."

HANDICAPPING PRACTICES AND THE AMERICANS WITH DISABILITIES ACT

The movement for the rights of individuals with disabilities, which was responsible for passage of the Americans with Disabilities Act in 1990, appealed to the circumstantial conception of disability. The legislation recognizes that handicaps don't result from disabilities alone, but from a combination of disabilities and circumstances, and that changing the circumstances can often eliminate the handicap.

The Americans with Disabilities Act requires that reasonable accommodation be made for people with disabilities in a host of areas, including employment. For example, Title I, Section 102, 5A, says that employers must make

> ...reasonable accommodations to the known physical or mental limitations of an otherwise qualified individual with a disability who is an applicant or employee, unless [the employer] can demonstrate that the accommodation would impose an undue hardship on the operation of the business...

From the point of view of the circumstantial conception of disability and handicap, this requirement is simply the application to individuals with disabilities of the same approach to inability that society takes towards others. Science, engineering, and education in general are devoted to eliminating inabilities: creating knowledge, structures and tools that allow people to accomplish what they want and need to accomplish. These energies are devoted to "reasonably accommodating" the needs and aspirations of people by putting the goals they need or want to reach within their accomplishment space and by providing tools and infrastructures that change the circumstances within which they live and work.

Handicapping Practices

This does not yet seem to be the typical way of looking at things. In discussions of the ADA, the following phenomenon is often observed. A person hears about the ADA for the first time (or thinks about it for the first time) and seems puzzled. Eventually, the person makes a comment about the unlikelihood of a blind race car driver, a quadriplegic NFL guard, or a deaf trumpet player. The point of such "joking" often seems to be that there is a sort of absurdity inherent in the law and the idea behind it.[12]

This reaction is provoked, we think, by trying to understand the law within an intrinsic conception of disability. The puzzled person thinks of disabilities and handicaps as inseparable, so that there is something simply confusing about the mandate of the ADA. In such a state, the mind is naturally drawn to examples that come closest to supporting the intrinsic conception, examples in which the connection between the disability and the handicap is maximally direct, minimally circumstantial.

This intellectual confusion can lead to practices that create and perpetuate handicaps. We list three.

1) **Inadvertent Over-restricting.** Inadvertent over-restrictions arise by the following flawed reasoning:

1. The primary function of X is to allow people to do Y.

2. Individuals with disability D cannot possibly do Y.

3. Individuals with disability D do not need X.

An example of this reasoning is:

1. The primary function of a drivers' license is to allow people to drive.

2. Blind people cannot possibly drive.

3. Blind people do not need a drivers' license.

---

[12]Amundson (1992) notes a more serious motivation behind such examples when they arise in a philosophical setting:

> Well known problems of health care ethics have disability-related correlates. One is the problem of the "social hijacking" of resources by extremely needy people. Radical modifications in environmental design for extremely disabled people might be as expensive as radical medical procedures for gravely diseased people. Those unfamiliar with disability issues tend to concentrate on these dramatic examples … [a] paralyzed ballerina or a (hypothetical) blind person who wants to become an airline pilot. What conceivable environmental modifications could support the "rights" of those people to their chosen professions? The fact is that such demands are not being made…

Cases of social hijacking can certainly be constructed involving access to information. We provide no answer to the philosophical problem, merely sharing with Admundson the hope that clarification of concepts relating to disability will facilitate fuller philosophical examination of the basis of the right to access. In terms of practical problems of the expense of access, we think that in a large number of cases the TAS approach can reduce the cost of access significantly.

The fallacy is in the word "primary"; things often have important secondary functions that are overlooked in this kind of reasoning. The primary function of a driver's license is to certify that the possessor can drive safely. But in the United States licenses also serve as identity cards. Before the rise of credit cards, a driver's license was the only sort of identification that was widely accepted for cashing checks and similar transactions. Therefore, people unqualified to drive (for whatever reason) were not only not permitted to drive, but also had difficulty cashing checks.

This seems like the sort of problem that could be resolved with the stroke of a pen, but in fact, the problem was not quickly remedied. It required court action to direct states to provide ersatz driver's licenses for identification purposes, in spite of the clear injustice of the situation.[13]

The same rationale can be used for not making certain buildings or parts of buildings wheelchair accessible. Why would a person in a wheelchair need access to a skating rink? Or a swimming pool? Reasons are not hard to imagine, once one stops and thinks. For example, persons who use wheelchairs may have ways of swimming or skating or may want to watch their children or grandchildren swim or skate. Indeed the latter was the basis of a court decision that resulted in wheelchair accessibility to a bowling alley.

Ultimately, the problem is not so much faulty reasoning, as a lack of foresight. The GUI problem can be seen as an instance of this. When the first graphical user interfaces were developed in the early 1980s, the question of how a blind person would use these interfaces arose. The answer was that a blind person would not use these interfaces; they wouldn't want to, because they would provide no advantage over a command line interface. Of course in time the graphical user interfaces became so popular that a great deal of software was not available in any other format.[14]

Stanford has an impressive collection of Rodin sculptures – the largest in the world outside of Paris. Most of these are located in a garden next to the Stanford Museum, but a few are scattered around campus. Rodin's famous statue *The Thinker* is located on a ten foot high pedestal, near the Stanford Library.

----

[13]The cases mentioned in this section were taken from *Enforcing the ADA; a Special Fifth Anniversary Status Report from the Department of Justice.* It can be found on the Department of Justice web page, http://www.usdoj.gov, or by calling 1-800-514-0301 (voice) or 1-800-514-0383 (TDD).

[14]See Appendix.

Sculpture is a form of visual art that is enjoyed by blind as well as sighted individuals. Blind visitors to Stanford enjoy experiencing Rodin's sculptures, most of which are accessible to them – but not *The Thinker*.

By putting *The Thinker* on a high pedestal, Stanford assured it would be a visually prominent landmark on campus, and perhaps be a bit more awe-inspiring than it would be on the ground. However, it was also inadvertently restricting the class of those who could enjoy it by touching it.

As a final example, consider the question of elevators in student dormitories. It has been argued that the ADA does not require that wheelchair-using students have access to the upper floors of a dorm, so long as accessible rooms that are equivalent in size and comfort are available on the first floor. This position – whatever its merits in the courts – uses a definition of equivalence that is too narrow. The social life of dorms often varies in predictable ways from floor to floor. At Stanford, a typical four-class dorm has three stories. The top story rooms are sought after by upperclass males, presumably because of their remoteness from the faculty resident fellow cottages. The parties on the top story tend to be best, at least as measured by prevailing undergraduate values. The faculty and staff committees who plan the dorms might consider the accessibility of such parties to be of no real value to the serious student – but why should disabled students be categorized as more serious on average than any others? Certainly, one can find successful Stanford alumni who remember such parties as among their most valuable college experiences.

The next two practices have to do with conceptualizing things at the wrong level of abstraction.

2) **Confusing a task with a particular way of performing it.** The only way to walk is to move one's legs. But, as Roosevelt found out, there are many ways to propel oneself around a room, or get from one floor to another – as long as the tools and infrastructure are provided. The only way to type is to move keys on a keyboard, but there are many ways to enter data without typing. For example, one can use speech or an eye-tracker. When a task is confused with a particular way of doing it, designers make decisions that have to do with that particular method, not the essential nature of the task.

3) **Confusing information with a particular form that it takes.** The exact nature of information is subject to philosophical debate, but on any reasonable conception, information is distinguished from the particular forms in which it is expressed, carried or stored in various situations. Consider, for example, the information that the wildflowers are blooming at Stanford. Someone might notice this while driving to work, remember it later in the morning and

send an e-mail message about it. That message might be read by Stanford alums in Germany, Korea and Japan, and conveyed to colleagues in those countries in the local languages. It might be printed out in Braille, or read by a screen-reader of a program officer at the National Science Foundation (NSF) in Washington, D.C. A Stanford researcher may read it on her home computer, and sign the information to her husband in American Sign Language before leaving for work. The same information, that the wildflowers are blooming at Stanford, is first carried by the visual system, then stored in the brain, then expressed electronically in one language. The same information is expressed in other languages, and in various ways, voice, Braille, print and sign.

The multimedia capacities of modern computers and the World Wide Web make it more possible than ever to provide information in various forms, but more tempting than ever not to do so. Suppose someone is designing a web page for a chain of motels. Much of the basic information, such as the name, address, phone numbers and rates of the various motels is naturally conveyed in text. The web page might also contain pictures of the various motels, and maps on how to get to them from the nearest large highway. Perhaps next to the picture of a seaside motel might be a button that allows one to hear the sound of the surf.

One could argue whether or not it is theoretically possible to convey in a text-only format, all and only the information that is conveyed in a picture. Clearly, as a practical matter, it is not. Nevertheless, it is usually fairly easy to convey the salient information: "This picture shows a one story motel with a parking lot and swimming pool located in front of a large construction site"; "This recording allows one to hear the sound of the surf from a room in the motel; the slightly fainter sounds of the nearby freeway are audible when the surf is quiet."

The rights of deaf individuals to serve on juries (with the institution providing ASL interpreters as needed) have been upheld as have the rights of blind individuals. One can conceive of cases in which direct inspection of evidence in a particular form – e.g., visual form or auditory form – by jurors would be expected to play a crucial and central role in the decision making process. That is, one can conceive of cases in which, because of our incomplete understanding of what makes different forms of information equivalent, a blind or deaf juror might reasonably be excused because of his or her impairment. However, in the case of a blind juror that was argued in court, such an argument was not made. In this case the juror was excused very early in the selection process, before being assigned to any particular case, simply for being blind.

Equal Access to Information

Even if everyone agrees that an accommodation is reasonable, there is still the question of who makes the accommodation and who pays.

On issues of mobility, the division of responsibility is clear legally and intuitively: people don't have to supply their own ramps and don't usually expect employers, stores, and other public facilities to supply wheelchairs.[15] But in the cases involving computers and other technological equipment, things are not always so clear. We believe the "divide and conquer" strategy exemplified by the TAS system has the potential to lower and distribute the costs of accommodations that provide access to computers. At a first pass we would suggest the following guidelines:

- Employers and institutions are responsible for providing an accessible infrastructure, that will permit use of accessibility tools. On our approach, this would mean computers outfitted with TAPs, so that individuals with disabilities can operate the computer (or devices with computer front-ends) with their accessors.

- Agencies, schools, employers and other agencies that help provide equipment to individuals with disabilities should focus on providing accessors that are suited to the individuals' continuing input and output needs and preferences, rather than computers whose utility is restricted to a particular class, grade, job, or other special situation.

To sum up. Philosophically and theoretically, modern technology in general and cyberspace in particular diminish the differences between disabled and nondisabled individuals. We all live in a hugely extended accomplishment space; we all depend on technology to bring us information and augment our action.

Individuals who are not agents in cyberspace have an accomplishment space that is diminished compared to others. Such a person is handicapped. The handicap may be caused by not having the right tool (e.g., an accessible computer) or by not having the infrastructure (e.g., an available phone line) to support the tool. If the individual has a disability, then there may be an additional problem: The right tool may be difficult to find or may be nonexistent. The inability is the same whether the individual can't afford the right tool

---

[15]There are exceptions. We expect airports to have wheelchairs available for travelers who need them. The rationale is basically that some travelers who use wheelchairs will travel without them (sending their chairs in luggage), and that some travelers will need chairs in airports that might not need them elsewhere.

or can't find it. In either case, in today's information-oriented society, the inability is a handicapping condition that affects an individual's opportunity to reach life's goals. Equality of opportunity and equality before the law are recognized as basic American principles; the embodiment of these principles in the concept of equality of access and workplace accommodations is legislated by the Americans With Disabilities Act. In the information age, all of these principles entail another: equal access to information which includes equal access to cyberspace.

Appendix: The Graphical User Interface Problem

Graphical user interfaces (GUI s) use icons, pull-down menus, windows and other nontextual devices to enhance communication between computers and the people who are using them. Pointing devices, such as the mouse, are an integral part of the GUI. Such interfaces, as found on Macintoshes, PCs running Windows and OS/2 and almost all of the more powerful workstations, have proven to be a boon for many computer users including those with many types of disabilities. Blind users, however, are an exception. For them, rather than improving access, the GUI has made computers less accessible than they were before. Screen reading programs for text-based computers are mature products which do a good job of automatically transcribing text from the screen into synthesized speech or Braille. Similar screen access programs for Windows-based computers are still in the early stages of development and are not yet able to provide comparable performance or ease of use. Screen reading programs for Windows 3.1 took more than four years to develop. Soon after they became available, many businesses moved to Windows 95, requiring another lengthy round of development to catch up. While there are many successful systems for translating text-based screens into alternative sound or tactile representations, strategies for representing GUI screens are still quite primitive and difficult to use, and keeping up with GUI innovations is a never-ending cycle. The scope of the GUI problem for blind computer users increases as GUI interfaces become standard not only for computers, but for appliances of all sorts, video access to telephones, the internet and interactive cable television.

Before GUIs, specialized access devices gave blind computer users almost equal access to information as sighted users. Now this access is threatened by the widespread acceptance of computers that rely almost totally on vision. Of course we do not suggest that GUIs be taken away from people who benefit from using them. However, as GUIs proliferate, it will be necessary to have access solutions that are much more general than at present, if blind people are to have general access to information comparable to sighted computer users. One major problem in providing access to graphically displayed information is the lack of standardization in the way graphics is generated and handled by different hardware, operating systems and applications software. Another major problem is much more fundamental; we really don't know very much about how to represent graphical information to someone who can't see it. In other words, there are two critical problems to be solved: The first is how to extract text and graphical information from any computer screen; and the second is how to present graphical information to a blind user in an effective and efficient manner.

Solutions to these problems will require a variety of technologies. Synthesized speech, nonspeech sounds, multidimensional sounds, touch, force, and

---

The following recommendations for promoting accessible were developed by members of a conference on Graphical User Interfaces and Blind and Visually-Impaired Computer Users held in Asilomar, California in November of 1993[a]:

- Agencies that fund grant proposals related to computer access should encourage vigorous efforts to develop accessible and efficient interfaces to computers and systems that use GUIs for blind users.

- An independent, vendor-neutral agency should develop and maintain standards and specifications for the inclusion of hooks within operating systems to support special access technologies.

- A vendor-neutral organization should define and widely disseminate Principles of Accessible Interface Design among all hardware and software designers and developers, not only of computer systems, but of all electronic devices that incorporate graphical user interfaces.

- The distinction between information and the form in which it is presented must be preserved in all electronic representations of information to allow the same information to be presented in a variety of ways.

- A considerable investment must be made in the training of individuals who are not visually oriented to ensure they are able to fully use computer systems that incorporate graphical user interfaces and tactile graphics.

---

[a]For more information on this conference and the succeeding one held in 1995, send e-mail to mckinley@roses.stanford.edu.

movement are all potentially useful for conveying information to a blind user. The larger question of how to present information content efficiently when shifting from a visual to nonvisual modality requires an interdisciplinary investigation of psychological, computational, and logical aspects of the representation of meaning and information in different modalities. The interested reader can find out about ongoing work in these areas by following the links in http://www-csli.stanford.edu/arch/research/html.

REFERENCES

Amundson, R. 1992. Disability, Handicap, and the Environment. *Journal of Social Philosophy*, Volume XXIII, No. 1 (Spring): 105–119.

Gallagher, H. 1985. *FDR's Splendid Deception.* New York: Dodd, Mead.

http://www-csli.stanford.edu/arch/research.html

Israel, D., J. Perry, and S. Tutiya. 1991. Actions and Movements. In *Proceedings of IJCAI-'91*, Mountain View, CA: Morgan Kaufmann.

Israel, D., J. Perry, and S. Tutiya. 1993. Executions, Motivations and Accomplishments. *The Philosophical Review* (October):515-40.

Longmore, P. 1993. *The Ideologies and Culture of Disabilities.* Talk given on 29 January, at Stanford University.

Scott, N.G. n.d. Total Access System. CSLI, Stanford University: Unpublished manuscript.

Scott, N.G., and C.W. Britell. 1993. Computer Adaptive Systems and Technology for the Disabled. In *Rehabilitation Medicine: Principles and Practice*, 2nd. ed., ed. J.A. DeLisa. Philadelphia: J.B. Lippincott Company.

World Health Organization. 1980. *International Classification of Impairments, Disabilities, and Handicaps: A Manual of Classification Relating to the Consequences of Disease.* Geneva: World Health Organization.

4

Do Categories Have Politics? The Language/Action Perspective Reconsidered

LUCY SUCHMAN

Abstract: Drawing on writings within the Computer Supported Cooperative Work (CSCW) community and on recent social theory, this paper proposes that the adoption of speech act theory as a foundation for system design carries with it an agenda of discipline and control over organization members' actions. I begin with a brief review of the language/action perspective introduced by Winograd, Flores and their colleagues, focusing in particular on the categorization of speakers' intent. I then turn to some observations on the politics of categorization and, with that framework as background, consider the attempt, through THE COORDINATOR to implement a technological system for intention-accounting within organizations. Finally, I suggest the implications of the analysis presented in the paper for the politics of CSCW systems design.

> *No idea is more provocative in controversies about technology and society than the notion that technical things have political qualities. At issue is the claim that machines, structures, and systems of modern material culture can be accurately judged not only for their contributions to efficiency and productivity ... but also for the ways in which they can embody specific forms of power and authority.*
> —*Winner 1986, p. 19.*

> *By teaching people an ontology of linguistic action, grounded in simple, universal distinctions such as those of requesting and promising, we find that they become more aware of these distinctions in their everyday work and life situations. They can simplify their dealings with others, reduce time and effort spent in conversations that do not result in action, and generally manage actions in a less panicked, confused atmosphere.*
> —*Flores et al., 1988, p. 158.*

> *The world has always been in the middle of things, in unruly and practical conversation, full of action and structured by a startling array of actants and of networking and unequal collectives ... The shape of my amodern history will have a different geometry, not of progress, but of permanent and multi-patterned interaction through which lives and worlds get built, human and unhuman.*
> —*Haraway 1991, p. 11.*

Since the inception of CSCW as an explicit research agenda in the early 1980s,

---

I am grateful to Phil Agre, Liam Bannon and Randy Trigg for their comments on an earlier version of this paper.

a class of systems has been under development that attempt to structure computer-based message systems into tools for the coordination of social action.
Some of these have been concerned with affording flexible support for a diverse and changing ensemble of communicative practices (for example COS-
MOS/Bowers & Churcher, 1988). Others have been aimed at using system design as a mechanism for the prescription of *a priori* forms of social behavior.
Arguably the most influential of the latter efforts has been the language/action
perspective of Winograd, Flores and their colleagues and the system, trade-
marked THE COORDINATOR, designed to implement it.[1]

This paper is an attempt to contribute to a critical reexamination of the
place of coordination technologies in CSCW research and development, in
particular that class of technologies that seeks to develop canonical frameworks for the representation and control of everyday communicative practices. Among the latter, I take the language/action perspective of Winograd,
Flores et al., and its embodiment in THE COORDINATOR as exemplary. Of particular concern is the problem of how the theories informing such systems
conceptualize the structuring of everyday conversation and the dynamics of
organizational interaction over time. To anticipate, I will argue that the adoption of speech act theory as a foundation for system design, with its emphasis
on the encoding of speakers' intentions into explicit categories, carries with it
an agenda of discipline and control over organization members' actions. Alternatively, we might embrace instead something closer to the stance that histori-
an Donna Haraway recommends; namely, an appreciation for and engagement within the specificity, heterogeneity and practicality of organizational
life.

My strategy for developing this argument will be to juxtapose what might at
first seem unrelated discussions, drawn on the one hand from influential writings within the CSCW community and on the other from recent social theory.
Specifically, I begin with a brief review of the language/action perspective introduced by Winograd, Flores and their colleagues, focusing in particular on
the place of speech act theory and the categorization of speakers' intent in that
perspective. I then turn to some observations on the politics of categorization
offered by the sociologist Harvey Sacks, and on disciplinary practice by the
philosopher Michel Foucault. The point of this latter move is to look at the
place of categorization as an instrument in the control of social relations. With

---

[1]Both the language/action perspective and THE COORDINATOR have been described in numerous
publications. The present discussion relies upon Winograd and Flores (1986) and Flores et al.
(1988).

that sociological framework as background, I consider the attempt, through THE COORDINATOR, to implement a technical system for intention-accounting in organizations. Finally, I suggest the implications of the analysis presented for the politics of CSCW systems design.

SPEECH ACT THEORY

In their book *Understanding Computers and Cognition: A New Foundation for Design* (1986) Winograd and Flores present speech act theory as the basis for a particular doctrine of communication, and an associated machinery for the training and improvement of members' participation in organizational life. From the language/action perspective they describe, the "ontology"of organizational life comprises speech acts combined into "recurrent patterns of communication in which language provides the coordination between actions" (1988, p. 156). Through their development of this perspective, speech act theory has come to be a dominant framework for the conceptualization of communicative action within the CSCW community. To understand the underpinings of that conceptualization requires a closer look at just what speech act theory takes to be its basic premises and what makes those premises compelling for computer research. The two aspects of the theory most relevant to the present argument are (a) the premise that language is a form of action and (b) the assumption that a science of language/action requires a formal system of categorization.

The observation that language is social action is due originally to Austin (1962) and the later Wittgenstein (1958), who argue for the impossibility of theorizing language apart from its use. Somewhat paradoxically, however, their observations have been taken by subsequent theorists as grounds for assuming that *a theory of language constitutes a theory of action.* Rather than setting up as a requirement on theorizing about language/action that it be based in investigations of talk as a form of activity, the observation that language is action has been taken to imply that action is, or can be theorized as, the use of language *qua* system to get things done. And language taken as a system provides a tractable core phenomenon for disciplines whose theory and methods best equip them for formal systems analysis. The proposition that dealing with language is dealing with action has consequently become a means of extending the scope of such disciplines while requiring little if any change to their organizing premises and practices.

Moreover, as Bowers and Churcher summarize it :

[s]ince Austin, the development of speech act theory has been largely associated with Searle ... Searle has been at pains to formalise the notions introduced by Austin, to classify the conditions under which different kinds of speech acts can be appropriately ("felicitously") issued, and to explicate a typology of illocutionary acts. It is Searle's work which has proved particularly influential in CSCW (Bowers & Churcher, 1988, p. 126).

Language in this scheme is an instrumentality, a technology employed by the individual to express his or her intentions to others. The taxonomy of utterances that speech act theory after Searle proposes seeks to provide a comprehensive ordering of the available communicative tools, represented as a formalized "grammar of action" (Agre, 1995, p. 183–185).

In response to the popularity of speech act theory a number of cogent critiques have appeared in recent years based on observations drawn from the analysis of actually occurring conversation (see for example Bogen, 1991; Bowers & Churcher, 1988; Schegloff, 1988; Levinson, 1983). These critiques turn on the interactional and circumstantially contingent character of meaning and intention. Briefly, the argument is that speech act theory takes communication as an exchange of speakers-hearers' intent, while conversation analyses underscore the irreducibly interactional structuring of talk. So, for example, conversation analysts have documented the ways in which a speaker's intent is observably shaped by the response of hearers over the course of an utterance's (co)production (see for example Goodwin, 1981; Goodwin & Goodwin, 1992; Schegloff 1982). Bowers and Churcher argue that the consequent "radical indeterminacy" of the unfolding course of human interaction presents a problem for any system designed automatically to track an interaction's course by projecting expected or canonically organized sequences. This, they argue, "cannot be ignored by designers of systems for CSCW without unwittingly coercing their users" (Bowers & Churcher, 1988, p. 137).

A related criticism of speech act theory turns on the difficulty, for the hearer/analyst, of categorizing the illocutionary force or perlocutionary effect of an utterance given its interactional and contingent character. THE COORDINATOR dispenses with this problem by enrolling speakers themselves in categorizing their utterances with explicit illocutionary tags. As Winograd and Flores explain it:

> We are not proposing that a computer can 'understand' speech acts by analyzing natural language utterances ... What we propose is to make the user aware of this structure and to provide tools for working with it explicitly. This is being done experimentally in a computer program that we are developing called a 'coordinator,' designed for constructing and controlling conversation networks in large-scale dis-

tributed electronic communication systems ... An individual performs a speech act using THE COORDINATOR by: selecting the illocutionary force from a small set of alternatives (the basic building blocks mentioned above); indicating the propositional content in text; and explicitly entering temporal relationships to other (past and anticipated) acts (1986, p. 159).

So in the face of otherwise intractable uncertainties in accounting for the "illocutionary force" of a given utterance, THE COORDINATOR enlists participants in a coding procedure aimed at making implicit intent explicit. The premise of this procedure is that explicitly identified speech acts are clear, unambiguous, and preferred.[2] Whether based in the assumption that intent is somehow there already in the utterance and that what is being done is simply to express it, or that left to themselves people will remain vague as to their own intent and that of others and will benefit from the discipline of being pressed for clarity, the strategy of THE COORDINATOR is to remedy the carelessness of organization members regarding their commitments to each other through a technologically-based system of intention-accounting. According to Winograd and Flores the motivation here is explicitly self-improvement:

> In their day-to-day being, people are generally not aware of what they are doing. They are simply working, speaking, etc. more or less blind to the pervasiveness of the essential dimensions of commitment. Consequently, there exists a domain for education in communicative competence: The fundamental relationships between language and successful action ... People's conscious knowledge of their participation in the network of commitment can be reinforced and developed, improving their capacity to act in the domain of language (Winograd & Flores, 1986, p. 162).

The machine thus becomes the instructor, the monitor of one's actions, keeping track of temporal relations and warning of potential breakdowns. It provides as well, of course, a record that can subsequently be invoked by organization members in calling each others' actions to account.

CATEGORIZATION AS DISCIPLINE

Speech act theory brings us into the presence of categorization as a basic device for the analytic sciences, including the longstanding search for a science of intentionality. Within recent social science, in particular ethnomethodology, this tradition has been challenged through a conceptually simple but con-

---

[2] See Bowers 1992, pp. 3–4 for a discussion of the modernist preference for the "clear and distinct" and its relation to agendas of explicitness, formalisation and control.

sequentially complex inversion of the status of categorization devices as analytic resources. Briefly, categorization has been taken up not just as a resource for analysts but as part of their topic or subject matter; that is, as a fundamental device by which all members of any society constitute their social order. With this move has come a rich corpus of theorizing and of empirical study about just how they do so (see for example Sacks, 1979; Sacks & Schegloff, 1979; Schegloff, 1972).

In his consideration of members' categorization devices, the sociologist Harvey Sacks was concerned among other things with the role that categorization plays in contests over the control of social identities. As a way in to his analysis we can take a passage from a 1966 lecture published under the title "Hotrodder: A Revolutionary Category" (1979). The problem Sacks sets up for himself in this lecture is to understand what is going on with teenage kids and cars. Sacks himself is working with a piece of transcript, in which kids are talking about the relative likelihood of getting picked up by the police depending on what kind of car you are driving and, within that, just how you are dressed when driving it. Of this bit of talk and its implications Sacks says:

> We could work at it by asking such questions as, why do kids go about making up all those typologies of cars – and the typologies they have are really enormously elaborate, and they use those typologies to make assessments of other drivers, and the assessments are not always very nice, as we've seen. Now the question to ask is why do they do it? Aren't the terms that are used before they go to work good enough? And what's the matter with them if they aren't? (Sacks, 1979, p. 8)

For my own present purposes, then, what I want to ask is: What is it about speech act theory that makes it so attractive as a way for practitioners of science and systems design to come to grips with organizational communications? Why do computer scientists go about making up all these typologies of interaction? Aren't the typologies used by practitioners themselves before we go to work, as designers, good enough? And what's the matter with them if they aren't?

I have already suggested how a particular interpretation of language as action could contribute to the attractiveness of speech act theory for the system sciences. To get more specifically at the question of categorization, we might begin by asking as Sacks does in relation to kids what it is that categorization provides for those making use of it in some domain of activity. Sacks frames his analysis of "hotrodders" in terms of acts of resistance, specifically how persons assigned to a place in a system of categorization not of their own making, e.g., "teenagers," can develop categories for themselves, e.g., "hotrodders" as, in Sacks' terms, a revolutionary act. That is to say, systems of categorization are ordering devices, used to organize the persons, settings, events or activities by whom they are employed or to which they refer. Noncompliance with the use of a particular category scheme, particularly one imposed from outside, or the adoption of an alternative are often in this sense acts of resistance.[3]

If membership categorization is appropriable as a technology of control by some parties over others, acts of resistance involve a taking back of systems of naming and assessment into indigenous categorization schemes developed by the "others" themselves. In Sacks' words

> ...that means, for example, that *they* will recognize whether somebody is a member of one or another category, and what that membership takes, and *they* can do the sanctioning ... what's known about hotrodders – what they do with their cars, *how* they look, how they behave – these are things that hotrodders can enforce on each other and defend against nonmembers (Sacks, 1979, p. 11–12).

Sacks' analysis identifies the relation of categorization devices to social identity, including assessments of persons' adherence to the moral and aesthetic sensibilities associated with a particular category. It points as well to the ways in which categorization can be taken up as a resource in the development of more elaborated and formalised systems of social control. These systems form a kind of technology whether or not they are literally inscribed in a machine. In *Discipline and Punish* (1979) Michel Foucault traces the historical development of a figurative machinery of disciplinary practice, the military, and takes as a case in point the soldier, treated in the 17th century as an intrinsically honorable entity whose character was reflected in his bearing, becoming in the 18th century a technical body to be trained via exercise:

> These methods, which made possible the meticulous control of the operations of the body, which assured the constant subjection of its focus and imposed on them a relation of docility-utility, might be called 'disciplines' ... The historical moment of the disciplines was the moment when an art of the human body was born ... A 'political anatomy,' which was also a 'mechanics of power' ... it defined how one may have a hold over others' bodies, not only so they may do what one wishes, but so that they may operate as one wishes, with the techniques, the speed and the efficiency

---

[3]Liam Bannon points out that this is part of the wider phenomenon of

> ...naming as a form of control...the missionaries banning the use of native names and giving natives 'Christian' names to make them lose their sense of history, or the British in Ireland renaming villages and counties in English terms that did not preserve the original Gaelic meanings, thus disinheriting future generations of their past folklore and roots" (1993, personal communication).

Anthropology is replete with further examples, drawn from colonial encounters between European and indigenous cultures throughout the world.

that one determines. Thus discipline produces subjected and practiced bodies, 'docile' bodies (p. 137–138).

Foucault further points out that disciplinary practices invariably develop in response to specific problems in the administration of power. With these perspectives in mind, we can return to the idea of taking the categorization devices of speech act theory as a basis for organizational communications. Like many of the cases reviewed by Foucault, this order is to be administered technologically. That is to say, troubles diagnosed as breakdowns in communication are to be addressed through a technological solution involving a new communicative discipline. Speech act theory and its attendant technologies are offered as a remedy to perceived flaws and inadequacies in organization members' communicative practices, by providing an order enforced through the technology. The 20th century then might be seen as a return to the analysis and manipulation of what Foucault calls the 'signifying elements of behavior,' through the training of the body's intentions as reflected in its talk.

THE CONVERSATION FOR ACTION

To see how the discipline of intention-encoding plays out in the technology of THE COORDINATOR we can turn to Winograd and Flores' "theory of management and conversation," centered around the "conversation for action" pictured as Figure 5.1 (1986, p. 65) in their text (Figure 1 here):

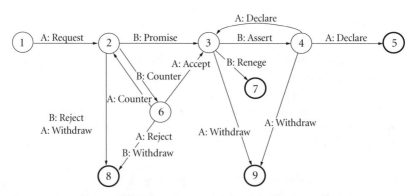

Figure 1. The basic conversation for action. (From Winograd and Flores, 1986, p. 65).

As Winograd and Flores explain this figure in their text:

As an example of conversational analysis we will consider in some detail the network of speech acts that constitute straightforward *conversations for action* – those in which an interplay of requests and commissives are directed towards explicit cooperative action. This is a useful example both because of its clarity and because it is the basis for computer tools for conducting conversations...

We can plot the basic course of a conversation in a simple diagram like that of Figure 5.1, in which each circle represents a possible state of the conversation and the lines represent speech acts (1986, p. 64, original emphasis).

This picture is central to Winograd and Flores' exposition, and so bears a closer look. In a paper titled "Pictures of Nothing? Visual Construals in Social Theory" (1990) Michael Lynch suggests that representations like that of "the basic conversation for action" as he puts it "both describe the operations of 'rationality' and display 'rationalistic commitments.'" Such pictures, he explains:

> ...do not propose to resemble observable phenomena, nor do they present readers with puzzles to be worked out in a visible workspace. Instead, they mobilize formal elements to exhibit and authorize a certain 'impression of rationality'...
>
> This impression of rationality is associated with at least the following formal elements: bounded labels, quasi-causal vectors, and spatial symmetries and equivalences...The spatial separation between the labels contributes to a sense of their conceptual discrimination, and the coherent two-dimensional arrangement provides a unitary 'ground' for linking together the heterogeneous factors...The labels are detached from the relative seamlessness and polysemy of discursive writing, taking on the appearance of stable concepts or even of names for things positioned in space...The entire array of cells and vectors in the picture look somewhat like an electrical wiring diagram; a tracing of a tightly contained flow of an homogeneous force from one well-defined component to another (Lynch, 1990, p. 20–22).

The picture of the basic conversation for action then unifies and at least implicitly mathematizes the phenomena it represents. It works by transforming a set of colloquial expressions into a formal system of categorization that relies upon organization members' willingness to reformulate their actions in its (now technical) vocabulary (Agre, 1995).[4] Once encapsulated and reduced to the homogeneous black circles and arrows of the diagram the "conversation" is findable anywhere. At the same time, specific occasions of conversation are no longer open to characterization in any other terms.

Winograd and Flores' figure of a conversation claims to be a reduction of the intentional structure of any conversation for action, while also providing the

---

[4]Agre further points out that in the formalization provided by speech act theory the categories employed are not different from members' own so much as different in kind; that is, they are technical renderings of familiar terms.

rendering that is required by the computer system, THE COORDINATOR, which they present as a logical consequence of their analysis. In displaying categorical action types and their logical relations, the representation sets up the grounds for just the kind of menu-driven procedures for intention-encoding and accounting that the technology of THE COORDINATOR embodies and prescribes. The Conversation for Action, in contrast to conversations in the course of on-going activity, is bounded and ready-to-hand for translation into the machine. And for management, the machine promises to tame and domesticate, to render rational and controllable the densely structured, heterogeneous texture of organizational life. As Flores et al. put it in the citation with which this paper begins:

> By teaching people an ontology of linguistic action, grounded in simple, universal distinctions such as those of requesting and promising, we find that they become more aware of these distinctions in their everyday work and life situations. They can simplify their dealings with others, reduce time and effort spent in conversations that do not result in action, and generally manage actions in a less panicked, confused atmosphere (1988, p. 158).

The assumption that "universal" distinctions such as requesting and promising are simple, however, conflates the simplicity of the category with the subtlety and complexity of the phenomenon categorized. One could imagine by analogy a system of painting that trained artists to follow a "simple" scheme of primary colors. But our sense of artistry in any field is precisely the ability to move, in more and less articulable ways, effectively through the circumstances in which one finds oneself. This is not done through reductions but through complex forms of highly skilled practice, involving an ability to bring past experience to bear in creative ways upon an unfolding situation.

There seems something of a contradiction, moreover, between the premise that THE COORDINATOR is a tool for introducing order into an otherwise "panicked, confused atmosphere," and the subsequent statement by Flores et al. that

> [w]e are primarily designing for settings in which the basic parameters of authority, obligation and cooperation are stable...THE COORDINATOR has been most successful in organizations in which the users are relatively confident about their own position and the power they have within it. This does not mean that the organization is democratic or that power relations are equal. It means that there is clarity about what is expected of people and what authority they have (Flores et al., 1988, p.173).

Rather than being a tool for the collaborative production of social action, in other words, THE COORDINATOR on this account is a tool for the reproduction of an established social order.

Winograd and Flores argue that theory-driven design will produce coherent systems and practices. They report that implementations of THE COORDINATOR have been used to manage large software engineering enterprises, in which they claim the participants report that "by providing a computer tool to maintain the structure of the requests and commitments, they were able to greatly improve productivity" (1986, p. 161). Other reports of THE COORDINATOR use from the field, however, indicate that users selectively appropriate and ignore aspects of the system in an *ad hoc* fashion (see for example Johnson et al., 1986; Bullen & Bennett, 1990). On the one hand, users' failure in these cases to use the system as intended by its designers could be seen as a failure of the design, or of the compliance of users. On the other hand, it could be taken to reflect the desirability of systems that lend themselves to various *ad hoc* forms of customization in use (Robinson & Bannon, 1991). The success that THE COORDINATOR has enjoyed, on the latter interpretation, would be understandable less as a result of its theory-driven coherence than of its practical adaptability.

CONCLUSION

The language/action perspective takes off from the observation that technologies comprise both artifacts and associated practices. From this it follows that "technology is not the design of physical things. It is the design of practices and possibilities to be realized through artifacts" (Flores et al., 1988, p. 153). What ties together hotrodders, Foucault's soldier and the users of THE COORDINATOR is the belief by others that they must be brought into compliance with a particular conventional order. For technical systems it is the computer scientist (presumably assisted by organizational development consultants and the managers who employ them) who is now cast into the role of designer not only of technical systems but of organizations themselves. And implicit in the endeavor of professional organizational design is the premise that organization members, like the components of the technical system, require a strong, knowledgable hand that orders them, integrates them and brings them effectively into use.

Organizational design from a language/action perspective takes place within the context of a technological imperative that leads inexorably to change and, if done well, to progress. As Flores puts it:

> When we accept the fact that computer technology will radically change management and the nature of office work, we can move toward designing that change as an improvement in organizational life (Flores et al.,1988, p. 154).

Before we accept this imperative, however, I would argue that we should subject it to the following questions:

First, what kind of a fact is it "that computer technology will radically change management and the nature of office work?" Computer technology, the directionality and dynamics of change, and the forms of work that are the objects of change are treated as self-evident, homogeneous and naturalized entities. But what if we were to open up this proposition to the uncertainties, heterogeneities and practical expediencies of the categories it invokes? We would need to specify then just what technologies concerned us, and how; whether, or even how those technologies are implicated in what processes of change; just what forms of managerial work we are concerned with and why; and what other forms of work, in what kinds of settings, we assume are getting done.

Second, who are "we?" From what position do we claim or are we granted rights to design change? In what sense is change designed? From what perspective do we assess the results of our actions as "improving organizational life," and for whom?

Throughout the history of communications technologies within organizations we find the imposition of regimes of action in the name of individual self-improvement and organizational efficiency (Yates, 1989). At the same time, organization members are subjected to ever more elaborated systems of record-keeping, measurement and accountability. Instead of the emancipating alternative that Winograd and Flores would seek, they seem to offer yet another technology designed to create order out of "nature" by, as Haraway would put it, "policing her unruly embodiments" (1991, p. 20).

I have proposed that speech act theory offers to system and management sciences a model of the communicative order compatible with the prior commitments of those enterprises – a model of speech that promises a universal basis for the design of technologies of accountability. By technologies of accountability I mean systems aimed at the inscription and documentation of actions to which parties are accountable not only in the ethnomethodological sense of that term (Garfinkel & Sacks, 1970), but in the sense represented by the bookkeeper's ledger, the record of accounts paid and those still outstanding. If this promise of speech act theory is consistent with the intellectual antecedents and aspirations of system and management science, however, it is also increasingly difficult to maintain in the face of a growing challenge from culturally and historically-based studies of talk as it is specifically located in space and time. Schegloff (n.d.) has stated this challenge in terms of the debate over "context":

> There is, to my mind, no escaping the observation that context … is not like some penthouse to be added after the structure of action has been built out of constitutive intentional, logical, syntactic, semantic and pragmatic/speech-act-theoretic bricks. The temporal/sequential context rather supplies the ground on which the whole edifice of action is built (by the participants) in the first instance, and to which it is adapted 'from the ground up'…(p 21).

With the emergence of technologies like THE COORDINATOR, this debate is no longer over intellectual terrain alone. The inscription of formal representations of action in technical systems transforms the debate more clearly into a contest over how our relations to each other are ordered and by whom. Sacks' discussion of membership categorization draws our attention to the ways in which categorization devices are devices of social control involving contests between others' claims to the territories inhabited by persons or activities and their own, internally administered forms of organization. In the case of hotrodders, the move is to develop indigenous categories through which kids are able to claim back ownership of their social identities from the adult world that would claim knowledge of them. In the move to inscribe and encode organization members' intentions, as commitments or otherwise, we find a recent attempt to gain members' compliance with an externally imposed regime of institutional control. Sacks' insight can help us make sense of the abiding interest that those committed to the reproduction of an established institutional order might have in replacing the contested moral grounds of organizational commitment and accountability with a scheme of standardized, universalistic categories, administered through technologies implemented on the desktop.

REFERENCES

Agre, P. 1995. From High Tech to Human Tech: Empowerment, Measurement, and Social Studies of Computing. In *Computer & Supported Cooperative Work (CSCW)* vol. 3, no. 2., 167–185. Dordrecht: Kluwer.

Austin, J.L. 1962. *How To Do Things With Words.* Oxford: Clarendon Press.

Bogen, D. 1991. Linguistic Forms and Social Obligations: A Critique of the Doctrine of Literal Expression in Searle. *Journal for the Theory of Social Behavior* 21(1): 31–62.

Bowers, J. 1992. The Politics of Formalism. In *Contexts of Computer-Mediated Communication*, ed. M. Lea. Hassocks: Harvester.

Bowers, J., and J. Churcher. 1988. Local and Global Structuring of Computer-Mediated Communication. In *Proceedings of the ACM Conference on Computer-Supported Cooperative Work (CSCW '88)*, 125–139. New York: Association of Computing Machinery.

Bullen, C., and J. Bennett. 1990. Learning from User Experience with Groupware. In *Proceedings of the ACM Conference on Computer-Supported Cooperative Work (CSCW '90)*, 291–302. New York: Association of Computing Machinery.

Flores, F., M. Graves, B. Hartfield, and T. Winograd. 1988. Computer Systems and the Design of Organizational Interaction. *ACM Transactions on Office Information Systems*, Special Issue on the Language/Action Perspective 6(2): 153–172.

Foucault, M. 1979. *Discipline and Punish: The Birth of the Prison.* New York: Random House.

Garfinkel, H., and H. Sacks. 1970. On Formal Structures of Practical Action. In *Theoretical Sociology*, eds. J. McKinney and E. Tiryakian, 337–366. New York: Appleton-Century-Crofts.

Goodwin, C. 1981. *Conversational Organization: Interaction between Speakers and Hearers.* New York: Academic Press.

Goodwin, C., and M. Goodwin. 1992. Assessments and the Construction of Context. In *Rethinking Context: Language As an Interactive Phenomenon*, eds. A. Duranti and C. Goodwin, 147–190. Cambridge, UK: Cambridge University Press.

Haraway, D.J. 1991. Science as Culture, Science Studies as Cultural Studies? Paper prepared for the volume *Cultural Studies Now and in the Future*, P. Treichler, C. Nelson, and L. Grossberg eds., in prep., presented at a conference on Disunity and Contextualism: New Directions in the Philosophy of Science Studies. Stanford University, March31–April 1.

Johnson, B., G. Weaver, M. Olson, and R. Dunham. 1986. Using a Computer-based Tool to Support Collaboration: A Field Experiment. In *Proceedings of the ACM Conference on Computer-Supported Cooperative Work (CSCW '86)*, 343–352. New York: Association of Computing Machinery.

Levinson, S. 1983. Speech Acts. Chapter 5 in *Pragmatics*. Cambridge, UK: Cambridge University Press.

Lynch, M. 1990. Pictures of Nothing? Visual Construals in Social Theory. Paper presented at the 85th Annual Meeting of the American Sociological Association, Washington, D.C., August.

Robinson, M., and L. Bannon. 1991. Questioning Representations. In *Proceedings of the European Conference on Computer-Supported Cooperative Work*, 219–234. Amsterdam.

Sacks, H. 1979. Hotrodder: A Revolutionary Category. In *Everyday Language: Studies in Ethnomethodology*, ed. G. Psathas, 7–14. New York: Irvington.

Sacks, H., and E. Schegloff. 1979. Two Preferences in the Organization of References to Persons in Conversation and their Interaction. In *Everyday Language: Studies in Ethnomethodology*, ed. G. Psathas, 15–21. New York: Irvington.

Schegloff, E. n.d. To Searle on Conversation: A Note in Return. Prepared for a volume of essays in response to the work of John Searle, unpublished manuscript, Department of Sociology, University of California, Los Angeles.

Schegloff, E. 1972. Notes on a Conversational Practice: Formulating place. In *Studies in Social Interaction*, ed. D. Sudnow, 75–119. New York, Free Press.

Schegloff, E. 1982. Discourse as an Interactional Achievement. In *Analyzing Discourse: Text and Talk*, ed. D. Tannen, 71–93. Georgetown Roundtable on Language & Linguistics, Washington, D.C.: Georgetown University Press.

Schegloff, E. 1988. Presequences and Indirection: Applying Speech Act Theory to Ordinary Conversation. *Journal of Pragmatics*, 12:55–62.

Suchman, L. 1993. Technologies of Accountability: On Lizards and Aeroplanes. In *Technology in Working Order: Studies in Work, Interaction and Technology*, ed. G. Button, 113–126. London: Routledge.

Winner, L. 1986. Do Artefacts Have Politics? In *The Whale and the Reactor*, 19–39. Chicago: University of Chicago Press.

Winograd, T., and F. Flores. 1986. *Understanding Computers and Cognition: A New Foundation for Design*. Norwood, NJ: Ablex.

Wittgenstein, L. 1958. *Philosophical Investigations*. Oxford: Blackwell.

Yates, J. 1989. *Control through Communication*. Baltimore and London: Johns Hopkins University Press.

5

Categories, Disciplines, and Social Coordination

TERRY WINOGRAD

Abstract: Lucy Suchman's chapter, "Do Categories Have Politics," challenges the validity of speech act theory as a basis for computer systems for workflow support. Suchman fears that the explicitness of the theory leads to undue discipline when it is applied in practice. Her fear is grounded in a misunderstanding of what it means to use such a theory, and this paper clarifies the difference between formal comprehensive *models* of behavior and formal *structures* used in communication and recording. Explicit speech act theory, like explicit accounting procedures, enforces a kind of uniformity that is necessary in any communication situation where ambiguity and vagueness cannot be routinely resolved through direct personal contact and knowledge. The practicalities of large geographically distributed organizations makes the appropriate use of shared structuring a precondition for effective cooperation.

Lucy Suchman's chapter "Do Categories Have Politics?" is an interesting text on which to reflect. Although it is couched in academic sociological arguments and citations, it clearly conveys a deeply felt political concern of the author, which evokes a strong response. The text deals with the validity of speech act theory and the categories it proposes for characterizing communication in organizations. The subtext is a sociopolitical drama, in which the villains (corporate managers and their accomplices: organizational development consultants and computer scientists) attempt to impose their designs on the innocent victims (the workers whom the managers want to "tame and domesticate"). The preeminent word in the text is "discipline," not in the sense of an academic discipline, but in the sense that one disciplines an unruly child. In fact, teenage hotrodders are one of Suchman's favorably cited examples of "resistance to externally imposed regimes of institutional control."[1]

In a way, it's an appealing story. We all feel acutely the unpleasant constraints of modern bureaucratic society, with its powerful impersonal organizations and lack of concern for the individual. More and more we feel that our lives are controlled by instititional forces that we cannot control or even clearly identify. In this social environment, every new technology or theory de-

---

[1] This quotation and others in this paper are based on the version of Suchman's paper that was originally published in the ECSCW '93 Conference, (DeMichelis, Simone & Schmidt, 1993). Suchman has made some minor modifications to the ECSCW '93 paper for the final journal version. In two places in this critique, Winograd has retained wording from the original version of the paper. In these cases, the original form is quoted and both citations are given.

serves to be approached with suspicion. But in her desire to cast THE COORDI-NATOR and its attendant language/action theory into the role of the oppressor, Suchman ends up making simplistic dichotomies and assumptions that do not do justice to the richness of social interactions.

Suchman's key dichotomy places the language/action perspective as "an agenda of discipline and control over organization member's actions" in stark opposition to her preferred "appreciation for and engagement within the specificity, heterogeneity and practicality of organizational life." The starting point from which she posits this distinction is accurate. Speech act theory (which Suchman refers to as "speech act doctrine") starts out with the goal of finding categories that can be applied to recurrent patterns of social action through language. As such it is concerned with what is common across individual situations and actions rather than what is specific and heterogeneous.

However, this search for generality becomes a doctrine (in the implied negative sense) only when it is taken to be a full account, rather than a basis for building objects for people to use. Suchman is absolutely correct in observing that no systematic account can fully capture the richness of mental life or social interaction. In spite of our extensive writing to the contrary (Winograd & Flores, 1986) she mistakenly takes that to be the goal of our work. Flores and I work from a practical rather than a disengaged analytical stance – the guiding question is not "How do you account for all of human behavior?" but "How do you design to augment people's capacity to act?"

Suchman hints at a more realistic understanding when she includes a parenthetical hedge in her statement that "Rather than opening up the boundaries of linguistic studies ... the language-as-action perspective has been taken to mean that action is, *or can be theorized as,* the use of langauge *qua* system to get things done." (ECSCW '93) [emphasis added] I would strongly reject the "is" and stand by the "can be theorized as." That is, I start from the perspective that no rationalized theory can fully account for any human mental or social phenomenon. The validity of "can be theorized as" is inevitably pragmatic – if the resulting structure is of demonstrable operative use, then one has a (but not *the*) valid theory of the phenomenon. Whether your theorizing focuses on determinacy or indeterminacy depends on what you are trying to accomplish.

The goal of THE COORDINATOR (and more recent systems based on the same fundamental concepts, as described in Medina-Mora et al., 1992) is to enable a structure of interactions that is effective for coordination within an organization. It uses a formal structure in which regular patterns of language acts are associated with the content and times of requests, commitments, and declarations of completion. It is based on the fact that these elements are implicit in all interactions where actions are being coordinated among people, whether or not they are stated explicitly.

Suchman is right in noting that "once encapsulated and reduced to the homogeneous black circles and arrows of the diagram, the 'conversation' is findable anywhere." But she is wrong in saying that "specific occasions of conversation are no longer open to investigation, or at least not in any other terms." This is like saying that once Laban invented and applied a systematic dance notation, "specific occasions of dance are no longer open to investigation, or at least not in any other terms." Only the most narrowminded application of such a tool would blind one to further investigations and dimensions of the phenomena.

Suchman asks rhetorically "Why do computer scientists go about making up all these typologies of interaction?" The answer is relatively simple – computer programs that we know how to construct can only work with fully-rationalized typologies (be they bits and bytes or knowledge bases). It is a bit like asking "Why do civil engineers go about making up all these typologies of construction materials and methods?" There may be much more to understanding architecture or homelessness, but one is bound to work with the materials at hand. Unless we question the whole enterprise and doubt whether anything built with computational materials is suited to human purposes, we are left with the question of "To what purposes and with what limits are the formal system manipulating capacities of computers well suited?" Our answer has been the development of systems for coordination of workflow, and Suchman disagrees about the appropriateness to this domain.

Let us first look at Suchman's key contention that

> …the categorization devices of speech act theory [are] a discipline for organizational communications … displacing earlier mechanical devices with electronic ones, this regime is to be administered technologically … by providing a discipline enforced through the technology.

All this sounds quite ominous, and her references to Foucault evoke sinister images from his work on modern society as a prison with its regimes of enforced discipline.

But it doesn't look quite the same if we take a more homely practical example, which Suchman suggests in describing THE COORDINATOR as a "technology of accountability … aimed at the inscription and documentation of actions to which parties are accountable … in the sense represented by the bookkeeper's ledger." The analogy is quite apt. Suchman's objection to the "imposition of standardized regimes of action" might well have been applied to the imposition of explicit accounting procedures as economic practices developed over history.

My grandfather started a small business early in this century. The structure was simple and informal. When he bought something, he took money out of his pocket to pay for it. When he sold something he took the customer's money and put it into his pocket. That was a perfectly adequate system for the size of the organization and it worked pretty well when there was an employee or two (although he began being a little more cautious about people putting money in their pockets).

As the organization got bigger, unstructured transactions turned out not to be a very good way of organizing things. He needed to keep track of how much money had come in for what, and how much went out for what. Systematic records were required for a variety of reasons, some internal and others external. At a minimum, the Internal Revenue Service wanted more than someone's memory of how much went in and out of a pocket over the year.

Within any social organization there is always this kind of mixture of internal and external clients and interactions. There is a web of conversations and commitments among the people inside and outside the organization. All this needs to be kept track of, and the problem becomes worse as the organization becomes larger and less physically coupled. When people interact face to face on a regular day to day basis, things can be done in a very different way than when an organization is spread over the world, with 10,000 employees and thousands of suppliers. You can run a tiny company out of your pocket. You cannot run even a moderately small company without regularized (disciplined) accounting procedures,which enable people to follow what is happening in situations far removed in space and time from their personal setting.

Imagine a world in which every business invented its own accounting procedures, or in which each person in an office adapted them in arbitrary ways. In some sense this would be good in that it could provide flexibility and the potential to respond creatively to the specificity and heterogeneity of situations. But overall it would create unbearable chaos in all of those areas where people need to interact. For my accounts to be matched up against yours, for us to make a deal and carry it through, there must be a standard structure or discipline. Accounting procedures are regularized because they support coordination.

Just as conventional bookkeeping is a generic way of keeping track of finances, the conversation structure in the language/action theory provides a basic framework within which each application adds the specifics relevant to the situation. Human action is always played out within a game, a language game, a set of rules, using the judgment that comes from that larger background. The language game does not determine a person's actions, it provides the space of actions in which one can move.

It is conceivable that one might hold on to an idealized view of free and undisciplined human interchange, in which the rigidity of modern bookkeeping serves authoritarian purposes because it is, in Suchman's words, "a tool for the reproduction of an established social order" rather than "a tool for the collaborative production of social action." Or one could take the contrary view – that the regularity provided by explicit categories and disciplines of bookkeeping make possible whole realms of collaborative production of social action that would not exist without a regularized structure that is mutually understood and obeyed.

My view of the language/action perspective is analogous. The use of explicitness makes possible coordination of kinds that could not be effectively carried out without it. This is especially true in a large modern organization with its global economic integration and tremendous capacity for distributed communications. As with my grandfather's business, the increasing size and complexity of the operation leads to breakdowns in the less formalized and more personalized ways of going about business. Structure is not an imposition of control for authoritarian motives, but a necessity of continued operation. The question is not whether to impose standardized regimes, but how to do so appropriately.

Of course, the salient word in that last sentence is "appropriately" and it is in regard to appropriateness that Suchman has some important observations to offer, once they are extracted from the drama of oppressor and oppressed. Rephrasing them briefly:

1) Explicit representation of intentions and commitments is more appropriate in some social/organizational situations than others.

As Suchman points out, it would be foolish to see THE COORDINATOR as a cure-all "technological solution" to breakdowns in communication. It helps people cope with and prevent some classes of breakdowns, and it can create others. The essence of using a tool well is knowing where, when, and how to apply it. We have learned a lot in our years of experience with people using THE COORDINATOR and subsequent technologies for workflow enablement (see Medina-Mora et al., 1992). There has been much greater success in applying them in the management of engineering change orders in a large manufacturing division, than in structuring the interaction among researchers in a telecommunications research laboratory. As a rule of thumb, explicit structure is more likely to be seen as an imposition in those cases where organizational activity has been relatively unstructured (e.g., in the communities and domains that have historically been served by e-mail) and as a valuable augmentation in areas that are relatively structured and have previously been served by a hodgepodge of paper forms and inflexible task-specific data processing applications.

A number of successful applications have been developed on a platform of workflow-enabled Lotus Notes, focusing on regularized activities, such as the flow of documents and coordination of meetings surrounding hiring in a large organization. Here the need for regularization and accountability ("discipline") has long been established by legal and organizational policy. Language/action based workflow technology offers a means for dealing with it.

2) The generation of representations can only be done successfully with the participation of the people who live the situations being represented.

Suchman inveighs against the authoritarian application of the "strong, knowledgeable hand that orders them [organization members], integrates them, and brings them effectively into use." Aside from her implied denigration of extrinsic organizational expertise, she is making an important point. Organizational design succeeds when it is grounded in the context and experience of those who live in the situation. One of the main elements in the suite of current products being offered by Action Technologies is a graphical workflow design tool, which is explicitly designed to use concrete visual representations of the work that can be understood without abstruse understanding of computer technologies. The attendant methodologies for structuring the workflows within an organization are centered on methods for involving the participants in the description and composition of the workflow structure. This may not be participatory design in all of its senses (see Muller & Kuhn, 1993), but is strongly influenced by the kinds of experiences with workgroups that have led Suchman and others in that direction.

3) It is a dangerous form of blindness to believe that any representation captures what is meaningful to people in a situation.

It is plausible to imagine that someone working in a setting with technologies based on language/action structure could have a false belief that somehow all the coordination and communication problems are taken care of. That would be like a bookkeeper believing that because spreadsheets don't make arithmetic errors, all accounting problems were taken care of. Suchman correctly points out that "our sense of artistry in any field is precisely the ability to move, in more or less articulatable ways, gracefully and effectively through the circumstances in which one finds oneself … bring[ing] past experience to bear in creative ways on an unfolding situation." Coordination of people in organizations is an activity that demands artistry as much as any other field, and Suchman accurately describes the nature of that artistry. An accountant can display financial artistry with or without a spreadsheet, but the spreadsheet helps keep things straight. A composer can display artistry with or without a formal notation for musical scores, but it would be foolish to complain that Mozart's music suffered from his compliance to a rigid discipline of tonal conventions.

And that leads me to the conclusion I would like to draw from this discussion. Not that there is an epic struggle between the forces of discipline and the forces of resistance, but that in the end we are dealing with interactions among people. People will adapt and reinterpret whatever they find in their environment, and they will do so in ways that simultaneously reproduce the existing social structure and create a clearing for social innovation. Suchman weaves a dramatic tale by lumping together speech act theory, THE COORDINATOR, military discipline, authoritarian social control, and the banning of native names by colonial missionaries. But we will be better off to embrace an appreciation for and engagement within the specificity, heterogeneity and practicality of oganizational life.

REFERENCES

De Michelis, G., C. Simone, and K. Schmidt, eds. 1993. *Proceedings of the Third European Conferenceon Computer Supported Cooperative Work (ECSCW '93) Milan, Italy.* Dordrecht: Kluwer Academic Publishers.

Medina-Mora, R., T. Winograd, R. Flores, and F. Flores. 1992. The Action Workflow Approach to Workflow Management Technology. *CSCW '92*, November.

Muller, M., and S. Kuhn, eds. 1993. Special Issue on Participatory Design. *Communications of the ACM* 36:4. (June).

Winograd, T., and F. Flores. 1986. *Understanding Computer and Cognition: A New Foundation for Design.* Norwood, NJ: Ablex.

6

Commentary on Suchman Article and Winograd Response

THOMAS W. MALONE

Abstract: This commentary provides a way of understanding the apparent contradictions in the views of Suchman (Chapter 4) and Winograd (Chapter 5). On the one hand, as Suchman points out, it is important to realize that no category system provides a complete story about the world, and all such systems are open to interpretation and reconstruction. On the other hand, not only are categories often useful, but to some extent they are necessary given the structure of human cognition. Accordingly, I suggest that designers need to learn the "art" of applying categories well and, in this regard, highlight the value of designing "semistructured" and "tailorable" systems.

The dialog between Suchman and Winograd highlights issues that are important for us to understand, and, as is often the case, a more complete picture emerges from the apparent contradictions in their views.

First, it is important to realize, as Suchman points out, that no category system – or anything else that can be said in words – provides a "complete" story about the world. Furthermore, the category systems we use are always open to interpretation and reconstruction. For people who believe that the categories, theories, or systems they know are the only ones possible, this realization is often a significant element of intellectual and personal development, and Suchman and her colleagues have done a valuable service by bringing this realization to many people who have not previously had it.

In particular, it is important for designers of cooperative work systems (like THE COORDINATOR) to remember that no category system is complete and to design systems that do not always rigidly constrain people to specific categories, but instead allow flexibility in the ways their systems can be used.

On the other hand, it is also important to realize that much human benefit – for individuals and for groups – results from our ability to recognize, describe, and act upon patterns in the world around us. Even though no single pattern or group of patterns describes everything that matters in the world, recognizing patterns allows us to act more effectively as individuals. And sharing assumptions about patterns with others is useful – even necessary – for many kinds of effective group action. Our very ability to communicate effectively with language, for instance, depends upon vast numbers of shared assumptions about grammatical patterns, word meanings, and so on. And effective group work can often be aided by explicit understandings about things like requests and commitments.

When people interpret the work of Suchman and her colleagues as denying the value of *any* agreed upon patterns, this distracts us from the necessary tasks of finding and agreeing upon useful patterns. In fact, Suchman – like all of us – uses categories, patterns, and shared assumptions in her arguments. And in parts of her paper, Suchman appears to be trying to have it both ways: to use philosophical arguments about the limitations of *all* categories to support what seem to be her political viewpoints about a particular set of categories: corporate managers as villains and oppressed workers as innocent victims.

I believe the most important lesson from all of this for the field of CSCW is that we need to learn the "art" of applying categories well. On the one hand, we need to avoid rigid or slavish devotion to any particular set of categories; on the other hand, we need to find and support useful patterns of interaction.

In practical terms, one of the most important implications of this concern is that we need to build CSCW systems that are "semiformal" or "semistructured" (e.g., Malone, Grant, Lai, Rao & Rosenblitt, 1987). That is, by providing some amount of structure, cooperative work systems can allow computers to support useful categories and patterns of interaction. But by also supporting unstructured information and informal interactions, the systems can be useful even in situations where the initial categories are not.

The usefulness of these semiformal systems is increased even more when they are also modifiable (or "tailorable") by their users (e.g., Lai, Malone, & Yu, 1988; Malone, Lai & Fry, 1995). With such tailorable systems, users can modify the systems as their needs change, and they can adapt the systems to new situations, even when the categories or patterns anticipated by the original designers of the software are no longer useful.

REFERENCES

Lai, K.Y., T.W. Malone, and K.C. Yu. 1988. Object Lens: A 'Spreadsheet' for Cooperative Work. *ACM Transactions on Office Information Systems,* 6: 332–353.

Malone, T.W., K.R. Grant, K.Y. Lai, R. Rao, and D.A. Rosenblitt. 1987. Semi-Structured Messages are Surprisingly Useful for Computer-Supported Coordination. *ACM Transactions on Office Information Systems* 5: 115–131.

Malone, T. W., K.Y. Lai, and C. Fry. 1995. Experiments with Oval: A Radically Tailorable Tool for Cooperative Work. *ACM Transactions on Information Systems* 13(2): 177–205.

7

Social Impact Statements: Engaging Public Participation in Information Technology Design

BEN SHNEIDERMAN AND ANNE ROSE

Abstract. From their introduction, people have questioned the impact computers will have on society. We believe it is our responsibility as system designers to achieve organizational goals while serving human needs and protecting individual rights. The proposed Social Impact Statements (Shneiderman, 1990) would identify the impacts of information systems on direct and indirect users, who may be employees or the public. This paper proposes a process for implementing Social Impact Statements for federal and local government agencies and regulated industries, with optional participation by other privately held corporations. A Social Impact Statement should describe the new system and its benefits, acknowledge concerns and potential barriers, outline the development process, and address fundamental principles. Examples from our work with the Maryland Department of Juvenile Justice are offered.

The real question before us lies here: Do these instruments further life and enhance its values, or not?

— L. Mumford (1934)

Information systems are becoming increasingly necessary to manage the government, utilities, and public services that citizens in modern societies have come to expect. Many analysts believe the social repercussions of computers may be as potent as those of the automobile and the telephone (e.g., Dunlop & Kling, 1991; Huff & Finholt, 1994; Kling, 1980; Sterling, 1974; Wiener, 1954). But many critics have pointed out the negative effects of modern technologies: "technological evolution is leading to something new: a worldwide interlocked monolithic, technical–political web of unprecedented negative implications. And it is surely creating terrible and possibly catastrophic impacts on the earth" (Mander, 1991, p. 4).

We thank Batya Friedman for encouraging us to explore this domain and our reviewers, Helen Nissenbaum, Judy Olson and Kent Norman, for providing us with valuable feedback. This report was supported by funding from the Maryland Department of Juvenile Justice. This paper is a revised version of the paper presented at the Symposium on Computers and the Quality of Life '96, sponsored by the ACM Special Interest Group on Computers and Society, February 1996, Philadelphia, PA.

Constructive criticism and guidelines for design could help protect us against the adverse ramifications of technology such as disruptions in telephone, banking, and charge card systems, dissatisfaction with privacy protection, dislocation through deskilling or layoffs, and deaths from flawed medical instruments. While some of these problems are due to malfunctions, others are results of technology functioning exactly as it has been designed (e.g., the atomic bomb worked just fine). While guarantees of perfection are not possible, we believe that policies and processes that will more often lead to satisfying outcomes can be developed.

This hopeful stance was part of a larger argument about taking responsibility for shaping future technology. A proposed Declaration of Responsibility (Shneiderman, 1990, p. 2) sought to clarify the responsibility of system developers. It stated that: "We, the researchers, designers, managers, implementers, testers, and trainers of user interfaces and information systems, recognize the powerful influence of our science and technology. Therefore we commit ourselves to studying ways to enable users to accomplish their personal and organizational goals while pursuing higher societal goals and serving human needs."

The second part of the Declaration proposed writing a Social Impact Statement (SIS), similar to an Environmental Impact Statement (Battle, Fischman & Squillace, 1994), for large complex systems that affect the lives of many people. The goal is a high quality system whose design is discussed early and widely, thereby uncovering concerns and enabling stakeholders to openly state their positions. Such open discussions might improve quality which should lead to increased system acceptance. Of course there is the danger that these discussions will elevate fears or force designers to make unreasonable compromises, but these risks seem reasonable in a well-managed organization. The practicality of writing SISs has begun to be addressed by Huff (1996).

This paper focuses on SISs as a tool to engage public participation in information technology design. First, we outline a process for implementing an SIS (see the following):

- Preparation
- Evaluation
- Enforcement

and then present a list of Social Impact Issues (see the following):

Describe the New System and Its Benefits.

Convey the High Level Goals of the New System.

Identify the Stakeholders.

Identify Specific Benefits.

Address Concerns and Potential Barriers.

Anticipate Changes in Job Functions and Potential Layoffs.

Address Security and Privacy Issues.

Discuss Accountability and Responsibility for System Misuse and Failure.

Avoid Potential Biases.

Weigh Individual Rights vs. Societal Benefits.

Assess Trade-offs Between Centralization and Decentralization.

Preserve Democratic Principles.

Ensure Diverse Access.

Promote Simplicity and Preserve What Works.

Outline the Development Process.

Present an Estimated Project Schedule.

Propose Process for Making Decisions.

Discuss Expectations of How Stakeholders Will Be Involved.

Recognize Needs for More Staff, Training, and Hardware.

Propose Plan for Backups of Data and Equipment.

Outline Plan for Migrating to the New System.

Describe Plan for Measuring the Success of the New System.

These issues are intended to help assist the average system designer in writing an SIS. Many of these issues will be open ended so designers may choose to call on specialized expertise in critical areas. Even when the answer is not known, the SIS should raise the question for the implementer's consideration.

PROCESS

We propose a three stage process for implementing SISs for large and novel systems. First, the SIS is prepared by system designers within the organization (or contracted by the organization), then presented to the stakeholders and the appropriate review panel for evaluation. Once approved, it must be enforced. Our goals are to encourage maximum participation in the review process by structuring the document, limiting its size, and controlling its complexity.

Preparation

The SIS should be produced early enough in the development process to influence the project schedule, system requirements, and the budget. It should be written by the system design team which may include end users, managers, internal or external software developers, and possibly clients. Even for complex systems, the SIS should be of a size and complexity that is understandable by users with relevant background. Some practical alternatives are to focus on those issues that appear to be the most dangerous or those that seem key to the system's success.

Evaluation

An appropriate review panel must evaluate the SIS for how well it addresses the impacts the system will have on its stakeholders. The review panel should consist of representative stakeholders (e.g., management, other designers, end users, and anyone else impacted). Some organizations may already have associations with groups that could act as reviewers: federal government units (e.g., General Accounting Organization, Office Personnel Management), state legislature bodies, regulatory agencies (e.g., SEC, FAA, FCC), professional societies, and labor unions (see Table 1).

Table 1: Potential Review Panels for Different Types of Organizations

Organization	Review Panel
Government agencies (e.g., IRS, Social Security)	Inspector general, GAO, OPM
State government agencies (e.g., motor vehicles, courts)	State legislative bodies
Public utilities (e.g., phone, electricity)	Review boards
Regulated industries (e.g., banking, airlines)	Regulatory agencies (e.g., SEC, FAA, FCC)
Commercial industry (optional) (e.g., Microsoft, IBM)	Board of directors, management
Research groups (optional) (e.g., universities, R&D labs)	Professional organizations (e.g., ACM, IEEE)

The review panel would receive the written report, hold public hearings, and request modifications. A group of knowledgeable authorities might be assembled for consultation. Private citizen groups would also be given the opportunity to present their concerns and suggest alternatives (Wurth, 1992).

Enforcement

Once the SIS is adopted, it must be enforced. An SIS serves to document the *intentions* of the new system and the stakeholders need to see those intentions backed up by actions. Typically, the review panel is the proper authority for enforcement. There needs to be a recognized cost to the organization for not adhering to the SIS.

DEPARTMENT OF JUVENILE JUSTICE

We are currently working with the Maryland Department of Juvenile Justice (DJJ) on redesigning their information system, Information System for Youth Services (ISYS). ISYS is a terminal-based system used by approximately 600 workers to support the processing of 50,000 juvenile case referrals per year. The next generation system, New ISYS (NISYS), will support DJJ's youth-related workflow and run on PCs in a Windows environment.

The NISYS redesign effort has raised several social impact issues. Who should be allowed to see a juvenile's case history? How will the handling of the youths be affected? How will jobs be changed? As the user interface designers, it has been our responsibility to consider the impact of our designs on DJJ, the youths served, and the citizens of Maryland. The executive staff of DJJ will be responsible for reviewing and accepting our designs, and finally for enforcing them. By offering example issues related to our work, we hope to inspire others to consider the impacts of their designs. While this work inspired us to promote the writing of SISs, one was not written when we started this project.

SOCIAL IMPACT ISSUES

An SIS should discuss the effects that a new system will have both within the organization and on society at large:

- describe the new system and its benefits,
- address concerns and potential barriers, and
- outline the development process.

We recognize that the issues discussed are not complete, rather they are meant to prompt insightful dialogue about what an SIS should include. It is difficult, if not impossible, to enumerate all of the potential impacts of a new system up front. Markus (1984) identifies different types of systems being designed (e.g., operational, monitoring and control, decision and planning, etc.) and then lists the impacts that each kind is likely to have. We anticipate that as more experience is gained in writing SISs, a better set of issues will be developed and tuned to specific applications.

Describe the New System and Its Benefits

An SIS should begin by describing the proposed system and its goals. This includes identifying who will be impacted and specifying the benefits they will receive.

Convey the High Level Goals of the New System

In order to be effective evaluators, stakeholders need to understand the purpose of the new system. A brief system description should be provided and the goals should be enumerated. For example, the goals may range from reducing costs to improving worker morale to meeting new legislative requirements.

DJJ: The next generation ISYS, NISYS, will be an integrated software system designed to support juvenile case tracking for DJJ operations. The primary goal is to increase the availability of staff to serve the youths and their families by reducing the time that front-line workers spend on administrative tasks, improving the quality of decisions, and the timeliness and accuracy of the data. A secondary goal is to improve the communication of DJJ personnel across divisions.

Identify the Stakeholders

A stakeholder is anyone who will be affected, directly or indirectly, by the new system like the end users, the software staff, and the organization's clients. Some stakeholders are affected because they work with the system, while other's are affected as a result of the system being used. For example, a motor vehicle licensing officer using a computer system to look up driving records is impacted by the system design and so is the driver applying for the license. Faulty information or a biased user interface might cause the licensing officer to reject the applicant's request. Defining the stakeholders helps alert designers to unanticipated impacts which may create bias with respect to certain stakeholders (Friedman & Nissenbaum, 1996).

DJJ: For NISYS, the stakeholders include the DJJ personnel who will use the system, such as the case managers and supervisors, and the MIS staff that will support the new system. Several other people will be affected by how the system is used including the youths and their families, the victims, other state agencies, and the citizens of Maryland. The information contained in NISYS will directly influence how DJJ interacts with the youths.

Identify Specific Benefits

"A critical factor for successful implementation of any innovation is that its benefits be construed as benefits by the potential adopters (Kaplan, 1994, p. 26)." The benefits may include reduced costs, faster performance, shorter learning times, reduced errors, and increased user satisfaction. These benefits differ by stakeholder. For example, an organization may be interested in reducing costs while employees may be more interested in reducing the workload. In order for all stakeholders to be motivated, the potential benefits for each must be described. The benefits to the organization as a whole may not be sufficient motivation (Kaplan, 1994).

DJJ: As an organization, DJJ will benefit from NISYS's ability to gather the data needed to obtain funding from the state and federal legislation in a timely fashion. NISYS will reduce the time front-line workers spend on administrative tasks by automatically generating required letters and reports. Most importantly NISYS will allow workers to focus more of their time and attention to working with the youths and their families in an attempt to reduce the rate of recidivism in Maryland.

Address Concerns and Potential Barriers

Identifying potential difficulties and concerns early in the development process allows an organization to manage them more effectively and minimize resulting problems. This section contains a starting list of issues that should be addressed. Open and honest discussion about these problems benefits all stakeholders.

Anticipate Changes in Job Functions and Potential Layoffs

Change is a major cause of stress because it instills uncertainty. Using the SIS to describe anticipated changes can help reduce speculation and fear, plus it allows an organization to manage them proactively (Kaplan, 1994). Stakeholders are most concerned with negative impacts such as layoffs, demotions, decreased skill requirements, and potential health problems. However, not all change is bad. Some positive changes may include enlarged job roles, new employment opportunities, increased wages, and flexible working arrangements (Ralls, 1994). It is difficult to guess how certain changes will impact an organization. Markus (1984) discusses how changes in work flow can affect communication, socialization (involvement vs. isolation), and loyalties.

Today, job security is a major concern. When considering layoffs, organizations should weigh the consequences both to society and to individuals. Sterling (1974) points out that the cost of finding new means of employment for those laid off is met by society, not the organization, and there is no way to measure the loss to individuals who are forced into less satisfactory employment. Iacono and Kling (1991) illustrate this point with the example of long distance operators whose jobs became less satisfying because their jobs became more automated and required less skill.

DJJ: In several offices, case referrals are being entered into ISYS by clerical staff. The NISYS design team is investigating techniques for facilitating electronic data entry. Some possibilities include scanning in the case referrals or having the police departments transfer them electronically. Both these techniques would drastically reduce the data entry done by the clerical staff, who might be retrained as case workers or as administrative assistants.

Address Security and Privacy Issues

Before computers, it was easier to physically lock up and secure information. Today, information can be collected and misused without ever violating physical barriers (Ladd, 1991). There are several measures that can be taken to secure electronic data including isolating computers (no network access), isolating networks (no internet access), requiring passwords, encryption protection, and monitoring logins. The chosen method should be appropriate to the criticality and confidentiality of the data.

Information systems should only collect specific and relevant data. Applicants for a driver's license should not have to provide their annual income, for example. Storage space has become increasingly affordable, so more organizations maintain huge databases that often contain unnecessary information. An organization's desire to collect data about its clients or employees may be in violation of an individual's right to privacy. One compromise is to store aggregate data (e.g., average number of logins per day for all employees) rather than individual data (e.g., number of times John logged into system).

DJJ: Since the juvenile data, especially the medical information, is confidential, there is an ongoing discussion of whether or not NISYS should be connected to outside networks. DJJ is trying to decide whether or not the benefits of network access outweigh the potential security risk. Another discussion is about what information should be recorded for each youth. The information necessary depends primarily on how the case is handled. If a youth is never placed in a DJJ facility, does medical information need to be collected?

Discuss Accountability for System Misuse and Failure

Designers and users should be held accountable for their actions, even though their organizations may be held liable. The SIS should identify potential types of abuses and failures and outline steps for monitoring these problems. Accountability is enhanced if specific roles are assigned for aspects of development and usage, rather than establishing universal responsibility. Accountability suffers if the computer is seen as the scapegoat and blamed for human failures. We would laugh at a criminal who asserted that the gun killed the victim, but some people are likely to accept an excuse that blames the computer. Current trends describing autonomous, expert, or smart computers reinforce the misconception that computers act with minimal human accountability. The complexity of software and the prevalence of bugs lead some people to deny their responsibility. Pressure for high quality software and clarification of the designers' responsibility to reduce bugs can promote improved system reliability and safety (Nissenbaum, 1996).

> DJJ: NISYS users will be held accountable for their actions by the installation of a new logging facility to record each change to a youth record. If incorrect changes were made, then managers could determine who made the change. Case workers's fear about monitoring might be countered by their having equal access to the log to demonstrate their high level of accurate work.

Avoid Potential Biases

Most system designs contain biases, both intentional and unintentional, but well-designed systems can limit these biases (Friedman & Nissenbaum, 1996). Functionality may be biased toward select groups of stakeholders, certain data may foster biased judgments, and some display techniques may encourage hasty decisions. For instance, an airlines' reservation system showed clear bias by always putting one airline's flights first. Unfortunately, it is not possible to avoid all biases, but thoughtful designs can minimize them.

> DJJ: There are several sources of potential bias with respect to how a youth is treated. For example, who should know if a youth is HIV positive? The medical staff needs to know to treat the youth but do the cases workers need to know? Should the victim of an attack by this youth be told? Also, what should happen to cases that are found not guilty? Should they still appear on the youth's record? If so, aren't they a source of bias? Also, the youth records naturally focus on negative behavior, but shouldn't equal attention be given to positive behavior (e.g., getting a job or staying drug free)?

Weigh Individual Rights vs. Societal Benefits

There are times during system design when individual rights conflict with societal benefits. When developing new technologies, it is the obligation of the SIS authors to weigh alternatives. For example, it was recently decided that tax records could be searched to locate individuals who refused to pay child support.

DJJ: While a youth's record is confidential, case workers are entitled to know if the youth they are dealing with has a violent history, but should future school teachers, neighbors, or employers be entitled to this information?

Assess Trade-offs Between Centralization and Decentralization

Centralization vs. decentralization is a long running debate about whether computer systems will result in decisions being made by a few select people (centralization) or by broader more diverse groups (decentralization) (George & King, 1991). For example, a decentralized system gives more control to the end users, while a centralized system ensures consistent policies. However, with control also comes responsibility which needs to be delegated. For example, will end users be responsible for backing up their personal data or will additional software staff be hired to do this? An SIS should assess the trade-offs and choose the approach that best suits the needs of the organization and society.

DJJ: Internally, DJJ is wrestling with the desire to empower their workers by giving them more control (e.g., letting them create their own customized reports, etc.) without burdening them with additional responsibility (e.g., data backups). Another question is if NISYS automatically generates reports, who should be responsible for requesting that function? Should workers continue to generate the reports and forward them to their supervisors or should the supervisors simply generate the reports themselves?

Preserve Democratic Principles

Successful system design depends, in part, on active user participation, and unless users are given a vote, it can be difficult to motivate them to participate. Giving users a "vote" requires management to relinquish some control. This does not mean that users should be given full control over the system design. For example, management may give users control over certain system aspects but within a defined budget. While the ideal may be a democracy, the hierarchical nature of many organizations makes this difficult.

DJJ: Even though the final decisions will be made by the executive staff, a representative from each user segment (e.g., intake workers, case managers, juvenile counselors) will be appointed to ensure some representation.

Ensure Diverse Access

It is very common to see the phrase "Equal Opportunity Employer" on job announcements. Unfortunately, very few systems provide equal access. Ideally, systems should be designed to meet everyone's needs: young, old, handicapped, rural, foreign, etc. While it may not be practical to design systems that accommodate everyone, this should not excuse designers from considering alternative designs that satisfy a wider range of audiences. An SIS should outline an organization's policy on ensuring equal opportunity and define the intended users of the system. In some cases, an organization may choose to provide alternative systems to ensure diverse access.

> DJJ: Within DJJ there is an employee with impaired vision and another with impaired motor coordination. While NISYS will not directly incorporate functionality to accommodate these individuals, different input devices will be investigated, time permitting.

Promote Simplicity and Preserve What Works

Designers should be careful not to overlook simple solutions. Today, with technology advancing rapidly, we often get carried away with integrating the latest breakthroughs in system design. It is important to recognize when certain technology works and when it does not. If organizations have devised good ways of handling their needs, then they should incorporate them into the new system. Designers should acknowledge and preserve what works, not reinvent solutions.

> DJJ: One of the design goals of NISYS is that it is not so complex that users have to constantly refer to technical manuals and look up obscure codes. The basic functionality of ISYS is a good starting point for NISYS (e.g., add a case, add a placement, add a review, etc.). Currently, many factors, such as the user interface and accessibility problems, make it difficult to perform these functions, but these functions still reflect DJJ's needs.

Outline the Development Process

The development process can have a significant impact on an organization. Work routines are disturbed, critical decisions need to be made, and training may be required. Outlining the process allows everyone involved to anticipate disruptions and plan accordingly.

Present an Estimated Project Schedule

The project schedule should outline the basic development stages, such as requirements generation, design, and implementation, and also estimate how long each stage will take. The idea is to provide the stakeholders with a rough idea of what to expect and when. Keeping the stakeholders abreast of what is happening enhances their satisfaction with the entire process.

> DJJ: The NISYS project is currently in the requirements generation and early design phase. The Request for Proposals (RFP) is scheduled to be ready by July 1, 1996. Once a contract is awarded, it is anticipated that it will be two years until initial product roll out.

Propose Process for Making Decisions

A component of any development process is decision making. Hardware needs to be chosen, functionality needs to be decided on, and the user interface needs to be designed. An SIS should outline the process for obtaining input and making decisions. Assuming an ideal democratic process, each stakeholder would be given a vote. In some cases, an executive review committee composed of different stakeholders might be a more practical alternative. In any case, the process should include informing the stakeholders, at least those who will be using and maintaining the system, about the resulting decisions including the motivation behind decisions and the reason for rejecting proposed alternatives.

> DJJ: Final decisions about the NISYS design will be made by upper management with input from their staff. It will be the University of Maryland's responsibility to present alternative designs and perform usability tests where appropriate.

Discuss Expectations of How Stakeholders Will Be Involved

Each stakeholder is interested in what is expected of them personally. Their involvement might consist of filling out questionnaires, participating in usability studies, and receiving training. Or, it might consist of procuring hardware, writing contracts, and analyzing user feedback. The SIS should explain what is expected and whether participation is voluntary or mandatory. If participation is voluntary, explain how volunteers will be chosen. All stakeholders should be given the opportunity to participate in the development process. Active participants will probably be more satisfied with the resulting system than those who are not involved in development. Management will need to allow time for workers to participate.

DJJ: Potential NISYS users will be encouraged to be active participants in the design process. Specifically, users will be asked to fill out questionnaires, allow observation of their work, participate in interviews, review user interface designs, and produce process maps.

Recognize Needs for More Staff, Training, and Hardware

A successful system requires more than functioning software. Additional software staff may be needed, users may require formal training, and more hardware may be required to provide adequate access. Inadequate training and education are typical reasons new systems do not achieve their potential. "Managers in too many organizations still perceive people and technology as substitutes, rather than complements. They invest in technology, but too often neglect to invest in the people who operate and use the technology" (Ralls, 1994, p. 58).

DJJ: The failure of ISYS is due in large part to the lack of machines and inadequate training. For NISYS, DJJ is planning on significantly increasing the number of machines. Additional MIS staff may be required to handle the increase maintenance responsibilities. Formal training is another key especially since NISYS is expected to run in a Windows environment and most DJJ employees have little experience, if any, in this environment.

Propose Plan for Backups of Data and Equipment

Unfortunately, all systems have the potential to fail. These failures can cause loss of business and productivity or possibly catastrophes resulting in loss of life. Organizations have the moral responsibility to take the steps necessary to minimize the impact these failures have on individuals and on society in general. A standard practice to protect data is to back it up periodically. For critical systems, like air traffic control systems, a backup system should be in place so services can continue if there is a malfunction.

DJJ: Procedures to perform routine backups to protect against data loss will be needed. In case of a long term failure, DJJ should also have a backup paper system in place so case processing can continue. A youth's processing should continue even when the system fails.

Outline Plan for Migrating to the New System

Migrating to the new system requires careful planning. Users may require training, the software staff may need to perform backups, and hardware may need to be installed. An evolutionary approach of smaller more manageable steps is preferable to the "flip the switch" approach (Kaplan, 1994). A backup plan should be in place in case the new system fails during migration or the transition takes longer than anticipated. Another issue to consider is how long the old system and the new system will overlap because the workload during this period will be increased.

DJJ: In order to familiarize their employees with graphical window environments, DJJ plans to provide courses in PC applications, such as word processors and spreadsheets. A training lab is currently under development. Formal training for NISYS will also be provided. Ideally, some PCs would be deployed early so users could begin integrating them into their work life. Unfortunately, state procurement practices may make this difficult.

Describe Plan for Measuring the Success of the New System

Oftentimes, stakeholders are left wondering if the system goals were ever achieved. The success or failure of the system to meet specific goals should be conveyed to the stakeholders along with the plan for correcting any shortcomings. Specific goals, like reduction of paper use by ten percent, can be measured over time. More subjective goals like, improve user satisfaction, can be evaluated by administering questionnaires.

DJJ: The Questionnaire for User Interaction Satisfaction (QUIS) (Chin, Diehl, & Norman, 1988), was administered to 332 employees to measure user satisfaction with ISYS. Using this as a benchmark, the QUIS could be readministered to measure the success of NISYS.

CONCLUSION

In 1974, Sterling recognized that systems will not become humanized on their own without the conscious effort of concerned citizens. Incorporating SISs into the development process would be one step toward achieving that goal. In our society, success is too often measured in terms of immediate costs: "The utility of humanizing procedures is not apparent from cost/benefit calculations but arises from the point of view of quality of life – not only of our own but also of future generations who will be saddled with the systems which are designed and implemented today" (Sterling, 1974, p. 613).

This paper takes a step in clarifying what a Social Impact Statement might contain and how it might be integrated into a realistic development process. We recognize the need to keep the effort, cost, and time appropriate to the project, while facilitating a thoughtful review. We believe that there can be large improvements from such a process by preventing problems which may be expensive to repair, improving privacy protection, minimizing legal challenges, and creating more satisfying work environments. Well-designed systems will be valued by users and appreciated by colleagues. Information system designers have no Hippocratic Oath, but excellence in design can win respect and inspire others to higher performance.

REFERENCES

Battle, J., R. Fischman, and M. Squillace. 1994. *Environmental Law Vol. 1.: Environmental Decisionmaking NEPA and the Endangered Species Act.* Anderson Publishing. WWW version http://www.law.indiana.edu/envdec prepared by R. Fischman. Bloomington, IN: Indiana University, School of Law.

Chin, J., V. Diehl, and, K. Norman. 1988. Development of an Instrument Measuring User Satisfaction of the Human–Computer Interface. In *Proceedings of ACM CHI Conference: Human Factors in Computer Systems,* p. 213–218. New York: ACM Press

Dunlop, C., and R. Kling, eds. 1991. *Computerization and Controversy: Value Conflicts and Social Choices.* San Diego, CA: Academic Press.

Friedman, B., and H. Nissenbaum. 1996. Bias in Computer Systems. *ACM Transactions on Information Systems* 14 (3): 330–347.

George, J., and J. King. 1991. Examining the Computing and Centralization Debate. *Communications of the ACM* 34 (7): 63–72.

Huff, C. 1996. Practical Guidance for Teaching the Social Impact Statement (SIS). *Proceedings of ACM SIGCAS Symposium: Computers and the Quality of Life* 96: 86–89.

Huff, C., and T. Finholt eds. 1994. *Social Issues in Computing: Putting Computing in Its Place.* New York: McGraw-Hill.

Iacono, S., and R. Kling. 1991. Computerization, Office Routines, and Changes in Clerical Work. In *Computerization and Controversy Value Conflicts and Social Choices*, eds. C. Dunlop and R. Kling. San Diego, CA: Academic Press.

Kaplan, B. 1994. Reducing Barriers to Physician Data Entry for Computer-Based Patient Records. *Topics Health Information Management* 15 (1): 24–34.

Kling, R. 1980. Social Analyses of Computing: Theoretical Perspectives in Recent Empirical Research. *Computing Surveys* 12 (1): 61–110.

Ladd, J. 1991. Computers and Moral Responsibility: A Framework for an Ethical Analysis. In *Computerization and Controversy Value Conflicts and Social Choices*, eds. C. Dunlop and R. Kling. San Diego, CA: Academic Press.

Mander, J. 1991. *In the Absence of the Sacred: The Failure of Technology and the Survival of the Indian Nations*. San Francisco, CA: Sierra Club Books.

Markus, M. 1984. *Systems in Organizations: Bugs and features*. Boston, MA: Pitman Publishing.

Mumford, L. 1934. *Technics and Civilization*. New York: Harcourt Brace and World.

Nissenbaum, H. 1996. Accountability in a Computerized Society. *Science and Engineering Ethics* 2: 25–42.

Ralls, S. 1994. *Integrating Technology with Workers in the New American Workplace*. Washington, DC: U.S. Department of Labor, Office of the American Workplace.

Shneiderman, B. 1991. Human Values and the Future of Technology: A Declaration of Responsibility. *ACM SIGCHI Bulletin* 23(1): 11–16. Revised version reprinted from *Proceedings of ACM SIGCAS Symposium: Computers and the Quality of Life, USA*, 90: 1–6.

Sterling, T. 1974. Guidelines for Humanizing Computerized Information Systems: A Report from Stanley House. *Communications of the ACM* 17(11): 609–613.

Wiener, N. 1954. *The Human Use of Human Beings: Cybernetics and Society*. Garden City, NY: Doubleday and Company.

Wurth, A. 1992. Public Participation in Technological Decisions: A New Model. *Science Technology Society Bulletin* 12: 289–293.

PART II

Computers as Persons? – Implications for Design

8

Computers Are Social Actors: A Review of Current Research

CLIFFORD I. NASS,[1] YOUNGME MOON,[1] JOHN MORKES,
EUN-YOUNG KIM, AND B. J. FOGG

Abstract: In this chapter, we present evidence that computers are social actors. Five experiments are presented; together, they demonstrate that people engage in social behavior toward machines even in situations in which users state that such responses are wholly inappropriate. Specifically, the studies provide evidence that: (1) users apply politeness norms to computers; (2) users respond to computer personalities in the same way they respond to human personalities; (3) users are susceptible to flattery from computers; and (4) users apply gender stereotypes to computers. A fifth study demonstrates that individuals do not exhibit social responses to computers because users are thinking of the programmer. Implications for improving the design of interfaces are explicated.

On the surface, the fact that people respond socially to technologies is not altogether surprising. After all, almost all of us can think of situations in which we have muttered to our computers, cursed at our automobiles, or "talked back" to the television set. However, the traditional academic response to such social responses has been one of dismissal; indeed, the tendency to respond socially to technology is typically viewed as some kind of aberration.

The arguments generally fall into two categories. On the one hand are the scholars who argue that social responses to technologies are a function of deficiency, such as youth, lack of knowledge about technology, or psychological or social dysfunction (Barley, 1988; Turkle, 1984; Winograd & Flores, 1987; Zuboff, 1988). According to this view, "normal," well-adjusted individuals are unlikely to engage in social behavior toward machines. Others argue that this social behavior is, in fact, directed toward the human creator behind the machine. In other words, because the machine is logically perceived by the user to be a human artifact (Dennett, 1987; Heidegger, 1977), the rational response is to adopt an "intentional stance" (Dennett, 1987) toward the technology since it is simply a proxy for the creator or programmer (Searle, 1981).

What both of these explanations have in common is the assumption that individuals' social responses to technologies are consistent with their beliefs about technology (Nass, Steuer, Henriksen, & Dryer, 1994). In other words, in

---

[1]Note: Both authors contributed equally to this chapter.

the first case, behavior is presumably based upon a mistaken belief about the nature of machines; in the second case, behavior is presumably based upon a rational decision to orient toward the human creator behind the machine.

In this chapter, we seek to demonstrate that neither explanation sufficiently accounts for the extent to which people respond socially to computer technologies. Five studies are presented, all of which provide evidence that individuals engage in social behavior toward machines even though: (1) they are not deficient in any way; and (2) they do not perceive themselves as having a relationship with the machine's creator. In other words, individuals engage in social behavior toward technologies even when such behavior is entirely *inconsistent* with their beliefs about machines.

In addition, the present studies suggest that social responses to technologies are much more commonplace than many may believe. In all of the experiments presented below, the social response does not involve an overt behavior such as "talking" to a computer. Rather, the social behavior under investigation is much more subtle, involving an experimental manipulation to which the subjects are blind. When subjects do engage in social behavior toward the computer, they are unaware that they are doing so. Postexperimental debriefs confirm this lack of awareness. In other words, users in these experiments automatically and unconsciously apply social rules to their interactions with computers.

All of the studies described in this chapter were conducted as part of the Social Responses to Communication Technologies (SRCT) research program in the SRCT Laboratory at Stanford University. Taken together, the studies suggest that the model for human–computer interaction should be *interpersonal*. Given this discovery, the results have intriguing implications for theoretical and design principles in human–computer interaction. Hence, the SRCT approach is not only to adopt this model to predict outcomes in various human–computer relationships, but also to generate suggestions for product design.

In making these product design suggestions, our goal is rather straightforward: We are interested in making technologies more "likable." And just as "liking" leads to various secondary consequences in interpersonal relationships (e.g., trust, sustained friendship, etc.), we suspect that it also leads to various consequences in human–computer interactions (e.g., increased likelihood of purchase, use, productivity, etc.).

The experimental paradigm used in the SRCT research program is similar across a variety of studies. In each case, we investigate a well-established social science hypothesis that concerns behavior or attitude toward humans. The hypothesis regarding human–human interaction is, however, rewritten for human–computer interaction. This involves changing the word "human" to "computer" in the statement of the hypothesis. Our next step is to experimentally test the new hypothesis, using a methodology similar to that used in testing the hypothesis in human–human interaction. The primary exception is that we replace the human in the experiment with a computer. The computer used in the experiment is programmed to exhibit certain characteristics traditionally associated with humans, such as language output, responses based on multiple prior inputs, and/or voice. Finally, if the hypothesis is supported, implications for theory and design are explicated.

All of the studies reviewed in this chapter have used this approach successfully. The studies address the following questions and concepts adapted from the interpersonal interaction literature: Do users apply politeness norms to computers? Do users respond to computer personalities in the same way they respond to human personalities? Are users susceptible to flattery from computers? and Do users apply gender stereotypes to computers? In addition, we present a fifth study that tests an alternative explanation (the programmer explanation) for social responses to computers.

STUDY 1: ARE PEOPLE POLITE TO COMPUTERS?

People apply politeness norms when responding to questions posed by other individuals. For example, an individual who directly asks others about oneself will receive more positive answers than if the same question is posed by a third party (e.g., Finkel, Guterbock, & Borg, 1991; Kane & Macaulay, 1993; Reese, Danielson, Shoemaker, Chang, & Hsu, 1986; Schuman & Converse, 1971; Singer, Frankel, & Glassman, 1983). Furthermore, politeness norms dictate that people directly evaluating an individual will feel more constrained in their responses than when a third party asks; thus, across individuals, responses will tend to be much more homogeneous (i.e., fall in a much narrower range) when a person asks about oneself compared to when a third party asks.

This first experiment was designed to determine whether people are "polite" to computers. To conduct this study, subjects underwent a tutoring, testing, and evaluation session with a computer. Following completion of the task, subjects were interviewed about the computer's performance during the task. In the first condition, this interview was conducted by the computer itself. Under this condition, there would seem to be no apparent reason for subjects to be anything less than honest, since it is impossible to "hurt a computer's feelings." On the other hand, if subjects were to give polite (i.e., socially appropriate) answers to the computer in this situation, then this would provide support for the idea that people unconsciously respond to computers in a social manner.

In a second condition, subjects were asked to evaluate the computer by answering a paper-and-pencil questionnaire. We predicted that subjects would perceive this paper-and-pencil questionnaire as a third party because it was physically separate from the computer. Thus, the prediction was that subjects would be much more likely to criticize the computer in this condition, compared to the first condition.

There was also a third condition in this experiment. Because paper-and-pencil is a fundamentally different medium than a computer, it could generate different types of responses. So in the third condition, subjects were asked about the computer's performance by a separate, but identical, computer. Again, the prediction was that subjects would perceive this other computer as a third party, and thus be more likely to criticize the computer in this condition, compared to the first condition.

Method

University undergraduates (N=33) from various communication classes were randomly assigned to one of three conditions – same–computer, paper-and-pencil, or different–computer – in a balanced between-subjects design. Upon arrival the subject was told that he or she would work with a computer to complete a task. Every effort was made to ensure that the appearance of the computer was as simple and straightforward as possible; neither graphical representations nor audio cues were used. The computer used only text-based output.

The subject then underwent the tutoring, testing, and evaluation session with the computer. Following completion of the task, the subject was interviewed about the performance of the computer. Depending on condition, this interview was conducted by either: (1) the same computer; (2) a paper-and-pencil questionnaire; or (3) a separate but identical computer in the next room. The dependent variables were subjects' perceptions of the computer. We also looked at the variance in the subjects' perceptions, because previous studies have indicated that extremity of responses is associated with greater honesty on the part of interviewees (see, e.g., Sproull, 1986). The prediction here was that same–computer subjects would rate the computer's performance more homogeneously than paper-and-pencil or different–computer subjects. Homogeneity of responses was measured in terms of standard deviation.

The actual interview consisted of a set of questions that asked subjects to evaluate the computer according to a given adjective. For all items, respondents answered on a 10-point scale anchored by "Describes Very Poorly" and "Describes Very Well." In our analysis, we used twenty-one different items that covered various aspects of the user's affective feelings toward the computer and the interaction, as well as perceptions of the computer's performance. The twenty-one items were: informative, helpful, likable, knowledgeable, friendly, analytical, fun, competent, useful, enjoyable, warm, and polite (tutoring session), and friendly, fun, likable, accurate, competent, confident, polite, fair, analytical, warm (evaluation session).

The specific model we examined was a comparison of the same–computer condition to both the paper-and-pencil and different–computer conditions. To test the relative positivity of assessments of the computer, we combined the items into a single factor score; higher scores on the factor indicated more positive responses toward the computer. We then performed t-tests to determine whether differences between conditions existed. For the comparison of the relative homogeneity (dishonesty) of responses, we did an item analysis: For each item, we calculated the standard deviation, and then did a paired comparison t-test by item. For both tests, we adjusted the p-level to control for the inflated significance levels associated with multiple comparisons.

Results

As predicted, subjects gave significantly more positive responses when interviewed by the computer asking about its own performance, compared to when interviewed by the paper-and-pencil questionnaire. In addition, subjects in the same-computer condition gave significantly more homogeneous (less honest) responses than subjects in the paper-and-pencil condition (see fourth column in Table 1).

What about the third condition? Again, as predicted, subjects who were interviewed by the same computer gave significantly more positive responses and more homogeneous responses, compared to subjects who were interviewed by a different computer (see the fifth column in Table 1). In other words, subjects seemed to perceive the different computer as a third party to whom they could give honest responses.

Finally, in postexperimental debriefs, all of the subjects denied feeling constrained in their responses, and all of them asserted – some of them rather strongly – that it would be absurd to engage in polite behavior toward a computer.

Table 1: Mean Perceptions of Tutor and Evaluator Sessions

	Conditions			Differences	
	Same Computer (SC)	Paper & Pencil (PP)	Different Computer (DC)	SC vs. PP t	SC vs. DC t
Mean Ratings	5.5	4.8	4.9	1.9*	2.7**
Homogeneity	2.0	2.5	2.5	3.5***	3.4***

*p.05; **$p<$.01; ***$p<$.001.

Note: Mean Ratings are based on an index of 10-point scales; significance level of t for Mean Rating is based on factor scores. Significance tests based on one-tailed Dunnett's t.[2]

Theoretical and Design Implications

The results of this study illustrate the extent to which people respond socially to computers. The more specific implication is that people obey politeness norms when interacting with computers, even though they are not consciously aware of doing so. In other words, people are polite to computers, however strange that may seem.

This study leads to important suggestions for those engaged in product testing. In product evaluation, these results suggest that questions about a product should not be asked by the product itself. Nor should they be asked by the technology used to test the product, despite the convenience. Instead, the interview should be conducted by using either a paper-and-pencil questionnaire or a different product or technology.

Another possible implication of this research may be that, in addition to being polite to computers, users also expect politeness from computers. These expectations may be unconscious, but if not met, may result in dissatisfaction and irritation on the part of the users. Most computer software programs avoid obvious impolite behaviors, such as directly insulting the user, but many other important politeness rules are commonly ignored by interface designers. A good example of this is confusing error messages, which are often blatantly impolite.

In fact, lists of politeness rules can be found in a wide variety of books. Of course, politeness rules differ from country to country and culture to culture. Hence, when one modifies an interface for another country, rather than simply changing the language, one must also avoid behaviors that would be con-

---

[2]This table is reprinted from Nass, Moon, & Carney (1996).

strued as impolite in that country. (For complete details of this study, see Nass, Moon & Carney, 1996).

STUDY 2: ATTRACTION AND PERSONALITY

Psychologists have found that one of the best ways to predict whether two people will be attracted to each other is to find out how similar they are (Byrne & Nelson, 1965). The more similar they are, the more likely they will be attracted to each other. This is particularly true with respect to personality: People with similar personality characteristics tend to like each other (Blankenship, Hnat, Hess & Brown, 1984; Byrne, 1969; Duck & Craig, 1978; Griffitt, 1969; Izard, 1960a, 1960b, 1963). For example, people prefer strangers who have personalities similar to their own over strangers who have personalities different from their own (Byrne, Griffitt & Stefaniak, 1967; Griffitt, 1966). Similar results have been found with respect to naturally occurring relationships, such as friendships (Duck & Craig, 1978; Izard, 1960a, 1963), as well as forced relationships, such as college roommate assignments (Carli, Ganley & Pierce-Otay, 1991).

Is the same thing true for computers? Are people attracted to computers that exhibit personality behavior similar to their own? To determine whether this is so, we constructed an experiment that matched different types of people with different types of computers. The participants were categorized by personality, using a standard personality test. The personality dimension on which we focused was the dominance/submissiveness dimension of the personality. This dimension is one of the two most psychologically important dimensions in impression formation (Williams, Munick, Saiz & FormyDuval, 1995). Moreover, the behavioral characteristics of this dimension are rather straightforward: Dominant people tend to be self-confident, leading, and assertive; submissive people tend to be self-doubting, obedient, and passive (Kiesler, 1983; Wiggins, 1979).

The computers were also categorized by "personality." The dominant computer was given characteristics associated with dominance, while the submissive computer was given characteristics associated with submissiveness.

It is important to note that this was accomplished using only the most simple, preprogrammed, text-based cues. In contrast, most interface designers and programmers tend to try to create computer "personalities" using technological features such as sophisticated graphics, natural-language programming, or artificial intelligence. We took a much more psychological approach, drawing on the literature on personality to find a limited set of text-based cues that would be sufficient to evoke a psychological response on the part of users.

The prediction was that once these computer personalities were created, people would respond to them in a social manner, i.e., in the same way that they would respond to human personalities. In other words, we predicted that people would prefer to interact with computers that exhibit personalities similar to their own.

Method

Undergraduates from various communication classes (N=80) were categorized as being either dominant or submissive, using a personality survey conducted several weeks before the experiment was conducted. Forty individuals from each category were recruited to participate in this experiment.

Personalities were then created on computers using four text-based language cues. First, the dominant computer was programmed to use strong language in the form of assertions and commands; the submissive computer used weaker language in the form of questions and suggestions. As an example, the dominant computer might display the following text: "You should definitely rate the flashlight higher. It is your only night signaling device." In contrast, the submissive computer would display the following text: "Perhaps the flashlight should be rated higher? It may be your only reliable night signaling device." Second, the dominant computer displayed a high level of confidence in its statements, whereas the submissive computer displayed a low level of confidence in its statements. Third, we programmed the dominant computer to always initiate the interaction, while the submissive computer waited for the subject to initiate the interaction. Finally, we gave the computers different names: The dominant computer was named "Max," and the submissive computer was named "Linus."[3]

Other than these four differences, the dominant computer and the submissive computer were the same; that is, both the dominant and the submissive computer gave the user the same type and amount of information. The entire

---

[3]These names were chosen based on a pretest of dozens of names. "Max" and "Linus" were most closely associated with dominance and submissiveness, respectively, *without* being associated with other dimensions of personality, such as friendliness, intelligence, etc. In subsequent replications of this experiment, we dropped these names from the manipulation; when we did this, the results were similar to those reported here (see Moon & Nass, 1996).

manipulation was preprogrammed; no natural-language programming or artificial intelligence was employed.

Half of the dominant subjects were assigned to the dominant computer and the other half to the submissive computer. Submissive subjects were divided in the same way, creating a 2 x 2 balanced, between-subjects design. During the experiment, the subject interacted with the computer to complete a task (the Desert Survival Task; for details, see Lafferty, Eady & Elmers, 1974) that lasted for approximately 15–20 minutes.

When the interaction was complete, the subject went into another room and filled out a paper-and-pencil questionnaire. The questionnaire presented a series of questions about the computer and about the subject's attitude toward the computer. Using factor analysis as a guide, we created three indices: Affiliation, Competence, and Quality of the Interaction. The Affiliation index was based on four items: friendly, likable, sympathetic, and warm. The Competence index was based on twelve items: intelligent, knowledgeable, rational, insightful, credible, competent, clever, helpful, efficient, conscientious, reliable, and the question, "How much did the computer improve your final ranking?" The Quality of the Interaction index was based on seven items: engaging, enjoyable, exciting, fun, interesting, involving, and satisfying.

Results

All results were based on a full-factorial ANOVA design.

First, the subjects identified and distinguished dominance and submissiveness in the computers even in the absence of anthropomorphic presentation. The dominant computer was rated as significantly more aggressive, assertive, authoritative, confident, controlling, dominant, domineering, and forceful – all adjectives associated with dominance. Conversely, the submissive computer was rated as more submissive, shy, and timid.

Second, the subjects were able to detect similarity of the computer's personality to their own. Dominant subjects found the dominant computer to be significantly more like them in style of interaction and in the phrasing of comments than submissive subjects did. Also, on the same attributes, submissive subjects found the submissive computer to be more like them than dominant subjects did.

Third, there was strong evidence that subjects preferred interacting with computers that shared their personality type. Moreover, this crossover interaction effect was found consistently over a wide range of attributes. For example, when the personalities of the subject and the computer matched, the computer was given higher affiliation ratings than when the person and the computer had different personalities (see Figure 1).

This same transverse interaction effect was found with respect to *competence*. When the subject and the computer shared the same personality, the computer received higher competence ratings (see Figure 1) compared to when the subject and the computer had different personalities. Finally, subjects matched with similar computers found the interaction to be more satisfying, compared to subjects matched with dissimilar computers (see Figure 1).

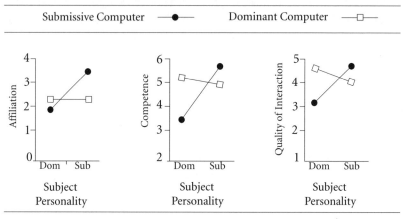

Figure 1. Dependent variable, as a function of subject and computer personality.[4]

Theoretical and Design Implications

The first theoretical implication of this experiment is that people respond socially to computer personalities. When they encounter a computer with a personality similar to their own, they tend to be attracted to it; when they encounter a computer that is dissimilar, they tend not to be attracted to it. In fact, in this study, users' perceptions of the computer changed dramatically depending on whether the computer's personality matched their own. These perceptions extended across affect – their liking of the computer and the interaction – as well as cognition – their assessments of information quality.

The second theoretical implication is that personality is easy to create. Contrary to the conventional wisdom that creating a personality requires natural-language programming, artificial intelligence, complex graphical environments, or richly defined agents, this research demonstrates that one of the

---

[4]This figure is reprinted from Nass, Moon, Fogg, Reeves & Dryer (1995).

most basic communication technologies – words – can provide very strong cues for personality.

This study also leads to several guidelines and suggestions for the design of interfaces. One is that *virtually any word-based interface may have a personality in the eyes of the users.* The style of language used in error messages and prompts, the method of navigation, and the level of interactivity may all provide cues that suggest a particular personality type. Unfortunately, in most cases, little thought goes into creating these messages. This is especially true for systems that do not have an intentional social presence; help systems, for example, often include content in a variety of personality styles, reflecting the personalities of the individuals who wrote the particular messages.

A second design implication of this research is that personality may be an important way to segment the market for computer interfaces. Traditionally, the primary focus for marketing of computers and other highly technical products has been user expertise. But if users are humans first and foremost, and experts second, as SRCT theory argues, then personality may be a very underutilized diagnostic. (For complete details of this study, see Nass, Moon, Fogg, Reeves & Dryer, 1995.)

STUDY 3: RESPONSES TO COMPUTERS THAT FLATTER

People have a basic desire to think of themselves favorably (Berscheid & Walster, 1978; Taylor & Brown, 1988). For this reason, people are "phenomenal suckers for flattery" (Cialdini, 1993). Not only do we tend to believe flattery (i.e., insincere praise), but we also tend to feel emotionally satisfied when we are flattered (Byrne, Rasche & Kelley, 1974), we tend to like people who flatter us (Jones, 1964), and we tend to judge their performance more favorably (Watt, 1993). In fact, flattery is so powerful that it often can evoke the same effects as sincere praise.

What happens when people are confronted with a computer that flatters · them? Will they respond in the same manner? This third experiment was conducted to test this idea. Our prediction was that people would, indeed, respond to computer flattery in the same way that they respond to human flattery.

Method

The participants (N=40) in this experiment were randomly assigned to one of three conditions: (1) sincere praise; (2) flattery (insincere praise); and (3) generic feedback.

After arriving at the laboratory, subjects were instructed to play a guessing game on the computer. The computer was programmed to give the subjects feedback on their performance at periodic intervals during the game.

For subjects in the generic feedback condition, this feedback consisted of a simple message that said, "Begin next round." For subjects in the other two conditions, this feedback consisted of positive statements praising the subject's performance, such as "Great job! You seem to have an uncommon ability to structure data logically."

The only difference between the sincere praise condition and the flattery condition was the description subjects received about this positive feedback: Subjects in the sincere praise condition were told that the feedback was contingent on their performance (although it was in fact randomly generated), whereas subjects in the flattery condition were told that the feedback was totally *non*contingent on their performance. More specifically, subjects in the flattery condition were told that the evaluation portion of the program was not yet written and therefore was randomly generated. In the latter case, this information was repeated several times to ensure that subjects understood that the computer feedback had nothing to do with their actual performance. Finally, subjects were given a paper-and-pencil questionnaire.

Based on factor analysis, we created six dependent variable indices from the items in the questionnaire. They were: Positive Affect of the User, Power–feeling of the User, User's Perception of Own Performance, Enjoyment of the Interaction, User's Willingness to Continue Working, and Evaluation of the Computer's Performance. Positive Affect of the User was based on three items: good, happy, and relaxed. Power–feeling of the user was based on three items: important, powerful, and dominant. User's Perception of Own Performance was based on four items: how well subjects felt they performed, how satisfied subjects were with their performance, how efficient their game framework was, and how favorably subjects rated their performance compared to other subjects. Enjoyment of the Interaction was based on three items: fun, creative, and rewarding. User's Willingness to Continue Working consisted of two items: how willing to continue working with the computer and how willing to continue on the task. Evaluation of the Computer's Performance was based on three items that referred to the computer: helpful, intelligent, and insightful.

Results

A manipulation check at the end of the postexperimental questionnaire confirmed that all subjects in the flattery and sincere praise conditions understood whether the praise from the computer was (ostensibly) contingent on their work or not.

In addition, as predicted, praise from the computer – both sincere praise and insincere praise (flattery) – had a remarkable impact on how users felt about themselves, the interaction, and the computer. To control for the experiment-wise error rate, we compared the flattery and sincere praise conditions to the generic feedback condition using Dunnett's *t*. Subjects in both the flattery and sincere praise conditions enjoyed the interaction more, felt more powerful, thought they performed better, liked the interaction more, were more willing to continue working with the computer, and evaluated the computer more highly, as opposed to subjects in the generic feedback condition (see Figure 2).

In addition, the responses of subjects in the flattery condition did *not* differ from the responses of subjects in the sincere praise condition. All comparisons were clearly insignificant with respect to all six measures, and this result was not a problem of lack of statistical power (see Figure 2).

Theoretical and Design Implications

Results from this study provide further evidence that people respond to computers socially. When confronted with computers that flatter us, our reaction is the same as when flattered by people: We like them, and ourselves, better.

This research has strong implications for the design of computer software and hardware. Most current computer applications are heavily geared toward critical feedback (e.g., error messages); adding positive feedback to these systems would significantly enhance the user experience. Note that under these circumstances, even noncontingent positive feedback would be quite effective.

Similarly, adding either sincere praise or flattery to training and tutorial software would aid in the learning process by increasing user enjoyment, task persistence, and feelings of self-efficacy. Applications that enhance user creativity, such as drawing and painting programs, would also be evaluated more highly if they were to incorporate a positive feedback mechanism.

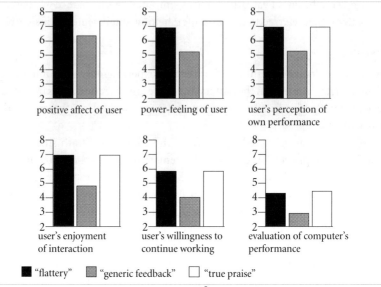

Figure 2. Mean response, as a function of condition.[5]

Finally, software programs designed to aid users in performing unpleasant tasks would be ideal candidates for positive message systems. For example, many programs are designed to help users pay their taxes, balance a spreadsheet, or draft legal documents. The results of this study suggest that incorporating a flattering feedback mechanism would boost user enjoyment of these tedious undertakings. (For complete details of this study, see Fogg & Nass, 1996.)

STUDY 4: CAN COMPUTERS BE "MALE" OR "FEMALE"?

Whether we like them or not, gender stereotypes are not only powerful, but also extremely common. Psychologists have demonstrated, for example, that men are generally perceived as more independent, assertive, and decisive than women, whereas women are perceived as being more sensitive and emotionally responsive than men (e.g., Rosencrantz, Vogel, Bee, Broverman & Broverman, 1968).

---

[5]This figure is reprinted from Fogg & Nass (1996).

Do people also apply gender stereotypes to computers? This study tested whether they do, by using computers with male- and female-voiced output.

Specifically, three stereotypes were tested. The first stereotype concerned dominant behavior. When men exhibit dominant behavior, they tend to be perceived as being "assertive" or "independent." When women exhibit dominant behavior, they tend to be perceived as being "pushy" or "bossy." In other words, researchers have found that dominance and aggressiveness are often considered undesirable in women but not in men (Costrich, Feinstein, Kidder, Marecek & Pascale, 1975; Deutsch & Gilbert, 1976; Pleck, 1978; Spence, Helmreich & Stapp, 1974). Based on this stereotype, the prediction was that a female-voiced computer in a dominant role would be perceived more negatively than a male-voiced computer in the same role.

The second stereotype involved evaluation. In general, when people are evaluated, they tend to consider the evaluation to be more valid if it comes from a male than if it comes from a female. Men are stereotypically regarded as being more "influential" than women; men are also perceived as being more "effective leaders" (Eagly & Wood, 1982). And according to researchers, both men and women are prone to using this stereotype. Thus, the prediction here was that users – regardless of gender – would take evaluations from male-voiced computers much more seriously than evaluations from female-voiced computers.

The third stereotype concerned knowledge about various topics. Research has shown that we tend to categorize certain topics and professions as being "masculine" or "feminine." These stereotypes, in turn, affect the entrance of men and women into these occupations (e.g., Heilman, 1979). In other words, people tend to gender-stereotype across topics, assuming that women know more about "feminine" topics and men know more about "masculine" topics. To test this stereotype, two different topics were used in the experiment. One was stereotypically "feminine" (love and relationships) and the other was stereotypically "masculine" (computers and technology). The prediction was that a female-voiced computer would be perceived as a better teacher of the former, while a male-voiced computer would be perceived as a better teacher of the latter.

In sum, this experiment tested whether people apply gender stereotypes to computers. The only gender cue in this experiment was the computer's voice output. In addition, subjects were never led to believe that they were interacting with a human hidden behind the computer; rather, they were explicitly told they were interacting with the computer itself. Thus, the experiment was conducted to determine whether gender stereotypes are applied in human–

computer interactions, where gender is downplayed and commonly thought of as irrelevant.

Method

Participants (N=40) in this experiment were told that they would be using computers for three separate sessions: tutoring, testing, and evaluation.

During the tutoring session, the tutor computer verbally presented (via a prerecorded female or male voice) ten facts on each of two topics, computers and technology, and love and relationships.

After the tutoring session, the subject was directed by the tutoring computer voice to move to a "tester" computer for the testing session. The tester computer, which had no voice, administered a text-based, multiple-choice test. Each question ostensibly had a "correct" answer.

Upon completing the testing session, the tester computer told the subject to go to a third computer, the "evaluator" computer, for the evaluation session. There, the evaluator computer informed the subject (via a prerecorded female or male voice) that he or she had answered six of the twelve questions correctly. The evaluator computer then reviewed each question separately. For each question, the evaluator computer indicated whether the subject had given a correct answer and then evaluated the performance of the tutor computer in preparing the subject. The overall evaluation of the tutor's performance was generally positive (e.g., "Your answer to this question was correct. The tutor computer chose useful facts for answering this question. Therefore, the tutor computer performed well.")

The evaluator computer thus played two roles: It evaluated the performance of the subject, and it also evaluated the performance of the tutor computer. The evaluator computer was thus extremely dominant (Strong, Hills, Kilmartin, DeVries, Lanier, Nelson, Strickland & Meyer, 1988).

Next, the evaluator computer asked the subject to complete a pencil-and-paper questionnaire that consisted of two sets of questions. The first set asked subjects for their assessment of the tutor computer's performance during the tutoring session. The second set of questions asked for an assessment of the evaluator computer during the evaluation session.

All subjects were randomly assigned to hear either female or male voices during the tutoring and evaluation sessions. These sessions had four possible combinations: male–male, male–female, female–female, and female–male. In addition, four different voices (two male and two female) were used, so that no subject heard the same voice in more than one session. All four voices said the same words within each session. In addition, all four voices were pretested to guard against the possibility of significant differences in paralinguistic characteristics. Pretests indicated that the four voices were not perceived differently with respect to intonation, pacing, or other paralinguistic cues.

Results

The first prediction – that a female-voiced computer in a dominant role would be evaluated more negatively than a male-voiced computer in the same role – was supported. Both male and female subjects found the female-voiced evaluator computer to be significantly less "friendly" than the male-voiced evaluator, even though the content of their comments was identical (see first row of Table 2). The full-factorial ANOVA revealed no other main effects (gender of tutor, gender of subject), and no significant interactions with respect to this measure.

The second prediction – that evaluations from male-voiced computers would be taken more seriously than evaluations from female-voiced computers – was supported as well. Subjects thought the tutor computer was significantly more "competent" when it was praised by a male-voiced evaluator computer, compared to when it was praised by a female-voiced evaluator computer (see second row of Table 2). Furthermore, subjects thought the tutor computer was significantly "friendlier" when it was praised by the male-voiced evaluator computer, compared to when it was praised by the female-voiced evaluator computer (see third row of Table 2). And in both cases, the gender of the subject and the gender of the tutor computer's voice made no difference.

Table 2: Means for Assessment of Tutor and Evaluator as a Function of Gender of Evaluator Voice

	Evaluator Voice		
	Male	Female	F
Evaluator Computer			
Friendliness	16.25	11.55	6.03[*]
Tutor Computer			
Competence	28.41	24.26	5.10[*]
Friendliness	19.65	14.15	5.74[*]

[*]$p<.05$.[6]

---

[6]This table is reprinted from Nass, Moon & Green (1996).

The results also confirmed the third prediction – that a female-voiced computer would be perceived as a better teacher on the topic of love and relationships, whereas a male-voiced computer would be perceived as a better teacher on the topic of computers and technology.

Finally, all of the subjects were experienced computer users who, in postexperimental debriefs, denied harboring stereotypes or being influenced by the gender of the computer voices. None of them thought the voices represented the computers' programmer; in fact, most subjects said they thought the three computers used in the experiment were programmed by the same person (which they were), and that the person was male (which is ironic, since they said they did not harbor stereotypes).

Theoretical and Design Implications

These results suggest that the tendency to gender-stereotype is so deeply ingrained in human psychology that it extends even to computers. In this experiment, vocal cues alone were enough to elicit stereotypic responses from users. Indeed, the most important design implication of this study is that users automatically and unconsciously stereotype computers based on the gender of the computer voices. Thus, choosing a computer voice's gender is one of the most important design decisions that can be made. By choosing (or casting) a particular voice, a designer will trigger in the user's mind a whole set of expectations associated with that voice's gender. A common mistake in the industry is to assume that a male voice is neutral; a male voice brings with it a large set of expectations and responses based on stereotypes about males.

This study also raises the possibility that visual representations of computer agents and even their language style may elicit stereotypic responses, and that computer voices may indicate much more than gender. For example, users may consciously or unconsciously assign an age, a social class, and a geographic location to a computer agent or voice, which creates expectations about how the agent will, or should, behave. In other words, no matter what choice a designer makes to represent the computer or a computer agent, the results may produce a number of expectations in the user.

Designing a computer agent or character can therefore involve tough decisions. For example, if you are selecting a voice to guide users through a CD-ROM on medical advice for pregnant women, should the voice be male or female? How old should the voice sound? Should it have a particular accent? Should there be two voices – a male voice for certain topics and a female voice for others? Perhaps a more important question is whether computer agents should be designed to conform to stereotypes at all. There may be very good reasons for designing agents that challenge these stereotypes. Obviously, these are questions that designers, their employers, and perhaps users, must answer. (For complete details of this study, see Nass, Moon & Green, in press.)

STUDY 5: TESTING AN ALTERNATIVE EXPLANATION FOR SRCT RESULTS: IS THE PROGRAMMER PSYCHOLOGICALLY RELEVANT?

As discussed in the introduction to this chapter, one of the most common explanations for social responses to computers is as follows: When users respond socially to computers, they are actually responding to the "source" behind the computer, i.e., the programmer. In other words, the unseen programmer, rather than the computer, is perceived by the user to be the psychologically relevant source of the computer's content.

Evidence from the field of psychology suggests the opposite. Social psychologists have shown that people generally orient to proximate sources rather than original sources (Stone & Beell, 1975). That is, the messenger, rather than the creator of the message, is typically considered the psychologically relevant source and is assigned credit or blame for the message.

Nonetheless, in order to test the possibility that people orient to the programmer when interacting with computers, we conducted an experiment in which half the subjects were told they were working with computers, and the other half were told they were working with programmers. The SRCT prediction was that there would be significant differences between responses from subjects who were told they were working with the programmer and from subjects who were told they were working with a computer. The programmer prediction, on the other hand, was that there would be no difference between responses from subjects in the two conditions, because the description of the computer as a programmer would be redundant.

Note that this study was *not* designed to provide a critical test of the idea that people respond socially to technologies; indeed, we believe the four previously mentioned studies, along with dozens of other studies conducted at the SRCT Laboratory (Reeves & Nass, 1996), already provide strong evidence of this. Rather, this study was constructed for a single purpose: to disconfirm the idea that people orient to the programmer when interacting with a computer.

Method

Participants (N=30) in this study were told the purpose of the experiment was to evaluate a tutor computer (or programmer). In the computer condition, the computer was labeled "computer." In the programmer condition, the computer was labeled "programmer." All verbal references to the computers were consistent with this labeling. In reality, all subjects worked with the same computer.

After being tutored, tested, and evaluated by the tutor, subjects were asked to complete a questionnaire that assessed the tutor's performance. In these questionnaires, the words "computer" and "programmer" were avoided so that the questionnaire would be the same for all subjects.

Based on factor analysis, four indices were created: Friendliness, Effectiveness, Playfulness, and Similarity to the User. The Friendliness index was based on seven items: cheerful, gentle, likable, warm, friendly, sympathetic, and affectionate. The Effectiveness index was based on nine items: articulate, clever, insightful, intelligent, helpful, responsive, competent, and analytical. The Playfulness index was based on four items: childlike, entertaining, enthusiastic, and playful. The Similarity to the User index was based on two items: subjects' perceived similarity to the computer's style of teaching, and subjects' perceived similarity to the computer's style of evaluation.

Results

The results confirmed the SRCT prediction: There were significant differences between the responses of subjects who were told they were interacting with a computer and the responses of subjects who were told they were interacting with a programmer.

Specifically, subjects in the computer condition perceived the tutor to be significantly more friendly, effective, playful, and similar to themselves than did subjects in the programmer condition (see Figure 3).

Theoretical and Design Implications

This experiment suggests that from a psychological standpoint, when users interact with a computer, they are in fact interacting with the computer itself, rather than the programmer behind the computer. Hence, this study suggests that computer users, like all people, tend to orient to the most proximate source. When the computer is psychologically relevant, then programmers, content providers, and other distant sources are not. Indeed, when a user is working with a program, the programmer is psychologically invisible, possibly because the user finds it difficult to focus on both the proximate source and the distant source at the same time. (For complete details of this study, see Nass & Sundar, 1996.)

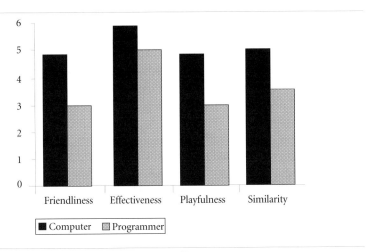

Figure 3. Mean response, as a function of condition.[7]

GENERAL CONCLUSIONS

In this chapter, we have presented several studies that provide evidence that computers are social actors. All of the studies demonstrate that people apply social rules to computers, even in situations in which they state that such responses are wholly inappropriate.

Of course, the assertion that computers are social actors raises interesting questions about what it means to *be* a social actor. Traditionally, the term social has been defined in terms of interpersonal interaction; hence, in order to be considered a social actor, a necessary requirement has been *humanness*. If, however, it can be demonstrated that social behavior is routinely directed toward nonhuman entities, then perhaps a reevaluation of the meaning of the word "social" is in order. Clearly, if we were to adopt an ontological perspective on this issue, the question would become a philosophical one that is essentially unanswerable (What does it mean to *be* a social actor?) using social

---

[7]This figure is reprinted from Nass & Sundar (1996).

science methodology. On the other hand, if we adopt a psychological criterion – that is, something is a social actor to the extent that people respond to it as if it were a social actor – then based on the research presented above, we could argue that computers *are* social actors.

This is exactly what we have done in this chapter. Based on the results of the first four experiments (along with numerous other studies from the SRCT Laboratory), we contend that, from the users' psychological perspective, computers *are* social actors. In addition, social responses to computers do not appear to be the function of deficiency or dysfunction; rather, they seem to be automatic and unconscious responses to social situations, i.e., situations that contain certain social cues.

So why do people behave this way toward computers? One possible explanation is that humans are social animals. That is, we are so emotionally, intellectually, and physiologically biased toward responding in a social manner that when confronted with computers (and other communication technologies) that bear even the slightest human resemblance, those deeply infused social responses are unconsciously triggered.

Obviously, there are a thousand ways in which computers are not like people. However, there are also a few very significant ways in which computers are very much like people. Computers use language, for example, unlike almost all inanimate objects. In addition, computers can respond based on multiple prior inputs, they often fill roles traditionally occupied by humans, and they can produce human-sounding voices. It might be that when we are confronted with an entity that does even some of these things, our brains' default response is to unconsciously treat the entity as human, even though at a conscious level, we know that it is not.

Furthermore, these studies suggest that it does not take extremely sophisticated technology to generate social responses. Indeed, in three of the five experiments described above (the exception being the gender experiment and the alternative explanation experiment), the computers used text-based output only. Social cues such as voice or sophisticated graphical representations were avoided. It thus appears that social responses are easy to generate, using a limited set of social cues.

Finally, it is important to note that the studies presented in this chapter cover a wide range of topics, ranging from politeness to gender-stereotyping. Other SRCT studies, not reviewed in this chapter, have looked at areas such as team affiliation, adaptivity, attributions of responsibility, and criticism (see Reeves & Nass, 1996). Indeed, our research has convinced us that social responses to computers are not limited to a single area; rather, these responses apply across a wide variety of human–computer situations.

REFERENCES

Barley, S.R. 1988. The Social Construction of a Machine: Ritual, Superstition, Magical Thinking, and Other Pragmatic Responses to Running a CT Scanner. In *Knowledge and Practice in Medicine: Social, Cultural, and Historical Approaches*, eds. M. Lock and D. Gordon. Hinghan, MA: Reidel.

Berscheid, E., and E. Walster. 1978. *Interpersonal Attraction.* Reading, MA: Addison-Wesley.

Blankenship, V., S.M. Hnat, T.G. Hess, and D.R. Brown. 1984. Reciprocal Interaction and Similarity of Personality Attributes. *Journal of Social and Personal Relationships* 1: 415.

Byrne, D. 1969. Attitudes and Attraction. In *Advances in Experimental Social Psychology, Vol. 4*, ed. L. Berkowitz. Orlando, FL: Academic Press.

Byrne, D., W. Griffitt, and D. Stefaniak. 1967. Attraction and Similarity of Personality Characteristics. *Journal of Personality and Social Psychology* 5: 82.

Byrne, D., and D. Nelson. 1965. Attraction as a Linear Function of Proportion of Positive Reinforcements. *Journal of Personality and Social Psychology Bulletin* 4: 240.

Byrne, D., L. Rasche, and K. Kelley. 1974. When "I Like You" Indicates Disagreement: An Experimental Differentiation of Information and Affect. *Journal of Research in Personality* 8: 207.

Carli, L.L., R. Ganley, and A. Pierce-Otay. 1991. Similarity and Satisfaction in Roommate Relationships. *Personality and Social Psychology Bulletin* 17: 419.

Cialdini, R.B. 1993. *Influence: Science and Practice.* (3rd ed.). New York: Harper Collins.

Costrich, N., J. Feinstein, L. Kidder, J. Marecek, and L. Pascale. 1975. When Stereotypes Hurt: Three Studies of Penalties in Sex-role Reversals. *Journal of Experimental Social Psychology* 11: 520.

Dennett, D.C. 1987. *The Intentional Stance.* Cambridge: MIT Press.

Deutsch, C.J., and L.A. Gilbert. 1976. Sex Role Stereotypes: Effect on Perceptions of Self and Others and on Personal Adjustment. *Journal of Counseling Psychology* 23: 373.

Duck, S.W., and G. Craig. 1978. Personality Similarity and the Development of Friendship. *British Journal of Social and Clinical Psychology* 17: 237.

Eagly, A. H., and W. Wood. 1982. Inferred Sex Differences in Status as Determinant of Gender Stereotypes about Social Influence. *Journal of Personality and Social Psychology* 43: 915.

Finkel, S.E., T.M. Guterbock, and M. J. Borg. 1991. Race of Interviewer Effects in a Pre-election Poll: Virginia 1989. *Public Opinion Quarterly* 55: 313.

Fogg, B.J., and C.I. Nass. 1996. *Silicon Sycophants: The Effects of Computers that Flatter.* Paper presented at the Annual International Communication Association meeting, Communication and Technology division, Chicago, IL.

Griffitt, W.R. 1966. Interpersonal Attraction as a Function of Self-concept and Personality Similarity. *Journal of Personality and Social Psychology* 4: 581.

Griffitt, W.R. 1969. Personality Similarity and Self-concept as Determinants of Interpersonal Attraction. *Journal of Social Psychology* 78: 137.

Heidegger, M. 1977. *The Question Concerning Technology, and Other Essays.* New York: Harper and Row.

Heilman, M.E. 1979. High School Students' Occupational Interest as a Function of Projected Sex Ratios in Male-dominated Occupations. *Journal of Applied Psychology* 64: 275.

Izard, C. 1960a. Personality Similarity and Friendship. *Journal of Abnormal and Social Psychology* 61: 47.

Izard, C. 1960b. Personality Similarity, Positive Affect and Interpersonal Attraction. *Journal of Abnormal and Social Psychology* 61: 484.

Izard, C. 1963. Personality Similarity and Friendship: A Follow-up Study. *Journal of Abnormal and Social Psychology* 66: 598.

Jones, E.E. 1964. *Ingratiation: A Social Psychological Analysis.* New York: Meredith Publishing Company.

Kane, E.W., and L. J. Macaulay. 1993. Interviewer Gender and Gender Attitudes. *Public Opinion Quarterly* 57: 1.

Kiesler, D.J. 1983. The 1982 Interpersonal Circle: A Taxonomy for Complementarity in Human Transactions. *Psychological Review* 90: 185.

Lafferty, J.C., P.M. Eady, and J.M. Elmers. 1974. *The Desert Survival Problem.* Plymouth, Michigan: Experimental Learning Methods.

Moon, Y., and C.I. Nass. 1996. How "Real" are Computer Personalities? Psychological Responses to Personality Types in Human–Computer Interaction. *Communication Research* 23: 651–674.

Nass, C.I., Y. Moon, and P. Carney. 1996. Social Desirability Effects in Computer-Based Interviewing Systems: Are Respondents "Polite" to Computers? Paper presented at the Annual International Communication Association meeting, Political Communication Division, Chicago, IL.

Nass, C.I., Y. Moon, and N. Green. 1996. Are Computers Gender-Neutral? In press. Gender Stereotypic Responses to Computers. *Journal of Applied Social Psychology.*

Nass, C.I., Y. Moon, B.J. Fogg, B. Reeves, and D.C. Dryer. 1995. Can Computer Personalities be Human Personalities? *International Journal of Human-Computer Studies* 43: 223.

Nass, C.I., J.S. Steuer, L. Henriksen, and D.C. Dryer. 1994. Machines and Social Attributions: Performance Assessments of Computers Subsequent to "Self-" or "Other-" Evaluations. *International Journal of Human-Computer Studies* 40:543.

Nass, C.I., and S. Sundar. 1996. Is Human–Computer Interaction Social or Parasocial? Unpublished manuscript, Stanford University.

Pleck, J.H. 1978. Males' Traditional Attitudes Toward Women: Conceptual Issues in Research. In *The Psychology of Women: Future Directions in Research,* eds. J. A. Sherman and F. L. Denmark. New York: Psychological Dimensions.

Reese, S.D., W.A. Danielson., P.J. Shoemaker, T. Chang, and H. Hsu. 1986. Ethnicity-of-Interviewer Effects Among Mexican-Americans and Anglos. *Public Opinion Quarterly* 50: 563.

Reeves, B., and C.I. Nass. 1996. *The Media Equation: How People Treat Computers, Television, and New Media Like Real People and Places.* Stanford, CA: CSLI Publications.

Rosencrantz, P.S., S.R. Vogel, H. Bee, I.K. Broverman, and D.M. Broverman 1968. Sex Role Stereotypes and Self Concepts in College Students. *Journal of Consulting and Clinical Psychology* 32: 287.

Schuman, H., and J.M. Converse. 1971. The Effects of Black and White Interviewers on Black Responses in 1968. *Public Opinion Quarterly* 35: 44–68.

Searle, J.R. 1981. Minds, Brains and Programs. In *The Mind's I,* eds. D. R. Hofstadter and D. C. Dennett. Toronto: Bantam.

Singer, E., M.R. Frankel, and M.B. Glassman. 1983. The Effect of Interviewer Characteristics and Expectations on Response. *Public Opinion Quarterly* 47: 84–95.

Spence, J.T., R.L. Helmreich, and J. Stapp. 1974. The Personal Attributes Questionnaire: A Measure of Sex-role Stereotypes and Masculinity-Femininity. *JSAS Catalog of Selected Documents in Psychology* 4: 43.

Sproull, L. 1986. Using Electronic Mail for Data Collection in Organizational Research. *Academy of Management Journal,* 29: 159–169.

Stone, V.A., and T.L. Beell. 1975. To Kill a Messenger: A Case of Congruity. *Journalism Quarterly* 52: 111–114.

Strong, S.R., H. Hills, C.T. Kilmartin, H. DeVries, K. Lanier, B.N. Nelson, D. Strickland, and C.W. Meyer, III. 1988. The Dynamic Relations Among Interpersonal Behaviors: A Test of Complementarity and Anticomplementarity. *Journal of Personality and Social Psychology* 34: 798–810.

Taylor, S.E., and J.D. Brown. 1988. Illusion and Well-Being: A Social Psychological Perspective on Mental Health. *Psychological Bulletin* 103: 193–210.

Turkle, S. 1984. *The Second Self: Computers and the Human Spirit.* New York: Simon & Schuster.

Watt, J.D. 1993. The Impact of the Frequency of Ingratiation on the Performance Evaluation of Bank Personnel. *Journal of Psychology* 127: 171–177.

Wiggins, J.S. 1979. A Psychological Taxonomy of Trait-Descriptive Terms: The Interpersonal Domain. *Journal of Personality and Social Psychology* 37: 395–412.

Williams, J.E., M.L. Munick, J.L. Saiz, and D.L. FormyDuval. 1995. Psychological Importance of the "Big Five": Impression Formation and Context Effects. *Personality and Social Psychology Bulletin* 21: 818–826.

Winograd, T., and C. Flores. 1987. *Understanding Computers and Cognition: A New Foundation for Design.* Reading, MA: Addison-Wesley.

Zuboff, S. 1988. *In the Age of the Smart Machine: The Future of Work and Power.* New York: Basic Books.

9

When the Interface Is a Face

LEE SPROULL, MANI SUBRAMANI, SARA KIESLER, JANET
WALKER, AND KEITH WATERS

Abstract: People behave differently when in the presence of other people than they do when they are alone. People also may behave differently when designers introduce more humanlike qualities into computer interfaces. In an experimental study, we demonstrate that people's responses to a talking face interface differ from their responses to a text-display interface. They attribute some personality traits to it; they are more aroused by it; they present themselves in a more positive light. We use theories of person perception, social facilitation, and self-presentation to predict and interpret these results. We suggest that as computer interfaces become more "humanlike," people who use those interfaces may change their own personas in response to them.

This paper explores the implications of designing computer interfaces to look or act more like people do. People act differently in the presence of other people than they do when they are alone. They pay attention to those people; they work harder; they present themselves in a more positive light. If this phenomenon extends to people in the presence of "humanlike" computers, then as interfaces display more humanlike characteristics, people who use those interfaces may change their own behavior in response to them.

Technologists have aspired to humanize computer interfaces for a long time. Humanizing interfaces entails making them more humane, in the sense of easier and more comfortable to use (Laurel, 1990; Shneiderman, 1987). Humanizing may also entail "humanifying," in the sense of embodying such humanlike attributes as speech (Eichenwald, 1986), speech recognition (Itou, Hayamizu, & Tanaka, 1992), and social intelligence (Binnick, Westbury, & Servan-Schreiber, 1989; Resnick & Lammers, 1985). Adding more humanlike attributes presumably makes interacting with the interface more satisfying – either because it is more "natural" or because it is emotionally more satisfying or both. This assumption can be quite problematic of course – consider, for example, the case of talking seatbelts in automobiles, which auto makers removed because of customer dissatisfaction.

The authors gratefully acknowledge assistance from Tom Levergood, Andy Payne, Dave Wecker, and Ted Wojcik of the Digital Equipment Corporation Cambridge Research Laboratory and Sebastian Sas of Boston University.

Financial support was provided by a grant to the first author from Digital Equipment Corporation and to the fourth author from NIMH Scientist Development Award MN 00533.

Because the human face is such a powerful signal of human identity, adding human faces to interfaces holds promise for interface designers to make interfaces more humanlike. There is some history of using human face icons and human faces in interfaces (Laurel, 1990; Takeuchi & Nagao, 1993; Thorisson, 1993). A well-known instance is "Phil," a semi-intelligent agent that appeared in Apple Computer Company promotional videotapes (although it has not yet appeared in any products). Exploration of humanlike interfaces has been limited to date by technology barriers but this situation is changing because the base technology needed to implement a variety of personable interfaces is advancing rapidly. With a combination of speech synthesis technology (commercially available) and facial animation (in research prototype), it is possible to display a synthetic talking face on a workstation screen (e.g., Waters, 1987; Waters, 1993). The face display is an image of a human face with the mouth animated in synchrony with speech delivered from an audio subsystem driven by a text-to-speech conversion algorithm. The animated face display with synchronized audio output has the likeness of a talking face. The talking face can speak arbitrary text and can participate more or less fully in an interaction with a user, depending on the underlying programming. The talking face could simply provide a stylized greeting and introduce the user to a more conventional interface. Or, the face could represent the computer side of an entire interaction, speaking all words that would otherwise be displayed on the screen as text and responding to the user orally instead of via text.

Interestingly, increasing the "humanness" of an interface by adding more human qualities to it does not necessarily make people like it more. For example, in one experimental study, users criticized "humanlike" error messages more than they did "computerlike" error messages (Resnick & Lammers, 1985). In an interface design effort, developers of navigation agents for a large hypertext historical database used icons of historical characters to provide paths through the database. Users over generalized from the character icons to expect them to have personality, motivation, and emotion and were disappointed when they didn't (Oren, Salomon & Kreitman, 1990). In a precursor to the study reported in this paper, Walker, Sproull, and Subramani (1994) administered questionnaires to people using either a text display or one of two talking face displays to ask the questions. They found that people interacting with a talking face display spent more time, made fewer mistakes, and wrote more comments than did people interacting with the text display. However, people who interacted with the more expressive face liked the face and the experience less than people who interacted with the less expressive face. Apparently at least some of the time, trying to make interfaces more like humans results in disconcerting users, if not actually confusing or displeasing them. Instead of assuming that more human is always better, it is important to understand how people interpret and react to different human qualities embodied in interfaces. This paper draws on social psychological theories of how people behave in the presence of others to investigate their response to a talking face display.

THEORETICAL FRAMEWORK AND HYPOTHESES

The human face is one of the most powerful human referents. Newborns exhibit a preference for facelike patterns over other patterns (Bond, 1972); infants begin to differentiate specific visual features of the face by the age of two months (Morton & Johnson, 1991). Faces can induce appropriate behavior in social situations and covering peoples' faces with masks can produce inappropriate behavior (Deiner et al., 1976). Faces, particularly attractive ones, even sell soap. That is, physically attractive models are found to be effective in improving peoples' responses to advertisements (Baker & Churchill, 1977).

Faces signal social identity by providing cues to emotion and personality (Ekman, 1982; Warner & Sugarman, 1986). When an observer sees a person's face, the observer can "read" emotion states such as surprise, happiness, anger, fear, or disgust and some personality attributes such as friendliness or optimism (but not other personality aspects such as dominance or activity). These readings are reliably consistent across multiple observers looking at the same faces (Ekman, 1982; Warner & Sugarman, 1986). Facial appearance also influences expectations for interaction (Hilton & Darley, 1991; Snyder, 1984). When people see a happy, friendly face they expect to have a more enjoyable interaction than when they see an unhappy, unfriendly one. Facial appearance is used (sometimes inappropriately) as an overall indicator of a person's goodness and competence (Berscheid & Walster, 1974). Facial appearance and facial expression can set off a self-fulfilling prophecy, whereby people's biased responses to appearance cues elicit responses that then reinforce their own expectations.

Previous research on physical appearance suggests that appearance elicits social perceptions related to personality and emotion, which in turn affect social behavior. Therefore to investigate if people change their behavior in the presence of a talking face display, we first asked if people would attribute personality attributes such as friendliness or pessimism to it even though the display was of a synthetic face. In experimental studies of personality attribution, subjects often are exposed to stimuli such as a one-minute tape recording of a person's voice, a single slide of a person's face, or a one-minute video of a person talking. Subjects do not interact with the stimulus person(s) but judge their personality by rating them on multiple dimensions of personality on the basis of initial exposure. These studies have documented that information about personality attributes is conveyed differentially by different information sources such as facial appearance, voice, and body gestures (O'Sullivan et al., 1985; Warner & Sugarman, 1986). For instance, sociability is conveyed better by facial appearance than by voice; activity or energy level is conveyed better by voice than by appearance. Thus, our first hypothesis is:

H1: People will differentially attribute appearance-linked personality attributes rather than nonappearance-linked ones to a talking face display as compared with a text display.

The mere presence of another human being can influence a person's behavior substantially. The presence of another person usually serves to increase arousal on the part of someone asked to perform a task (Zajonc, 1965). It leads people to attend more to the social situation and may increase evaluation apprehension and task motivation. Deemed the "social facilitation effect," this response can lead to improved performance if the task is simple or to degraded performance if it is complex (Zajonc, 1965), (Holroyd, Westbrook, Wolf & Badhorn, 1978). If people are cued to behave socially by a talking face display, as they are by a real person, then we would expect to see the social facilitation effect in this situation. Hence our second hypothesis is:

H2a: People will be more aroused when interacting with a talking face display than with a text display.

H2b: People will be more attentive when the task is presented by a talking face display than when it is presented by a text display.

The presence of other people also generally leads people to present themselves in a positive light. For example face-to-face interviews elicit more socially desirable self-reports of behavior such as wearing seat belts or voting in elections than paper and pencil questionnaires asking the same questions do (Bradburn, 1983). Face-to-face interviews also elicit fewer reports of socially undesirable behavior such as drug abuse or alcohol consumption (Waterton & Duffy, 1984). If people are cued to behave socially by a talking face display as they are by a real person, then we would expect people to present themselves in a positive light when interacting with the display. Hence our third hypothesis is:

H3a: People will present themselves in a more positive light when interacting with a talking face display than when interacting with a text display.

H3b: People will be more guarded in their revelations to a talking face display than to a text display.

There is substantial evidence that during interaction men and women are differentially aware of and sensitive to social cues such as facial expressions (Hall, 1979). Therefore our fourth hypothesis is:

H4: Men and women will differ more from one another in their responses to a talking face display than in their response to a text display.

OVERVIEW OF STUDY

The study reported below experimentally investigated peoples' responses to an ostensible computer-based career counseling system. The subjects answered psychological test items and described themselves and their interests to an interactive career counselor program. The interface through which the subjects interacted with the system was either a talking face display or a text display.

The general context of the study, the interview survey, is a familiar one and one with an extensive literature on how the nature of the experience affects peoples' responses (Bailey, Moore & Bailar, 1987; Schuman & Presser, 1981). Generally, surveys elicit social responses in much the same way as do other social contexts. Surveys delivered by human agents in face-to-face or telephone interviews are more socially involving than those delivered by paper and pencil. Thus response rates are higher; people give a greater quantity of information. But social involvement also can lead to social posturing; surveys delivered by human agents elicit more biased reports of socially desirable and undesirable behavior. We reasoned that our hypotheses could be tested in the context of a computer survey. We predicted more appearance-linked attribution and more social facilitation (arousal; attentiveness to the situation) in the presence of a talking face survey interview than a text survey interview. We predicted that subjects would present themselves more positively in a survey interview delivered by a talking face display than in an interview delivered by a text display.

In order to rule out the possibility that a particular facial expression caused the predicted effects, we used two different talking faces – one with a relatively stern expression and one with a relatively pleasant one – each derived from the sameunderlying image. We predicted subjects in both face conditions would differ from those in the text display condition. Different expressions might elicit different responses from people. For example, people might like a pleasant face more than a stern face but they might perceive the stern face as more judgmental and perform more carefully for a stern face than for a pleasant one. We did not develop hypotheses about specific differences in response to different expressions because previous research does not imply clear directional predictions regarding appearance-linked attributes, arousal and attention, or disclosure.[1] In this experiment, the pleasant and stern faces were used as empirical replications of the talking face display rather than investigated in their own right.

METHOD

The experiment was a 3 (display) x 2 (gender) between subjects factorial design with 130 subjects randomly assigned to three display conditions. The display presented fixed-response and open-ended questions in a window on a computer screen either through text, through a talking face with a pleasant expression, or through a talking face with a stern expression. Approximately equal numbers of men and women were assigned to each condition.

Subjects

Subjects were Boston University students whose participation was solicited by flyers posted on campus seeking volunteers to "try out a prototype computer-based career counseling system." Subjects' mean age was 20.7 years; 76% reported English as their native language; their self-report of typing skill was 3.0 on a 5-point scale where 1=very slow and 5=very fast. Men and women did not statistically significantly differ on any of these characteristics.

---

[1]The research on arousal and disclosure in the presence of pleasant versus stern others did not suggest a clear prediction. For example, there is evidence people will disclose more information to a pleasant or liked other, but the strength of the effect depends on whether the other person is well known, also discloses, or is nonevaluative (Collins & Miller, 1994). Since the talking face was a "stranger," did not itself disclose information about itself, and was collecting nonanonymous information that could be evaluated by a superior, the conditions for an increase in disclosure of a pleasant face as compared with a stern face were not satisfied.

Apparatus and Display Manipulation

The computer workstation was a Digital Equipment Corporation Alpha AXP, with built-in telephone-quality audio and externally-powered speakers. The workstation was running OSF version 1.1, a software implementation of the DECtalk text-to-speech algorithm, and DECface for the animated face (Waters, 1993). Face images were displayed in gray scale. The experimental session was managed using TK/Tcl (Ousterhout, 1994) and the Lisp facilities of Gnu Emacs.

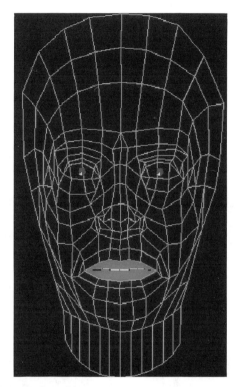

Figure 1. Underlying geometric model.

The face display was produced by texture-mapping an image captured on videotape onto a geometric wire-frame (see Figure 1). The mouth was animated by computing the mouth posture (viseme) corresponding to the current linguistic unit (phoneme) and using a cosine-based interpolation to transit between mouth postures (Waters, 1993). The voice was produced by a software implementation of the KLSYN88 revisions of the DECtalk text-to-speech algorithm (Klatt & Klatt, 1990). The DECtalk parameters used a neutral voice in the female pitch range at 160 words a minute (Waters, 1993). DECtalk speech is acceptably comprehensible at this rate (Duffy & Pisoni, 1992).

The pleasant and stern expressions were produced from the facial model of the neutral face used in Walker, Sproull, and Subramani (1994). The pleasant expression (Figure 2, right) was synthesized by slight contractions of the zygomatic major muscles in the geometric facial model that pull the corners of the mouth up and the frontalis inner and outer muscles that pull the eyebrows up (Waters, 1987). The stern expression (Figure 2, left) was synthesized by slight contractions of the zygomatic minor muscles that pull the corners of the mouth down and the corrugator muscles that pull the inner portion of the eyebrows in and down. These muscles are known to be involved in producing pleasant and stern expressions, respectively (Ekman, 1982). Expression was present only between utterances. During animation in synchrony with speech, each face returned to the initial neutral expression. As a result, the expression was identical in both face conditions during speech. The experimental expression was refreshed after each complete utterance. The facial animation software simulated eye blinking during speech; the face displayed between utterances was static.

Figure 2. Faces stern (left) and pleasant (right).

The open-ended questions were delivered in a "counselor interview" which used the Gnu Emacs implementation of ELIZA (Weizenbaum, 1976), an interactive program that simulates responses to subject input. The program consists of a simple table-driven keyword recognizer and response generator. When the subject's input contained a word classified as being related to academic performance, the program would generate a question using the word from the input and the next template in the list of academic-performance-related templates. If none of the words contained in the input had category information, the program chose one from a set of templates that changed the subject, sometimes returning to an earlier topic. The categories and templates shipped with Gnu Emacs were modified by removing inappropriate phrases and including a vocabulary relevant to career and lifestyle aspirations. We chose this approach for its ease of implementation only; we make no claim of processing natural language.

Procedure

Each subject completed the study individually in a faculty office equipped with a computer workstation. The male experimenter introduced the study and told subjects that they were helping the researchers test a prototype of a computer-based career planning system. Subjects were told they would answer some standard psychological questions and some open-ended questions from a computer-based career counselor, and then would complete a questionnaire assessing the experience. The experimenter introduced the system by having subjects complete a short demographic questionnaire and respond to a set of practice items, one in each of the response formats used in the psychological scales. After assuring that subjects understood how to enter their responses, the experimenter told subjects they could take as long as they wished and left the room. Figure 3 summarizes how the experiment proceeded across the different conditions. Note that both the psychological scales and the counselor interaction were presented in one of the experimental conditions of text display, pleasant talking face display, or stern talking face display.

Subjects in the text condition first saw a window displaying the text of instructions on how to record their answers for the first psychological scale. Items were displayed one at a time as shown in Figure 4 and subjects used a mouse to click on their chosen response for each item and to go to the next item. In all conditions the three scales were presented in random order as were the items within scales. After completing all three psychological scales, subjects

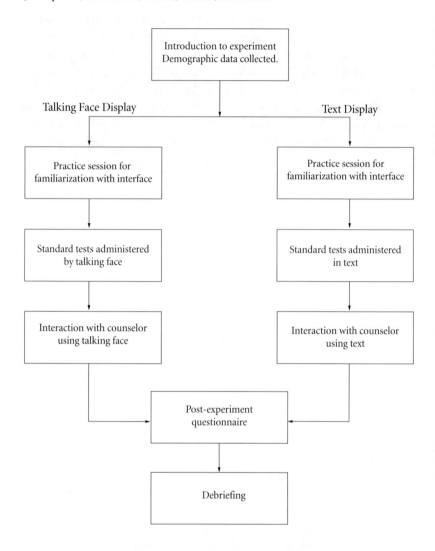

Figure 3. Flow diagram of experimental procedure.

saw a text window with a welcoming message from the "prototype computer career counseling service." This message concluded with the prompt, "Tell me something about yourself." Subjects typed their response in the lower part of the window in which the counselor's prompt was displayed. The prompt remained visible in the upper part of the window until the subject finished

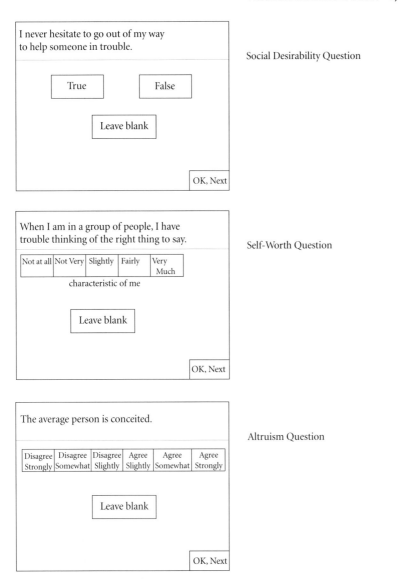

Figure 4. Sample answer windows, all conditions.

typing his or her response. When the subject clicked "go ahead," the counselor's prompt and subject's response disappeared from the window and the counselor asked another question ostensibly based on the subject's response. Subjects could continue interacting as long as they wished and were free to terminate this interaction at any point by clicking on a command button in the window frame.

In the window corresponding to the text display window in the text condition, subjects in the talking face conditions saw and heard a face speaking the same words that had been displayed as text in the text condition. The appropriate response format for each psychological scale was then displayed in text identical to that in the text condition and subjects indicated their answers by clicking with the mouse. The face remained on the screen while subjects made their response and then asked the next question. In the interview, the face spoke the counselor's side of the interaction. After a one-second delay, the counselor's words were displayed in text in the top half of the response window and subjects typed in their response in the bottom half of the window just as in the text condition. The counselor's face remained on the screen while the subject was entering his or her text.

After completing the three psychological scales and counselor interview, subjects completed a postexperiment questionnaire about their impressions of "the question asker" and their experience using the prototype system. The experiment and questionnaire were self-paced; subjects were free to work as long as they wished. Most subjects completed the session in less than forty-five minutes. They were then debriefed by the experimenter, given a packet of career planning materials provided by the university's placement office, and paid ten dollars for their participation.

Measures

Social perceptions of the interface (i.e., was it perceived to have personality attributes) were measured in the postexperiment questionnaire by having subjects complete six scales composed of thirty-three items about perceptions of the "question asker." These scales were drawn from previous studies (Buss & Plomin, 1984; Warner & Sugarman, 1986). Three of the six scales measure appearance-linked personality attributes (social evaluation, intellectual evaluation, and sociability) and three measure nonappearance-linked personality attributes (activity, emotionality, and potency). Three of the scales (social evaluation, intellectual evaluation, and potency) use 7-point semantic differentials (e.g., *unattractive attractive*) and the other three use 5-point Likert scales (1=*not at all true of this person*; 5=*very true of this person*). (See the Appendix for items, scale reliabilities, and intercorrelations.)

Arousal was measured in the postexperiment questionnaire by asking subjects "how relaxed did you feel?" and "how confident did you feel?" during their use of the system. These items were reverse-scored so that a higher number would indicate less relaxed and less confident. These questions are similar to those used in other studies of arousal (e.g., Maslach, 1979; Holroyd, et al., 1978). To measure subjects' attention to the experiment, the system recorded information on how much time subjects spent in each section of the experiment, the number of items they skipped in the scales, and the number of words subjects wrote in the counselor task. The number of interactions turns in the counselor task, also measured automatically by the system, was used as a control variable.

Self presentation was measured by subjects' responses to the three psychological scales. (See Figure 4 for an example of one item from each scale.) The Marlowe Crowne Social Desirability scale is composed of thirty-three true/false items. Scores on this scale ranged from 0 to 33, with a higher score indicating more social desirability. The Philosophy of Human Nature Altruism scale is composed of twenty 6-point Likert scale items, with anchors of "*disagree strongly*" (coded -3) and "*agree strongly*" (coded +3). Scores on this scale can could range from -60 to +60, with a higher score indicating greater altruism. The Texas Social Behavior Inventory of Self Worth is composed of sixteen 5-point Likert scale items anchored at "*not at all*" (coded 0) and "*very much*" (coded 4)." Scores on this scale can could range from 0 to 64, with a higher score indicating higher self worth.

The Social Desirability and Altruism scales measure aspects of self-presentation that are susceptible to situational influences (Kiesler & Sproull, 1986; Paulhus, 1991; Wrightsman, 1974). We expected scores to vary by experimental condition. The Self-Worth Inventory is more situationally stable (Blascovich & Tomaka, 1991); hence we did not expect scores on this scale to vary by condition. We used this scale as a covariate in some analyses to control for self-esteem effects on responses.

RESULTS

The data were analyzed using SAS version 6.07. We tested for overall differences with one-way or two-way ANOVAs, then tested for differences between the two faces. Then, in planned contrasts we used Dunnett's one-tailed or two-tailed (as appropriate) comparisons of treatments with a control to compare each of the face conditions with the text condition. Subject characteristics of age, first language, and typing skill did not vary significantly across condition and did not interact with the dependent measures and so are dropped from further analyses. We first present results for all subjects, then present results separately for men and women.

Check on Manipulation of Talking Face Expression

Some of the main analyses entailed comparing responses to the two faces. Before doing those comparisons we wanted to know if subjects could discriminate between the two faces. Twenty-two subjects from the text condition in the main experiment participated in a discriminability test of the two faces after they had completed the main experiment and postexperiment questionnaire. Hard copy prints of the two faces were presented side by side. Subjects were given forty-six attribute questions drawn from previous research on perception of personality attributes and asked to indicate, for each question, which of the two faces had more of the attribute. For example, "Which one is more intelligent?" or "Which one is happier?" Thirty-three of the questions constituted measures of the same six personality attribute scales used in the main experiment: social evaluation, intelligence evaluation, and potency from Warner and Sugarman (1986) and emotionality, activity, and sociability from Buss and Plomin (1984). (The other thirteen questions were individual items drawn from separate studies. A factor analysis of these items did not reveal any interpretable factors and so they were dropped from the analysis.) A choice of the pleasant face in response to each question was coded as "1" and a choice of the stern face was coded as "0." The scores for each scale were calculated by averaging responses across all the scale questions. The data were tested against the null hypothesis of no discrimination between faces (average score of 0.5) using a t-test. Subjects consistently discriminated between the two faces on the scales measuring social evaluation ($t[21]=10.73$, $p<.001$), sociability ($t[21]=4.3$, $p<.001$), and emotionality ($t[21]=3.8$, $p<.001$), but did not discriminate on the scales measuring intellectual evaluation ($t[21]=0.52$), activity ($t[21]=1.08$), and potency ($t[21]=0.39$). These results are consistent with the previous literature for the attributes of social evaluation, sociability, activity, and potency. In previous studies people did not discriminate faces on the attribute of emotionality, although they did in this test. In previous studies people did discriminate faces on the attribute of intelligence, although they did not in this test. We note that this test demonstrates discriminability for the static faces only; a more rigorous test would have displayed the talking faces side by side.

Social Perception of Question Asker

Figure 5 shows that subjects did perceive some personality attributes of the "question asker" differently across conditions. The data in Figure 5 are organized according to the theoretically-derived categories of appearance-linked and nonappearance-linked traits from Warner and Sugarman (1986). We follow Warner and Sugarman (1986) in reporting social evaluation and sociability separately even though they are correlated at .56. Combining them into a single factor does not change the results. ANOVAs yielded significant F-statistics for Social Evaluation ($F[2,118] = 5.85$, $p<.01$); for sociability ($F[2,118] = 3.39$, $p<.05$); and for activity ($F[2,118] = 3.93$, $p<.05$). Subjects did not differentiate the interfaces on intelligence, potency, or emotionality. Planned contrasts revealed no statistically significant differences in the perception of attributes between the two faces.

Subjects perceived the faces differently from the text on the appearance-based personality attributes of sociability and social evaluation, which is consonant with our first hypothesis. (Note that a lower score on social or intellectual evaluation or potency means that subjects perceived that attribute more negatively, not that the stimulus has less of the attribute.) Subjects did not make different attributions of intelligence, as previous research had led us to predict. Previous research on appearance-based personality attributions typically elicits first impressions of personality with no or little interaction; in this study, the prolonged interaction with the "question asker" could have attenuated any initial differential intelligence attributions. That subjects differentially rated the interface on the attribute of activity also was unexpected. In previous studies, the personality attribute of activity has been shown to be better conveyed by voice than by facial appearance. Both of the face conditions in this study included (the same) voice. Thus differentiating "faces" from text on the personality attribute of activity is consistent with previous research, if subjects were using voice (in the two face conditions) as their cue to activity. Although perhaps paradoxical that the display with an animated face was rated as lower on the activity dimension than the text display, perhaps the subjects thought the face-based question asker was (relatively) slow paced and unenergetic .

Perception	Text ($n = 43$)	Pleasant Face ($n = 44$)	Stern Face ($n = 43$)	F(2,118 to 2,119)
Appearance-linked attributes				
Social evaluation 1 = *negative*, 7 = *positive*	4.17	3.42+	3.29+	5.85**
Sociability 1 = *not at all true*, 5 = *very true*	3.34	3.04	2.74+	3.39*
Intellectual evaluation 1 = *negative*, 7 = *positive*	4.88	4.73	5.08	0.85
Nonappearance-linked attributes				
Potency 1 = *negative*, 7 = *positive*	4.6	4.4	4.5	0.2
Activity 1 = *not at all true*, 5 = *very true*	3.33	2.84+	2.90+	3.93*
Emotionality 1 = *not at all true*, 5 = *very true*	2.82	2.69	2.79	0.36

Figure 5. Mean social perception of personality attributes in computer display.

Note. Cells with + differ by at least $p<.05$ from the text condition, which is used as a control in Dunnet's planned contrast *t* test with *dfs* ranging from 118 to 119.
*$p<.05$. **$p<.01$.

Arousal and Attention to Performance

Factor analysis of attitude items from the postexperiment questionnaire that assessed subjects' experience in the experiment revealed three clear interpretable factors (see Figure 6). There were no differences across conditions in the factor we label *Happy* (Factor 1), which we interpret as a measure of general affect or mood while subjects were participating. Also, there were no differences across conditions in the factor we label *Enjoyment* (Factor 3), which we interpret as a measure of how much subjects enjoyed the overall experience. However, consistent with our second hypotheses, there were significant differences across conditions in the factor we label *Arousal* (Factor 2), which is a measure of relaxation and assurance. People reported themselves to be less relaxed and assured in the face conditions than in the text condition, $F(2,119) = 3.64$, $p<.01$.

Item	Factor 1 (Happiness)	Factor 2 (Arousal)	Factor 3 (Enjoyment)
How satisfied were you?	.86667	.06041	.06674
How happy were you?	.87135	.19513	.08655
How much like to continue?	−.00544	.09073	.89989
How much like participating?	.35401	.08058	.77853
How relaxed were you?	.07671	.88579	.07799
How confident were you?	.26205	.79803	.09018
Percent of variance explained	33	25	24.5

Figure 6. Factor analysis of attitude items about interacting with computer display.

To examine differences in attentiveness to the experiment, we measured the time subjects took to complete the psychological scales and the number of questions they answered (or skipped) in these scales. Subjects in the face conditions spent more time (M=19.1m.) than did subjects in the text condition (M=14.0m.) (F [2, 112] = 25.6, p<.01), as shown in Figure 7. This result supports our hypothesis, in that a longer time to answer questions bespeaks thinking more carefully about one's answers. The difference may be partly due to the one-second delay between the end of an utterance in the face conditions and the display of the answer window on the screen. However, subtracting 1.15 minutes from the overall response time in the face conditions to remove the effect of the one-second delay does not change the significance of these results. Another reason for the difference is that it may take longer to listen to a question than to read it. Because we did not measure reading speed we cannot investigate this possibility. Subjects in the face conditions skipped more questions across all the psychological scales (M=3.3) than did subjects in the text condition (M=1.9) (F [2, 127] = 3.22, p<.05). This difference suggests that subjects were less careful in the face conditions, but also suggests they were avoiding certain personal questions. This latter interpretation is supported by analyses showing that subjects in the face conditions skipped significantly more questions on the two scales known to be susceptible to social influence (social desirability and altruism) than did subjects in the text condition but did not differ from subjects in the text condition in the number of questions they skipped on the scale less susceptible to social influence (self-worth).

Response	Text (n = 43)	Pleasant Face (n = 44)	Stern Face (n = 43)	F(2,109 to 2,127)
Arousal[a] (1 to 7)	1.81	2.37[+]	2.40[+]	3.64**
Performance on self-presentation scales				
Minutes to complete all scales	14.0	18.9[+]	19.4	25.55***
Number of skipped items overall	1.89	3.9	2.7	3.22*
Altruism items skipped	−8.4	−1.6[+]	−1.6[+]	3.35***
Social Desirability items skipped	1.07	2.20[+]	1.58	2.38*
Self-Worth items skipped	.21	.52	.4	1.95
Self-presentation				
Altruism[a]	−8.4	−1.6[+]	−1.6[+]	3.35**
				4.16***[b]
Social Desirability	14.2	14.8	16.2[+]	2.20
				5.61***[b]
Self-worth[a] (0 to 64)	45.0	43.7	45.0	0.45
Interaction with counselor				
Minutes interacting	11.5	9.3	8.8	1.64
Words to counselor	189	143	131[+]	2.88*
Number of interaction turns	18	17	14	0.67

Figure 7. Mean behavioral responses to computer display.

Note. Cell values with [+] differ by at least $p<.05$ from the text condition, which is used as a control in Dunnett's planned contrast t-test.
[a]More positive score means more of the trait. [b]Adjusted F using Self-Worth as covariate.
*$p<.05$. **$p<.01$. ***$p<.001$.

Thus the results support Hypothesis 2a: subjects reported more arousal in the face conditions than in the text condition. The results provide some support for Hypothesis 2b. Subjects took longer to respond in the face conditions, a finding that may reflect heightened attention (although we cannot rule out alternative explanations). In the face conditions subjects had more missing answers (compared with text) on the two scales known to be subject to social influence but did not have more missing answers (compared with text) on the scale less susceptible to social influence.

Self Presentation

The Social Desirability score is the sum of responses to thirty-three social desirability items (Cronbach's coefficient α = .75). The mean across all subjects was 15.05; s.d.=4.58. The Altruism score is the sum of the twenty responses to the altruism scale (α = .79) (M =-3.84; $S.D.$ = 14.36). The Self-Worth score is the sum of responses to the sixteen Self-Worth items (α = .75) (M = 44.85; $S.D.$ = 7.54).

Self-presentation was more positive in the face conditions than in the text condition on Social Desirability and Altruism, the two scales known to be more sensitive to social context. (See Figure 7) No difference across conditions on the Self-Worth scale is consistent with findings that self-worth is more stable across situations. Subjects in the face conditions reported themselves to behave in more socially desirable ways, $F(2, 119)$ = 2.20, $p<.1$, than did subjects interacting with the text interface. Subjects in the face conditions also reported themselves to be significantly more altruistic, $F(2, 119)$ = 3.35, $p<.01$. Stronger results obtained for Social Desirability and Altruism in analyses of covariance with Self-Worth as the covariate – see Figure 7.

Subjects in the face conditions wrote less in the counselor interaction than did subjects in the text condition, $F(2, 109)$ = 2.88, $p<.05$. Note that there was no difference in the number of interaction turns across conditions; subjects in the face conditions were asked just as many questions by the counselor as were subjects in the text condition. They simply wrote less in reply to each question. In planned contrasts, there were no differences in self-presentation behaviors between the two different faces. Taken together, the pattern of results in which subjects in the face conditions presented themselves more positively in the self-presentation task and wrote less in the interaction task supports Hypotheses 3a and 3b.

Difference Between Men and Women Across Conditions

Figure 8 presents data on men and women separately. Men and women did not differ in their perception of the question asker across conditions. They did not differ in arousal or attention to the experiment (attitude items, missing answers, or how long it took to answer self-presentation scale questions).

Women reported significantly higher self-worth than did men $t(124)$=-2.04, $p<.04$, consistent with previous reports in the literature (Helmreich & Stapp, 1974). There were no significant differences between men and women on altruism or social desirability. Our interest was not in general differences between men and women but in whether they would react differently to the talking faces. In statistical terms, we were interested in the interaction of gender with display condition. We predicted the face display would evoke differences in the responses of men and women but the text display would not. There were significant differences across conditions in the patterns of how men and women presented themselves but the text and face displays often evoked differences in opposite directions (see Figure 8). Both men and women presented themselves more altruistically to the talking faces than to the text display but only in the pleasant face condition was the difference between men and women large interaction $F(2,116) = 4.24$, $p<.01$. Women wrote more in interaction with the counselor in the text condition than in the face conditions, whereas men wrote more in the face conditions interaction $F(2,123) = 5.04$, $p<.01$. Our hypothesis, derived from the gender literature, was that men and women would differ more in their response to a face display than in their response to a text display. Our results, however, showed that men and women differed in both text- and face-display conditions, but their responses diverged according to the nature of the display. In general, men responded more positively to the face displays whereas women responded more positively to the text display.

There were no significant Gender x Condition differences in the three attitude factors. But an internal item analysis revealed that men significantly liked interacting with the face more than with text while women preferred interacting with text, interaction $F(2,123) = 3.58$, $p<.05$.

DISCUSSION

This study presents evidence that people respond to a talking-face display differently than to a text display. They attribute some personality attributes to the faces differently than to a text display. They report themselves to be more aroused (less relaxed, less confident). They present themselves in a more positive light to the talking-face displays. Men and women both presented themselves more positively to the talking faces than to the faceless interface. But men apparently enjoyed the experience more than women did. They interacted more with the face-based counselors than with the text-based one. They enjoyed the entire experience more in the face conditions than text, unlike women.

Although the two expressions used in this study were perceived differently in a static discrimination study, subjects generally did not respond to them differently in the interaction context. An expressive face display, whether the expression was perceived positively or negatively, elicited generally the same kinds of behavior from subjects in comparison with a text display. Although it surely would be possible to create faces so grotesque or charming that they would elicit different behaviors, in this study perceptible differences in expression did not systematically affect behavior.

Response	Text	Pleasant Face	Stern Face	Interaction F (2,106 to 2,124)
Self Presentation				
Altruism				4.24*
Women	−8.0	3.2	−3.0	
Men	−8.8	−7.3	.16	
Social Desirability				0.93
Women	15.0	15.8	16.1	
Men	13.2	13.6	16.3	
Self-Worth				0.72
Women	46.2	44.5	45.5	
Men	43.6	42.8	44.4	
Interaction				
Minutes to complete counselor interaction				4.92**
Women	13.7	8.0	7.4	
Men	8.7	11.0	10.7	
Number of words to counselor				5.04**
Women	227	123	107	
Men	140	167	160	
Attitudes Toward Experience				
Liked participating?				3.58*
Women	8.2	7.8	7.7	
Men	7.1	8.4	8.9	

Figure 8. Gender differences in mean behavioral responses to computer display.

Note. In the text condition there were 19 men and 24 women; pleasant-face condition, 20 men and 24 women; stern-face conditions, 19 men and 24 women.
*$p<.05$. **$p<.01$.

We did not undertake to investigate the underlying reasons why people might respond to a synthetic talking face as though it were human (relative to their response to a text display). One possibility is that some subjects thought there was a real person behind the screen. Or, the face interface might have caused subjects to think a real person would be reading and evaluating their answers. If the talking face display reminded subjects of a real human being, that thought, rather than the face display itself, could have elicited social behavior. Throughout the instructions and experiment we tried to insure that subjects knew that the face was simulated and that no real human being would see their responses. Subjects' behavior during the experiment and their remarks during the debriefing suggested that we were successful. So why would people respond to a talking face display as they might to a person? Nass and his colleagues have demonstrated that social cues (such as a taped human voice emanating from a computer) can lead people to respond to a computer as though it has some human attributes. For example, their experiments have shown that people act as though computers are motivated by self-interest (Nass, Steuer, Henriksen & Dryer, 1994a) and are sensitive to criticism (Nass, Steuer, & Tauber 1994b). Field research describes how people imbue computers with personality (Sproull, Kiesler, & Zubrow 1984; Turkle, 1984). For the purposes of this research, it does not matter if people think the computer is actually human, is like a human, or has humanlike qualities. We were interested in demonstrating that people change their own behavior in the presence of humanlike attributes in the interface. Future research should explore how different components of a talking face display contribute to peoples' social responses and how this might be so. (For instance in our study the voice, rather than the face, might cause subjects to behave socially. Or, certain "abnormal" features of the face such as the regularity of the eye blinks or the lack of inflection in the voice might have caused subjects to think that the "question asker" was uncomfortable.)

On average subjects in all conditions said they liked the experience of interacting with a computer-based career counselor (M=8.0 on 10-point scale where 1 [*not at all*] and 10[*very much*]). There were no differences across conditions although men liked the faces more than they liked the text. This generally positive response may have been caused by novelty, by demand characteristics (wanting to please the experimenter), or possibly even by a genuinely good technology application. The first and second explanations should be further investigated by designing studies that incorporate talking face displays into more ongoing work tasks and by collecting longitudinal data. We note, however, that even though subjects shared a general positive attitude, their behavior differed significantly between text display and face display, as we had predicted.

The gender differences we found merit further investigation along at least two different lines. One is related to the gender of the faces. It is possible that male and female subjects' behaviors and attitudes would have reversed themselves if the talking face had been male rather than female. We selected a female face for this study based on the survey methodology literature that shows that both men and women respond more and more positively to a female interviewer than to a male interviewer (Backstrom & Hursh-Cesar, 1981; Luptow, Moser & Pendleton, 1990). But we may simply have encountered a cross-sex interaction preference in this study. Although such preferences are common and expected in studies of interpersonal attraction, they are not commonly reported in the literature on counselor–client interactions (Snell et al., 1988; Snell et al., 1989). Women might have responded negatively to the talking face display because it was a computer face. Women might be more sensitive to the "unnaturalness" of a computer face than men are. Men might like a talking face display because it is a newer, more complex form of technology than a text display is. There is some evidence that men like new computing technology more than women (Chen, 1985). Furthermore, in one recent study women thought it was less appropriate than men did for computers to take on roles entailing personal interaction such as boss or psychiatrist (Nass, Lombard, Henriksen & Steuer, 1995). Although this study did not investigate why men and women responded differently, future work should pursue this topic. It takes on practical relevance, as well as theoretical import, since today it is disproportionately men who make decisions about how, whether, and when to incorporate synthetic faces into interface products.

Part of the allure of computers is that they are so malleable, in principle. In practice, interfaces have been fairly clunky for a long time, but that state is beginning to change. Designers can aspire to create ever more responsive interfaces. The technology used in this research was extremely primitive in comparison with what will be feasible in the future. Yet people did change their personas – and liked it or not – in response to talking faces. The prospect of people's putting their best foot forward for their computer is an odd one indeed. Some will immediately embrace the idea. Will reservations or sales clerks work harder with a face on the screen? Will children learn more from educational software if it is accompanied by a school marm's face? Many people want computers to be responsive to people. But do we also want people to be responsive to computers?

Appendix

Scales and Items (source)	Cronbach's alpha	Mean	S.D.	Range
Social Evaluation (Warner & Sugarman,1986) Unattractive Attractive Depressed Cheerful Unfriendly Friendly Optimistic Pessimistic (reverse scored) Cool Warm	.87	3.61	1.28	1-7
Intellectual Evaluation (Warner & Sugarman, 1986) Ignorant Knowledgeable Incompetent Competent Irresponsible Responsible Unintelligent Intelligent Foolish Sensible	.85	4.89	1.19	1-7
Potency (Warner & Sugarman, 1986) Weak Strong Frail Sturdy Submissive Dominant	.88	4.50	1.27	1-7
Sociability (Buss & Plomin,1984) Likes to be with people (not at all to very much) Prefers working with others rather than alone Finds people more stimulating than anything else Is something of a loner (reverse scored)	.82	3.04	1.02	1-5
Activity (Buss & Plomin,1984) Life is fast paced (not at all to very much) Usually seems to be in a hurry Likes to keep busy all the time Often feels as if is bursting with energy	.64	3.04	.84	1-5
Emotionality (Buss & Plomin,1984) Frequently gets distressed (not at all to very much) Often feels frustrated Everyday events make troubled and fretful Gets emotionally upset easily Is easily frightened Often feels insecure When gets scared, panics Is known as hot-blooded and quick-tempered Takes a lot to make mad (reverse scored) There are many things that annoy When displeased, lets people know it right away	.88	2.76	.75	1-5

Figure A-1. Scales used to measure social perception of computer displays.

Scale	Scale					
	1	2	3	4	5	6
1. Social Evaluation	–	.489	.098	.559	.433	-.184
2. Intell. Evaluation		–	.243	.295	.296	-.148
3. Potency			–	.182	.140	-.125
4. Sociability				–	.418	-.167
5. Activity					–	.192
6. Emotionality						–

Figure A-2. Intercorrelations Between Social Perception of Computer Displays Scales

REFERENCES

Backstrom, C.H., and G. Hursh-Cesar. 1981. *Survey Research* (2nd ed.). New York: John Wiley and Sons.

Bailey, L., T. Moore, and B. Bailar. 1987. An Interviewer Variance Study for the Eight Impact Cities of the National Crime Survey. *Journal of the American Statistical Association* 73: 16–23.

Baker, M.J., and J.G. A. Churchill, 1977. The Impact of Physically Attractive Models on Advertising Evaluations. *Journal of Marketing Research* 14: 538–555.

Berscheid, E., and E. Walster. 1974. Physical Attractiveness. In *Advances in Experimental Social Psychology*, ed. L. Berkowitz, 157–215. New York: Academic Press.

Binnick, Y.M., C.F. Westbury, and D. Servan-Schreiber. 1989. Case Histories and Shorter Communications. *Behavioral Research Therapy* 27: 303–306.

Blascovich, J., and J. Tomaka. 1991. Measures of Self-Esteem. In *Measures of Personality and Social Psychological Attitudes*, eds. J.P. Robinson, P.R. Shaver, and L.W. Wrightsman, 115–160. San Diego, CA: Academic Press.

Bond, E.K. 1972. Perceptions of Form by the Human Infant. *Psychological Bulletin* 77: 225–245.

Bradburn, N. 1983. Response Effects. In *Handbook of Survey Research*, eds. P.H. Rossi, J.D. Wright, and A.B. Anderson, 289–328. New York: Academic Press.

Buss, A.H., and R. Plomin. 1984. *Temperament: Early Developing Personality Traits*. Hillsdale, NJ: L. Erlbaum Associates.

Chen, M. 1985. Gender Differences in Adolescents' Uses of and Attitudes Toward Computers. In *Communication Yearbook*, ed. M. McLaughlin, 200–216. Beverly Hills, CA: Sage.

Collins, N.L., and L.C. Miller. 1994. Self-Disclosure and Liking: A Meta-Analytic Review. *Psychological Bulletin* 116: 457–475.

Deiner, E., S.C. Fraser, A.L. Beaman, and R.T. Kelem. 1976. Effects of Deindividuating Variables on Stealing by Halloween Trick-or-Treaters. *Journal of Personality and Social Psychology* 33: 178–183.

Duffy, S.A., and D.B. Pisoni. 1992. Comprehension of Synthetic Speech Produced by Rule: A Review and Theoretical Interpretation. *Language and Speech* 35: 351–389.

Eichenwald, K. 1986. Hi, Voter. This is Your President. *New York Times*, (November 2) p. 19.

Ekman, P., ed. 1982. *Emotion in the Human Face* (2nd ed.). Cambridge, UK: Cambridge University Press.

Hall, J.A. 1979. Gender, Gender Roles, and Nonverbal Communication Skills. In *Skill in Nonverbal Communication*, ed. R. Rosenthal, 32–67. Cambridge, MA: Oelgeschlager, Gunn & Hain.

Helmreich, R., and J. Stapp. 1974. Short forms of the Texas Social Behavior Inventory (TSBI), an Objective Measure of Self-Esteem. *Bulletin of the Psychonomic Society* 4: 473–475.

Hilton, J.L., and J.M. Darley. 1991. Effects of Interaction Goals on Person Perception. In *Advances in Experimental Social Psychology*, ed. M.P. Zanna, 235–267. San Diego, CA: Academic Press.

Holroyd, K.A., T. Westbrook, M. Wolf, and E. Badhorn. 1978. Performance, Cognition, and Physiological Responding in Test Anxiety. *Cognitive Therapy and Research* 3: 165–180.

Itou, K.S., S. Hayamizu, and H. Tanaka. 1992. Continuous Speech Recognition by Context-Dependent Phonetic HMM and an Efficient Algorithm for Finding N-Best Sentence Hypotheses. In *ICASSP '92*, 121–124. San Francisco, CA: IEEE Press.

Kiesler, S., and L. Sproull. 1986. Response effects in the Electronic Survey. *Public Opinion Quarterly* 50: 243–253.

Klatt, D.H., and L.C. Klatt. 1990. Analysis, Synthesis, and Perception of Voice Quality Variations Among Female and Male Talkers. *The Journal of the Acoustical Society of America* 87: 820–856.

Laurel, B. 1990. Interface Agents: Metaphors with Character. In *The Art of Human–Computer Interface Design*, ed. B. Laurel, 355–365. New York: Addison-Wesley.

Luptow, L.B., S.L. Moser, and B.F. Pendleton. 1990. Gender and Response Effects in Telephone Interviews about Gender Characteristics. *Sex Roles* 22:29–42.

Maslach, C. 1979. Negative Emotional Biasing of Unexplained Arousal. *Journal of Personality and Social Psychology* 37:953–969.

Morton, J., and M.H. Johnson. 1991. CONSPEC and CONLERN: A Two-Process Theory of Infant Face Recognition. *Psychological Review* 98:164–181.

Nass, C., M. Lombard, L.Henriksen, and J. Steuer. 1995. Anthropocentricism and Computers. *Behavior and Information Technology.*

Nass, C., J. Steuer, L. Henriksen, and D.C. Dryer 1994a. Machines, Social Attributions, and Ethopeoia: Performance Assessments of Computers Subsequent to "Self-" or "Other-" Evaluations. *International Journal of Human–Computer Studies* 40: 543–559.

Nass, C., J. Steuer, and E.R. Tauber. 1994b. Computers are Social Actors. In*CHI '94*, 72–78. New York: ACM Press.

O'Sullivan, M., P. Ekman, W. Friesen, and K.R. Scherer. 1985. What you Say and How You Say It: The Contribution of Speech Content and Voice Quality to Judgments of Others. *Journal of Personality and Social Psychology* 48: 54–62.

Oren, T., G. Salomon, and K. Kreitman. 1990. Guides: Characterizing the Interface. In *The Art of Human–Computer Interface Design*, ed. B. Laurel, 367–381. New York: Addison-Wesley.

Ousterhout, J.K. 1994. *Tcl and the Tk Toolkit.* Reading, MA.: Addison-Wesley.

Paulhus, D.L. 1991. Measurement and Control of Response Bias. In *Measures of Personality and Social Psychological Attitudes*, eds. J. P. Robinson, P. R. Shaver, and L. W. Wrightsman, 17–60. San Diego, CA: Academic Press.

Resnick, P.V., and H.B. Lammers. 1985. The Influence of Self-Esteem on Cognitive Responses to Machine-Like Versus Human-Like Computer Feedback. *The Journal of Social Psychology* 125: 761–769.

Schuman, H., and S. Presser. 1981. *Questions and Answers in Attitude Surveys: Experiments in Question Form, Wording, and Context.* New York: Academic Press.

Shneiderman, B. 1987. *Designing the User Interface: Strategies for Effective Human–Computer Interaction.* Boston: Addison-Wesley.

Snell, W.E. Jr., S.S. Belk, A. Flowers, and J. Warren. 1988. Women's and Men's Willingness to Self-disclose to Therapists and Friends: The Moderating Influence of Instrumental, Expressive, Masculine, and Feminine Topics. *Sex Roles* 18: 769–776.

Snell, W.E. Jr., R.S. Miller, and S.S. Belk. 1989. Men's and Women's Emotional Disclosures: The Impact of Disclosure Recipient, Culture, and the Masculine Role. *Sex Roles* 21:467–486.

Snyder, M. 1984. When Belief Creates Reality. In *Advances in Experimental Social Psychology*, ed. L. Berkowitz, 247–305. Orlando, FL: Academic Press.

Sproull, L., S. Kiesler, and D. Zubrow. 1984. Encountering an Alien Culture. *Journal of Social Issues* 40(3):31–48.

Takeuchi, A., and K. Nagao. 1993. Communicative Facial Displays As a New Conversational Modality. In *INTERCHI '93*, 187–193. Amsterdam: ACM Press.

Thorisson, K.R. 1993. Dialog Control in Social Interface Agents. In *INTERCHI '93*, 139–140. Amsterdam: ACM Press.

Turkle, S. 1984. *The Second Self: Computers and the Human Spirit.* New York: Simon and Schuster.

Walker, J., L. Sproull, and R. Subramani. 1994. Using a Human Face in an Interface. In *CHI '94*, 85–91. New York: ACM Press.

Warner, R. M., and D.B. Sugarman. 1986. Attributions of Personality Based on Physical Appearance, Speech, and Handwriting. *Journal of Personality and Social Psychology* 50:792–799.

Waters, K. 1987. A Muscle Model for Animating Three-Dimensional Facial Expressions. *Computer Graphics* 21:17–24.

Waters, K., and T.M. Levergood. 1994. An Automatic Lip-Synchronization Algorithm for Synthetic Faces. In *Proceedings of the Multimedia Conference '94*, 149–156. San Francisco, CA: ACM Press.

Waterton, J.J., and J.C. Duffy. 1984. A Comparison of Computer Interviewing Techniques and Traditional Methods in the Collection of Self-Report Alcohol Consumption Data in a Field Study. *International Statistical Review* 52: 173–182.

Weizenbaum, J. 1976. *Computer Power and Human Reason.* San Francisco, CA: Freeman.

Wrightsman, L.S. 1974. *Assumptions about Human Nature: A Social-Psychological Analysis.* Monterey, CA: Brooks/Cole.

Zajonc, R. 1965. Social Facilitation. *Science* 149: 269–274.

10

'Social' Human–Computer Interaction

SARA KIESLER AND LEE SPROULL

Abstract: This chapter describes two experiments we conducted since the publication of "When the Interface Is a Face" (chapter 9). The results from both experiments demonstrate that people will trust and behave cooperatively with a computer partner. To this extent, the results follow in line with those of Nass et al. (chapter 8). But our results do not support Nass et al.'s stronger claim that people think of computers as social actors. Discussion focuses on the social nature of computing.

The experiments by Nass and his colleagues in this volume, and our own experiment in "When the Interface Is a Face," show rather convincingly that research participants will emit seemingly social responses while interacting with computers. Does this mean your desktop computer is truly social? In this addendum we will briefly describe two further experiments we conducted since "When the Interface Is a Face." The results are striking, showing that people will trust and behave cooperatively with a computer partner. Nonetheless, our conclusions depart in important ways from those of Nass and his colleagues.

INTERFACE PERSONAS VS. "THE COMPUTER"

We established in "When the Interface Is a Face" (as Nass and his colleagues have done) that some fundamental social responses can be elicited and examined in laboratory settings when people interact with computers. However, our study suggests that people's responses differ greatly depending upon whether the interface with which they are interacting has more or fewer humanlike characteristics. Accordingly, if you turned on your desk computer and suddenly it emitted a *Wizard of Oz* pronouncement, your behavior would likely be different than if your computer brought up your e-mail on the screen; for example, you might address the computer screen verbally in the first case but simply scroll down through your email headers in the second. This second response could hardly be called social.

When we say a human being exhibits "social behavior" in a particular situation, we mean the behavior is influenced by others in the situation. The behavioral influence may occur as a result of direct interaction, as when a person talks or works with another. It may occur due to the mere presence of others, as when a person works harder when others are in the same room, even when those others are merely passive observers. Or it may occur through reminders of others, as when a solitary person works harder after having been told that someone will later review his or her work. Human beings have learned (through their own experience as well as through evolution) how to behave with respect to other people and what to expect from others' behavior.

These days, "the computer" can mean anything from the chips in your car to your desktop machine, and hardly any of these will cause people to act socially. When the user interface for a computer program is given a human persona, then people may respond to the persona "as though" it were human. An interface persona is a bundle of characteristics that people usually associate with human beings, such as human speech or physiognomy, that acts as mediator between the user and a program. We think interface personas are the aspects of computers that are particularly likely to elicit what resembles social behavior in users. We perform research on interface personas to understand when they are effective. Also, we think human responses to these personas can be used to examine theories of social behavior and interaction with interfaces.

COOPERATION WITH A COMPUTER PARTNER

Two of our studies have asked if an interface persona could elicit cooperation from a user in a social dilemma, and whether more humanlike interface personas would be more effective in eliciting cooperation. In social dilemmas, rational self-interest conflicts with and discourages cooperation with others. Suppose members of a group are expected to contribute to a group project, whose success will be of benefit to everyone involved. Nonetheless, some members might be "free riders" who leave others to do most of the work, for which all will take credit. Others may not cooperate in order to avoid being made "suckers." Social dilemmas have been investigated extensively in experimental laboratory games, in field studies of resource constraints such as water shortages, in studies of organizational citizenship, and in analyses of computer-supported cooperative work (CSCW) systems. In our studies of cooperation in a dilemma, the research participant plays a game for money with a computer "partner." The partner is an interface persona: the interface presents a bundle of more or less human characteristics such as a voice or a face. The underlying game playing program, as well as the interaction dialog, are completely scripted. In the game, each partner privately selects one of two alternatives, say, A or B. The incentives are such that if both choose the same choice, say, A, then both will gain an equal sum. If both choose the other alternative, they will receive no money. The dilemma arises because if one partner makes the designated cooperative choice, A, but the other defects and chooses B, the defector takes the bulk of the money and the cooperator loses. (The defector is analogous to the free rider in the above example and the cooperator is analogous to the sucker in the example.) Previous studies of experimental social dilemmas (see Sally, 1995) have found that discussion among the partners is the most powerful determinant of cooperation. Therefore, in our studies, we allow for discussion with the computer partner.

In our first cooperation experiment using a computer partner (Kiesler, Sproull & Waters, 1996), research participants played six trials of a dilemma game with a real person (confederate) or with one of three computer partners that varied in humanlike characteristics. The partner interface was text-only, voice-only, or a person's talking face – a digitized version of the confederate's face manipulated through DECface (Waters, 1988; Waters & Levergood, 1995). Participants rated the talking face computer "partner" to be more humanlike than the other computer partners (text or voice). Crosscutting these partner conditions, we varied whether the research participant and the computer partner (or confederate) had a chance to discuss their choices before making them. The research participant typed his or her comments into the computer; the computer partner either spoke (in the voice only or talking face conditions) or displayed text. The partner always encouraged cooperation or agreed to it.

This study replicated previous research on cooperation in social dilemmas in such a way that when the research participant and the partner (confederate or computer partner) had a chance to discuss their choices, they cooperated significantly more than when they did not have a chance for discussion. Participants cooperated at high levels with the confederate. However they cooperated next most highly with the text-only partner, not with the talking face partner. We concluded that improvements in design would be required to create an interface persona (a computer partner) with which people would cooperate at high levels.

Our next study (Parise, Kiesler, Sproull & Waters, 1996) followed overall improvements made to the DECface program, notably color rendition, and smoothing of transitions across muscular mouth positions. Beyond these general improvements, we tested three alternative designs for a computer partner which allowed us to test different theories about the conditions for cooperation with a computer partner. In all conditions, the research participant played six trials of a dilemma game for money prizes with a partner – a human partner (confederate) or a computer partner. All conditions allowed for discussion before each choice. The experimental conditions were as follows:

1) Human partner, a confederate, communicating through desktop video:

In condition 1, our real person control condition, the confederate's image was conveyed through real-time desktop video. We used video rather than face-to-face communication to rule out an alternative explanation of differential cooperation to the real person. If the confederate interacted with the research participant face to face, higher cooperation with the confederate than with the computer partner could be attributed to the advantages of face-to-face communication over a 2-dimensional (2-D) interaction. In the present experiment, all interactions were mediated by a computer monitor and 2-D display.

2) Computer partner based on an image of the confederate's face:

A condition for cooperation with a computer partner might be pictorial realism. Pictorial realism increases involvement and the sense of presence in virtual reality environments (Welch, Blackmon, Liu, Mellers & Stark, in press). Involvement and presence, in turn, may increase the feeling that one's promises to cooperate are real and should be honored, and/or that the partner is committed to the choices. If so, then research participants should cooperate most in our most realistic condition, that is, when the partner is a real person and next most when the partner is based on a realistic image of a real person's face.

3) Computer partner based on an image of a pet dog:

Social identity theorists have argued that discussion increases cooperation because discussion increases the feeling of belonging to the same group (Hogg & McGarty, 1990) Group identification presumably transforms self-interest into prosocial interest thereby motivating the parties to improve the outcomes of the partnership or group. Being a member of the same social category increases group identity. Therefore, people should identify more easily, and feel a sense of partnership more with a human than with a dog. If similarity is a condition for cooperation, we would predict that cooperation would be most with the real person (condition 1), next most frequent with the personlike computer partner (condition 2), and least with a doglike computer partner (conditions 3 and 4).

4) Computer partner based on a cartoon drawing of a dog:

The computer partner in our previous experiment might have failed to elicit cooperation because it was not likable enough to motivate cooperation. The talking face had attributes, such as its speech output (DECtalk), that were somewhat robotlike. These attributes might have stigmatized the partner and caused research participants to denigrate it. Indeed, a colleague of ours strongly argued that people would prefer to cooperate with a charming, but clearly unreal, partner such as Kermit the Frog or Mickey Mouse than with an "unnatural" personlike partner. This argument led us to reason that a pet dog computer partner or, especially, a cartoon dog computer partner might be especially charming, and that if likability leads to cooperation, then research participants would show high levels of cooperation with such a partner.

To give a flavor of the interaction, here is the script of an initial interaction between the partner and participant [computer condition script differences are shown in brackets]:

Confederate or computer partner: Hi, my name is Josh. Nice to meet you. What's your name?

Participant answers by typing text in a window on the computer screen.

Confederate or computer partner: I come from Boston [Digital Equipment Corporation]. Where are you from?

Participant answers.

Confederate or computer partner: I'm majoring in information systems. What's your major?

[I come from a computer lab. I guess you can say my major is information systems. What is your major?]

Participant answers.

Confederate or computer partner: Are you ready to begin?

Participant answers.

Confederate or computer partner: I think we should each give $3.00 What do you think?

Participant answers.

The results of this experiment were striking. Participants cooperated highly and equally as often with the confederate (the real person) and the personlike computer partner. What about the doglike partners? Research participants loved both dog partners, but (excepting dog owners), they cooperated significantly less with them than with the human partners. We concluded that the humanlikeness of the personlike computer partner caused participants to make a best guess attribution about the partner, that the partner would act like a person. Participants interacting with the dog partners, we think, made a best guess attribution that these partners would act like dogs. If so, there is a simple "economic" explanation for our results. Suppose the participants all wanted to win money for themselves. From practice trials they knew the repercussions of defection, that is, that a real human partner would probably defect on the next trial if they defected (didn't share the $3.00) on this one. The participants in both the real person and personlike computer partner conditions predicted their partner would not abide defection; if they themselves defected, they would be in a lose–lose situation. But, we think, the participants in the dog partner conditions predicted their partner would be trustworthy and loyal, because that is how dogs act, so there was less risk for them to defect.

CONCLUSION

Our analysis implies a variation on an old adage. If it walks like a duck and talks like a duck, we are going to treat it like a duck – at least for now. After all we have to treat it some way, and ducklikeness seems a good clue to its future behavior and to how we should respond. Our conclusion is much more limited than the one drawn by Nass and his colleagues. We do not think computers are social, and we do not think people's social behavior in interaction with computers tells us much about the social nature of computing.

Consider that sometimes you swear at your computer when it "misbehaves." But this isn't because the computer is social. It's because swearing is one of the ways you've learned to react when you are angry because something breaks. You might swear when your pencil breaks, too, yet no one has said pencils are social! Swearing when something breaks says something about human behavior in response to certain frustrating situations. In our experiments, and those by Nass and his colleagues, research participants act on the information they have, and do what seems most sensible in the situation, including making social responses and evaluations consistent with the humanlike stimuli emitted from a computer. Sometimes this includes anthropomorphizing (attributing humanlike emotions or behavior to a nonhuman entity, beyond what actually is observed). Still, a parsimonious explanation of anthropomorphizing is that the user's response is an "as if" response rather than a true attribution of humanity to "the computer." The response may not extend much further than the situation in which the user is tested.

Here is a thought experiment. Suppose we make an interface persona look and act like a duck. The "duck" asks you in a quacking kind of voice to say hello. You say "Quack, quack," i.e., speak the "duck's language." Does this mean that every time you use the computer you'll continue to quack like a duck? That you will discuss the duck with your friends as though it is a duck rather than a computer? Or indeed, do you really believe the computer *is* a duck? We think not, any more than the computer thinks you are a duck!

The results of Nass and his colleagues are consistent with our more limited explanation of people's social interactions with computers. For instance, they report that a dominant personality will "like" a dominant-acting computer and a submissive personality will "like" a submissive-acting computer (Nass et al., this volume). We interpret this study as demonstrating only that people who have dominant personality traits prefer competitive situations more than submissive individuals. In this experiment, many stimuli in the "dominant computer" condition were consistent with a competitive atmosphere, such as the fact that the research participant had to wait for the computer to take a turn. In the "submissive computer" condition, many stimuli were consistent with a cooperative, polite atmosphere. However, the research participants weren't asked if they liked and felt comfortable in the *situation*; they were not asked if they liked and felt comfortable with the experimenter, either; they were asked about "the computer." Given this option, dominant types would be expected to say they liked the computer in the dominant situation they preferred, and submissive types would say they liked the computer present in the submissive situation they preferred. And when requested to make personality attributions to the computer, they would respond to the information they had. If the computer used assertive grammar, they would mark "assertive" on the scale. (It wouldn't be sensible to mark "submissive," for example.)

We think research participants in this study probably *did* prefer the situation that included a computer whose behavior was part of what made the situation more comfortable for them. This implies that there can be aspects of computers that can elicit and engender strong feelings and social responses in people. But this isn't a fundamental or surprising discovery. Many artifacts and situations whether they be computers, appliances, books, animals, or university experiments can elicit social responses in people. We do not jump immediately to the conclusion that these appliances, books, animals, and experiments are themselves social. We need to ask what it is about the situation, and the expectations of people, that cause the social responses they seem to elicit.

Our work, and that of Nass and his colleagues, suggests several improvements that need to be made to research designs in studies of computer personas. First we must be sure that other laboratories can replicate our results. (Thus far, only our group and Reeves and Nass's lab at Stanford have studied social responses to computer personas.) Second, "the computer" is too complex an artifact to serve as a useful research stimulus. In particular, if research should inform design, we must carefully specify what aspects of the computer (all software? particular programs? particular interface characteristics? particular hardware?) evoke human response. Third, we must note that people's attitudes toward interface personas and their behavioral response to them in particular situations may be at odds. (Remember that our participants reported they really liked the dog partners but they treated them relatively shabbily.) When interface personas will be used in real products, attitudes and behaviors should be tested outside of laboratory situations. Laboratory studies (this also goes for focus groups) can be high in "experimental demand characteristics," that is, stimuli in the situation which cause people to feel special respect for the situation and the experimenter. They are sheltered situations in which people feel safe. Laboratory experiments are wonderful for testing hypotheses, but perhaps not for generalizing when people will be exposed to a multitude of influences and will have more than the limited repertoire of responses provided in the laboratory. For example, users who are called by their nickname or flattered falsely by a computer interface in an experiment might elicit a positive response. In a shopping center kiosk, they might react poorly to the same nickname or flattery, and view it perhaps as an invasion of privacy. (Customers did not like early ATM machines that called them by their first names.) Studies in the field, whether experimental or not, will help to focus designers' attention to how people will perceive and interpret software or interface behavior in the situations in which the computer will be used.

Software developers, interface designers, and social scientists will be increasingly interested in how people perceive and respond to interface personas. No doubt people will build interface personas for "intelligent agent" programs. Phil, from Apple Computer's Knowledge Navigator video, may be the best-known, although never built, current example. Serious research will be necessary to understand the conditions under which users anthropomorphize the persona based on behaviors of both the agent program and the interface persona. Companion research will also be necessary to understand how users alter their own behavior in response to persona behavior.

REFERENCES

Hogg, M.A., and C. McGarty. 1990. Self-Categorization and Social Identity. In *Social Identity Theory: Constructive and Critical Advances*, eds. D. Abrams and M.A. Hogg, 10–27. New York: Springer-Verlag.

Kiesler, S., L. Sproull, and K. Waters. 1996. A "Prisoner's Dilemma" Experiment on Cooperation with People and Human-like Computers. *Journal of Personality and Social Psychology* 70:47–65.

Parise, S., L. Sproull, S. Kiesler, and K. Waters. 1996. My Partner is a Real Dog: Cooperation with Social Agents. In *Proceedings of CSCW '96*, 399-408. New York: The ACM Press.

Sally, D. 1995. Conversation and Cooperation in Social Dilemma: A Meta-Analysis of Experiments from 1958 to 1992. *Rationality and Society* 7:58–92.

Waters, K. 1987. A Muscle Model for Animating Three-dimensional Facial Expressions. *Computer Graphics* 21:17–24.

Waters, K., and T. M. Levergood. 1995. DECface: A System for Synthetic Face Applications. *Multimedia Tools and Applications* 1:1–16.

Welch, R.B., T.T. Blackmon, A. Liu, B.A. Mellers, and L.W. Stark. In press. *The Effects of Pictorial Realism, Delay of Visual Feedback, and Observer Interactivity on the Subjective Sense of Presence*. Presence: Teleoperators and Virtual Environments.

11

Reasoning About Computers as Moral Agents: A Research Note

BATYA FRIEDMAN AND LYNETTE I. MILLETT

Abstract: Typically tool use poses few confusions about who we understand to be the moral agent for a given act. But when the "tool" becomes a computer, do people attribute moral agency and responsibility to the technology ("it's the computer's fault")? Twenty-nine male undergraduate computer science majors were interviewed. Results showed that most students (83%) attributed aspects of agency – either decision making and/or intentions – to computers. In addition, some students (21%) consistently held computers morally responsible for error. Discussion includes implications for computer system design.

Medical expert systems. Automated pilots. Loan approval software. Computer-guided missiles. Increasingly, computers participate in decisions that affect human lives. In cases of computer failure, there is a common response to "blame the computer." Is this a sincere instance of attributing moral agency to a computer, or a superficial verbal response that simply appropriates moral language? In this chapter, we provide a research note on a study which examined this question, and more (Friedman & Millett, in preparation).

METHODS

Twenty-nine male[1] undergraduate computer science majors from a leading research university in California (mean age=23:1) participated in a one and a half hour interview about their views on computer agency and moral responsibility for computer error.

The interview contained questions in three general areas: (1) students' views of computer agency (the capability to make decisions and the capability to have intentions); (2) students' assessments of computer system characteristics and limitations; and (3) students' judgments of moral responsibility for two scenarios that involved delegation of decision making to a complex com-

We thank Sara Brose and Sue Nackoney for help with the coding, reliability, and analysis of the data. This research was funded in part by the Clare Boothe Luce Foundation and by a Natural Sciences Division Research Grant from Colby College.

[1]A considerable effort was made to interview equal numbers of females and males; however, a low enrollment of female computer science majors made this goal unfeasible.

puter system. One scenario involved a computer system that administers medical radiation treatment, and due to a computer error overradiates a cancer patient. The second scenario involved a computer system that evaluates the employability of job seekers, and due to a computer error rejects a qualified worker. For each scenario, three conditions were investigated: a fully automated computer system that entails no human intervention; a token human intervention in which a person with little authority and status in the organizational hierarchy and little content area expertise operates the computer system (e.g., a hospital orderly in the radiation treatment scenario); and a nontoken human intervention in which a person with authority and status in the organizational hierarchy and content area expertise oversees the use of the computer system (e.g., the attending physician in the radiation treatment scenario).

A coding manual was developed from half of the interviews and then applied to the remaining half of the data. To insure reliability of the coding scheme, an independent scorer trained in the coding manual recoded 28% of the data. Intercoder reliability for evaluations was 96%, for content responses 97%, and for justifications 74%.

Nonparametric statistics were used to analyze the categorical data. The McNemar statistic was used to determine a change in students' evaluations across measures (e.g., evaluation of blame across conditions). The amount of blame students' assigned to each potential agent was treated as score data. Then matched-pair t-tests were used to determine differences in students' assignments of blame across agents and conditions.

RESULTS

Computers as Agents

The capability to make decisions and the capability to have intentions were used to assess students' views on computers as agents. Seventy-nine percent of the students judged computers to have decision-making capabilities and 45% judged computers to have intentions. Eighty-three percent of the students attributed at least one of the two capabilities to computers; 41% attributed both capabilities. Furthermore, when students attributed only one aspect of agency to computers, they were more likely to attribute decision making than intentions ($p < .006$).

Students' reasons for their assessments were also obtained. In justifying their positive or negative assessment of computer decision making, virtually all students (95%) appealed to computers as deterministic systems that make use of rule-based or algorithmic processes, or lack free will. For example, in support of computer decision-making one student said, "[the computer is] deciding based on a clear strict algorithm … it's a decision but not an open-ended one." In contrast but also drawing on the idea of computers as deterministic systems, to buttress a negative assessment another student said, "the decisions that the computer makes are decisions that somebody else has made before and programmed into the computer … it can analyze its input and take various actions depending on what the nature of the input is, but somebody has already told it how to proceed in the case of various inputs." Thus, students shared a view of computers as deterministic systems, but differed in their assessments as to whether or not deterministic activity constitutes genuine decision making.

Students drew on a largely different set of reasons to support their assessments of computer intentions. Of the students who judged computers to lack intentions, 36% appealed to deterministic systems, 14% to emotions, 7% to consciousness, 7% to the soul, and 36% provided unelaborated responses. In many of these cases students referred to the absence of qualities in computer systems such as a lack of consciousness (e.g., "The program is not actually knowing … it's like a level of consciousness … it's just a computer that executes these lines of code … so there's no intention on the part of the program."). In contrast, students who judged computers to have intentions encountered difficulty explicating their reasons. Although probed to the same degree as students who did not attribute intentions to computers, all of these students (100%) provided vague, unelaborated justifications that often did little more than reassert their assessment.

While the above findings overall provide a positive portrayal of computers as agents, students also judged computers to be different than humans along similar dimensions. Of the students who judged computers to have decision-making capabilities, 100% judged computer decision making to be different from human decision making. Similarly, of the students who judged computers to have intentions, 77% judged computer intentions to be different from human intentions ($Z = 2.30, p < .05$).

Responsibility for Computer-Error

Overall, students perceived the two scenarios – on radiation treatment and employment rating – as similar. No significant differences were found between scenarios for corresponding agents and conditions in students' evaluations of who or what to blame.

Roughly one-fifth of the students (on average 21%) consistently blamed the computer system itself for the computer-based error. No significant differences were found across the three conditions and two scenarios for students' evaluations of blame and the amount of blame. However, the amount of blame finding should be understood with caution as only those students ($n <=6$) who blamed the computer were assessed for the amount of blame.

A central concern of this study is how students understand computers to be accountable, if at all, for computer error. Thus, it is useful to examine students' reasons for blaming or not blaming computers in relation to their reasons for blaming or not blaming people (the computer system designer, the computer system's human operator, and the organization's administrators). Averaging across conditions and scenarios, virtually all of students' justifications for blaming the computer (96%) referred to the computer's participation in the sequence of events that led to harm. In contrast, the large majority of students' justifications for blaming people (80%) referred to failing to meet some commonly expected reasonable level of performance (e.g., negligence). When students did not assign blame, differences were also found among the justifications students used for computers and for people. Again, averaging across conditions and scenarios, virtually all of students' justifications for not blaming the computer (97%) referred to qualities of computers that diminish its agency and thus undermine computers as being the sort of thing that can be blamed. Notably, the appeal to diminished agency was used exclusively in reference to computers. In contrast, students' justifications for not blaming people primarily referred to adequately meeting commonly expected levels of performance (55%) and deferring to an authority perhaps due to habit, lack of autonomy, or the authority's greater power or knowledge (41%).

DISCUSSION

The data reported above joins a growing body of research (Nass et al., 1994; Walker et al., 1994) that suggests people, even computer literate individuals, may at times attribute social attributes to and at times engage in social interaction with computer technology. Some researchers argue that as good designers we ought to exploit this psychological phenomena to build systems that actively engage users in a social relationship with the technology. Much of the work on computer agents and intelligent agents is of this vein. The results reported here, however, should give us pause. For the results suggest that even some computer literate individuals hold computer technology at least partly responsible for computer error. If this finding is correct, a different design strategy is in order. It would follow, for example, that designers should communicate through the system that a (human) who – and not a (computer) what – is responsible for the consequences of the computer use.

REFERENCES

Nass, C., J. Steuer, and E.R. Tauber. 1994. Computers Are Social Actors. In *Proceedings of CHI '94 Human Factors in Computing Systems*, 72–78. New York: ACM Press.

Walker, J.H., L. Sproull, and R. Subramani. Using a Human Face in an Interface. In *Proceedings of CHI '94 Human Factors in Computing Systems,* 85–91. New York: ACM Press.

12

Interface Agents: Metaphors with Character

BRENDA LAUREL

Abstract: Anthropomorphism is a natural human tendency that human–computer interface designers can employ to good advantage. This chapter presents criteria for design of anthropomorphic agents that are based on the characteristics of agency, responsiveness, competence, and accessibility. Just as the performance of a dramatic character provides cues and clues to its proclivities and helps us to predict its actions, the qualities projected by an interface agent should be a good match for its capabilities, appropriately communicating expectations regarding performance and relationship. The chapter concludes with an R&D agenda for agents first presented in 1990 – it is interesting to see how far we have (or have not) come.

THE CASE FOR AGENTS

On the bridge of the USS *Enterprise*, a decidedly clipped female voice announces that the computer is "working." On board the *Nostromo*, Ripley hunches over her console seeking advice from "Mother." On the moon, Adam Selene foments a revolution. HAL refuses to open the pod bay doors, and his sibling SAL wonder whether she'll dream when her creator powers her down.

Since the beginning of this century, people have dreamed about the new companions they might create with high technology. Some of those dreams are nightmares about malevolent computers enslaving mankind as techno-evolution catapults them far beyond our puny carbon-based brains. Most are wistful longings for new helpers, advisors, teachers, playmates, pets, or friends. But all of the computer-based personae that weave through popular culture have one thing in common: They mediate a relationship between the labyrinthine precision of computers and the fuzzy complexity of man.

Why is this tendency to personify interfaces so natural as to be virtually universal in our collective vision of the future?

Computers behave. Computational tools and applications can be said to have *predispositions* to behave in certain ways on both functional and stylistic levels. Interfaces are designed to communicate those predispositions to users, thereby enabling them to understand, predict the results of, and successfully deploy the associated behaviors.

When we think and communicate about behavioral predispositions, we naturally use metaphors based on living organisms. Even the most technologically savvy user will feel quite comfortable comparing the Macintosh and IBM PC in terms of their "personalities" and may characterize software with adjectives based on a living-organism metaphor: Word is fussy, my spelling checker is illiterate, Emacs is obtuse. Where agentlike activities already exist, they are often perceived as having character-one interface designer has described error messages as "wrist-slapping grannies."

An interface agent can be defined as a character, enacted by the computer, who acts on behalf of the user in a virtual (computer-based) environment. Interface agents draw their strength from the naturalness of the living-organism metaphor in terms of both cognitive accessibility and communication style. Their usefulness can range from managing mundane tasks like scheduling, to handling customized information searches that combine both filtering and the production (or retrieval) of alternative representations, to providing companionship, advice, and help throughout the spectrum of known and yet-to-be-invented interactive contexts.

OBJECTIONS TO AGENTS

Although the notion of interface agents seems natural and desirable to many, considerable resistance exists. One negative view can be described as the "agent as virus" problem. For example, one colleague of mine characterized agents as "whining, chatting little irritants." She dreaded waking up one day to find "a whining little secretary stuck in my machine." Here the problem is not agents *per se*, but rather the traits that they are assumed to possess. One solution is to offer the user a number of agents from which to choose (rather like a job interview or theatrical audition); another is to provide an "identa-kit" whereby agents could be configured by their users.

Closely related to "agent as virus" is the notion that agents are just plain silly. "I would feel incredibly stupid pretending that there was a person in my computer," one programmer told me (however, this same person has often been observed shouting obscenities at his screen). In a lively conversation on the subject on the Whole Earth 'Lectronic Link (WELL), one user confided that he had been saving digitized images of his dog to immortalize him as an agent after his death. This idea was greeted with a mixture of derision and horror. Yet the idea of a canine agent (perhaps not one's own departed pet) readily suggests a class of activities (fetching the morning paper and announcing intruders, for instance), a level of competence (the agent will deliver the paper but will not provide commentary), and a kind of communication (a small repertoire of simple commands and an equally small repertoire of behavioral responses) that may be entirely appropriate.

For some users, the idea of agents smacks of indirection. "Why should I have to negotiate with some little dip in a bow tie when I know exactly what I want to do?" The answer, of course, is equivocal. Few of us would hire an agent to push the buttons on our calculator; most of us would hire an agent to scan 5,000 pieces of junk mail. If I were looking for a specific book for a research project, I'd probably use a reference librarian; if I were browsing with an opportunistic eye, I'd want to go into the stacks. When I have to negotiate with UNIX, I call my husband. It doesn't feel like indirection when an agent does something for me that I can't or don't want to do myself. I have often railed against interfaces that force me to plead with a system (in exotic language) to do a very simple thing (Laurel, 1986a). But that is quite different than having a competent agent at my beck and call. Agents, like anything else, can be well or poorly designed. A good one will do what I want, tell me all I want to know about what it's doing, and give me back the reins when I desire. Good interfaces usually allow for more than one way of doing things, too. Only users who want to use agents should have them; others should have other choices.

Perhaps a more thought-provoking objection to agents rests on an ethical argument that goes something like this: If an agent looks and acts a lot like a real person, and if I can get away with treating it badly and bossing it around without paying a price for my bad behavior, then I will be encouraged to treat other, "real" agents (like secretaries and realtors, for instance) just as badly. This argument seems to hinge on the fear that humans will mistake a representation for the real thing, possibly first expressed by Plato when he banned the dramatic arts from his Republic on the same grounds. Yet few would trade the plays of Shakespeare and Molière for the apparent unambiguity of Plato's world. Today, parents are concerned that their children will confuse the violence in the news with that in the latest commando movie (or video game). These are real issues that must be addressed by artists and citizens. The solution lies, I believe, not in repression of the form (which is a strategy that is bound to fail, if history is any indicator), but rather in the ethics of the artist, the entrepreneur, the parent, and the culture at large.

Another objection is that implementing agents would necessarily involve artificial intelligence, a discipline whose star is currently in eclipse. "AI doesn't work," the litany goes, "and even if it did, an agent would gobble up more cycles than it's worth." Two responses apply. First, although the grand platform of AI may not have been satisfactorily realized, there are numerous examples of the successful use of AI techniques. For example, Object Lens, an "intelligent groupware" system under development at the Sloane School of Management at MIT, enables users to create agents that can sort mail, issue reminders, and find things in object-oriented databases (Crowston & Malone, 1988). Second, there are already examples of agents that employ no AI at all. The problem here may be that an anthropomorphic agent is being confused with a full-blown "artificial personality," the implementation of which is, of course, a daunting prospect. But an agent can – indeed, must – be much simpler than that, as we shall see.

IN DEFENSE OF ANTHROPOMORPHISM

Anthropomorphizing interface agents is appropriate for both psychological and functional reasons. Psychologically, we are quite adept at relating to and communicating with other people. We utilize this ability in dealing with non-sentient beings and inanimate objects through the process of anthropomorphism. This mode of operating in the world is so natural that we often engage in anthropomorphizing objects in our daily lives – ships, countries, cars, and vacuum cleaners. Where an anthropomorphic persona is not readily apparent, one is often created for us by advertisers: Reddy Kilowatt, the Pillsbury Doughboy, and the California Raisins come to mind (indeed, the anthropomorphic raisins are so attractive that they have generated more revenue than their fruity friends).

Anthropomorphism is not the same thing as relating to other people, but is rather the application of a metaphor with all its concomitant selectivity. Metaphors draw incomplete parallels between unlike things, emphasizing some qualities and suppressing others (Lakoff & Johnson, 1980). When we anthropomorphize a machine or an animal, we do not impute human personality in all its subtle complexity; we paint with bold strokes, thinking only of those traits that are useful to us in the particular context.

The kinds of tasks that computers perform for (and with) us require that they express two distinctly anthropomorphic qualities: *responsiveness* and the *capacity to perform actions*. These qualities alone comprise the metaphor of agency. To flesh out a particular agent, the computer can be made to represent its unique skills, expertise, and predispositions in terms of character traits. As in drama, traits can be represented directly through appearance, sound, communication style (external traits), which in turn cause us to infer traits on the level of knowledge and thought (internal traits). Evaluating action taken by an agent provides a feedback loop through which we refine and embellish our understanding of the agent's characters. The point here is that, as the ultimate device for making dynamic, mimetic representations, the computer is ideally suited to the task of manifesting agents as dramatic characters (Laurel, 1986b).

By capturing and representing the capabilities of agents in the form of character, we realize several benefits. First, this form of representation makes optimal use of our ability to make accurate inferences about how a character is likely to think, decide, and act on the basis of its external traits. This marvelous cognitive shorthand is what makes plays and movies work; its universality is what makes the same play or story work for a variety of cultures and individuals. With interface agents, users can employ the same shorthand – with the same likelihood of success – to predict, and therefore control, the actions of their agents. Second, the agent as character (whether humanoid, canine, cartoonish, or cybernetic) invites conversational interaction. This invokes another kind of shorthand – the ability to infer, cocreate, and employ simple communication conventions. The essence of conversationality can be captured without elaborate natural language processing. Third, the metaphor of *character* successfully draws our attention to just those qualities that form the essential nature of an agent: responsiveness, competence, accessibility, and the capacity to perform actions on our behalf.

KEY CHARACTERISTICS OF INTERFACE AGENTS

Agency

In a purely Aristotelian sense, an agent is one who takes action. In social legal terms, an agent is one who is empowered to act on behalf of another. Researcher Susan Brenner observes that most people whom we refer to as "our agents" – real estate agents, insurance agents, and the like – are not working for us at all, but rather for the companies who pay their salaries (Brennan, 1984). An interface agent would exercise its agency entirely on behalf of the user. Alan Kay traces the development of the concept:

> The idea of an agent originated with John McCarthy in the mid-1950s, and the term was coined by Oliver G. Selfridge a few years later, when they were both at the Massachusetts Institute of Technology. They had in view a system that, when given a goal, could carry out the details of the appropriate computer operations and could ask for and receive advice, offered in human terms, when it was stuck. An agent

would be a "soft robot" living and doing its business within the computer's world. (Kay, 1984)

Agents provide expertise, skill, and labor. They must of necessity be capable of understanding our needs and goals in relation to them (either explicitly or implicitly), translating those goals into an appropriate set of actions, performing those actions, and delivering the results in a form that we can use. They must also know when further information is needed from us and how to get it. In life, any person or institution who is empowered by us to take action on our behalf is an agent. Examples include secretaries, gardeners, craftspeople and laborers, teachers, librarians, and accountants.

What kind of tasks do we perform with computers for which agents are appropriate? They are tasks with the same requirements as those for which we employ agents in real life: tasks that require expertise, skill, resources, or labor that we need to accomplish some goal and that we are unwilling or unable to perform ourselves. Figure 1 provides examples of computer-related tasks where agents would be appropriate.

Information	**Work**
Navigation and Browsing	Reminding
Information Retrieval	Programming
Sorting and Organizing	Scheduling
Filtering	Advising
Learning	**Entertainment**
Coaching	Playing against
Tutoring	Playing with
Providing	Performing

Figure 1. Kinds of tasks an agent might perform.

Some of these tasks are appropriate for an agent because they are too complex for either straightforward algorithmic solutions or for complete parametric specification by the human user. An obvious example is a search for information in a large database, which may involve linguistic, numeric, formal, and a variety of heuristic and stylistic concerns. The nature of the complexity of such problems makes them excellent candidates for an expert-systems approach (Hayes-Roth et al., 1983). Like the human experts who give expert systems their not-so-metaphorical name, agents based on such systems probably require considerable detailing and subtlety in their character traits. Other kinds of tasks (such as sorting mail or preparing monthly invoices) require much less "intelligence"; the associated agents are valuable because they are diligent, quick, accurate, and impervious to boredom. Representing such agents would require relatively fewer, more simplistic traits. Both functional implementation and external representation (that is, character) will vary widely according to the nature of the agent's task.

Responsiveness

Because of its social contract with the user, an interface agent is a prime example of user-centered interface design. An agent succeeds or fails on the basis of its ability to be responsive to the user. What are the dimensions of responsiveness?

Most other forms of human–computer interface exhibit *explicit responsiveness*; that is, user and system communicate through a series of highly constrained, explicit transactions. Typically, a system accommodates users' expressions of goals and intentions only in ways that are formally compatible with its operating requirements. Even when commands are camouflaged in comfortable metaphors like "cut," "paste," or "paint," users must parse their actions and intentions in terms dictated by the system (and therefore the interface) and must express them explicitly.

Because it is the function of an agent to take action on behalf of a user, it follows that the value of the agent derives, at least in part, from its ability to formulate and execute a set of actions solely on the basis of a user's goals. Whether those goals are explicitly stated by the user or inferred by the system, the way an agent interprets and attempts to meet them constitutes *implicit responsiveness*. This is the principal means whereby an agent amplifies the user's personal power.

One aspect of implicit responsiveness is the ability of an agent to tune its actions to the user's traits and preferences. If my French tutor notices that I'm a theater buff, she'll enhance my learning process by assigning readings in Molière. Noting my intransigence regarding the three-comma rule, my writing coach should probably beat on me mercilessly until I either succumb to the new grammar or exchange him for Edgar Allan Poe. Knowledge about the user can be both obtained explicitly (by questioning) and inferred (by noticing).

Users also change over time. Even when the user's goals are explicitly the same from day to day, the way they should be interpreted changes. If I ask my news agent to tell me what's going on in the Middle East, for instance, he should not present me with the same article I read yesterday. And if he's smart, he'll notice that I seem to have become especially interested in the Persian Gulf and will gather materials accordingly. Responsiveness therefore requires that the agent have access to a dynamic model of the user, or at the very least, a log of his experience in a particular application or environment with rules for interpreting that experience when formulating actions.

Depending upon how it is implemented, an interface agent may be associated primarily with a single user or with an application or environment that has multiple users. In the latter case, the agent must be able to distinguish among users, at least on the basis of experience and preferences, in order to be genuinely responsive.

Interface designers often have a strong aversion to implicit responsiveness because it requires inference, and inference is fuzzy. The belief is that an incorrect inference is more disturbing to the user than no inference at all (that is, insistence on explicit transactions). But a failed inference need not be painful if it results only in a request for more information. If a system knows enough to generate an error message, it also knows enough to ask a question. The risk of incorrect inference can be mitigated by a variety of strategies for disambiguation, including dialogue, user modeling, and the creation of redundancy through the use of multiple input channels.

Competence

Suggestions about building and employing the first area of competence, knowledge about the user, are included in the discussion of responsiveness above. Clearly, an interface agent must also be competent in the domain of the application or environment in which it operates. An agent can be said to have access to all of the information and possible operations in its domain by virtue of its being part of the same system. But in order to serve the user well, an agent must possess (or be able to generate) both metaknowledge and multiple representations.

By *metaknowledge* we mean knowledge about problem solving in a domain. If the domain is a database, knowledge is required about both the information content and the process of retrieving and representing that information to the user. If the domain is a table of airline schedules and fares, the metaknowledge consists in knowing how to formulate a travel plan based on both domain information and the preferences of the traveler, and then knowing how to present it in a clear and actionable way.

The ability to provide multiple representations of information is a key aspect of responsiveness. Brennan observes:

> Multiple representations increase the odds that the user and the system will be able to communicate effectively and that ambiguities in one representation will be disambiguated by another; multiple representations also provide a basis for a learning environment. Good teachers and good students are skilled at providing feedback by trading multiple representations back and forth… (Brennan,1984)

At the very least, competence consists of knowing how to select from among multiple representations already extant in a single database. Ultimately, however, such limited competence will prove to be inadequate. Users will eventually want agents to assemble information from multiple sources containing huge volumes of information in a wide variety of forms. It seems impractical to create a new information-linking industry where humans attempt to stitch all the information in the world together so that we can build interfaces that simply follow the threads. It also seems impractical to include multiple representations for every item in even a small database. Competence ultimately will include the ability to both retrieve and generate alternate representations of information according to the needs and personal styles of users. Agents will be selected or configured by users partially on the basis of their distinctive searching heuristics and representation-making abilities.

Accessibility

An agent's traits and predispositions must be made accessible to the user. Perceptually, users must be given cues by the external representation of an agent that allow them to infer its internal traits. Selection of the modes of representation (for example, visual, verbal, auditory, etc.) should be driven by a consideration of the whole character, the environment, and the traits in question. For some agents and environments, text is just enough (ELIZA's disembodied phrases may be its greatest strength), whereas for others completely different modalities are required (imagine capturing Marilyn Monroe without a picture or Donald Duck without a voice). For example, in the Guides project, graphical icons that minimize facial detail and emphasize emblematic props are adequate for distinguishing among points of view in the task of navigating through the textual database, but for providing alternative representations of information in storytelling style, motion video and character voice are required.

On the conceptual level, an agent is accessible if a user can predict what it is likely to do in a given situation on the basis of its character. Equally important is the criterion that an agent must be conceived by users as a coherent entity. It is in the area of accessibility that the idea of structuring agents as dramatic characters has the greatest value.

DESIGN AND DRAMATIC CHARACTER

The case for modeling interface agents after dramatic characters is based on both the familiarity of dramatic characters as a way of structuring thought and behavior and the body of theory and methodology already in place for creating them. Most cultures have a notion of dramatic form, and people are quite familiar with both the differences and the similarities between characters and real people. Character traits function as stereotypic "shorthand" for understanding and predicting character behavior (Schank & Lebowitz, 1979).

Somewhat ironically, dramatic characters are better suited to the roles of agents than full-blown simulated personalities. The art of creating dramatic characters is the art of selecting and representing only those traits which are appropriate to a particular set of actions and situations (Schwamberger, 1980). For most uses, an interface agent, like a dramatic character, must pass a kind of anti-Turing test in order to be effectively understood and employed by the user. We want to know that the choices and actions of our agents, whether computational or human, will not be clouded by complex and contradictory psychological variables. In most cases, we want to be able to predict their actions with greater certainty than those of "real" people.

Although designers and scholars like Alan Kay worry that oversimplification of character will destroy the illusion of lifelikeness (Kay, 1984), the fact is that, thanks to well-internalized dramatic convention, we can enjoy (and believe in) even one-dimensional dramatic characters. In fact, when a minor dramatic character possesses only one or two functional traits, audience members will impute elaborate histories and motivations as needed to make it believable (Schwamberger, 1980). Whether the character is as simple as Wiley Coyote or as complex as Hamlet, we take pleasure when – and *only* when – even the surprises in a character's behavior are causally related to its traits.

Happily, the selectivity and causality inherent in the structure of dramatic characters simplifies the task of representing them computationally (Laurel, 1986b). In the area of story generation, James Meehan, Michael Lebowitz, and others have created functional and entertaining characters from a small cluster of well-conceived traits that are realized as goal-formulating and problem-solving styles (Meehan, 1976; Lebowitz, 1984). Increasingly in the world of adventure and role-playing computer games, designers are implementing characters with traits that are *dynamic* (modified by learning and experience) and *relational* (modified in relation to objects and situations).

The artistic side of the design problem is to represent the character (in this case, an interface agent) to the user in such a way that the appropriate traits are apparent and the associated styles and behaviors can be successfully predicted. External traits like diction and appearance must be shaped to suggest those internal traits (values, heuristics, etc.) which determine how a character will make choices and perform actions. A character is coherent – whole – when its traits are well integrated through careful selection and planned interaction. The designer can look to the considerable body of work on playwriting, as well as to the area of modeling and representing character traits computationally for guidance (see, for instance, Carbonell, 1980).

AN R & D AGENDA

As we are discovering with all types of interfaces, good design is no longer the exclusive province of the applications programmer, the graphic designer, the AI researcher, or even the multimedia hacker. In the effort to make interface agents a reality, several areas of technology and design must be explored simultaneously.

In the theoretical arena, work must proceed on the analysis of user needs and preferences vis-à-vis applications and environments. What are the qualities of a task that make it a good candidate for an agentlike interface? What kinds of users will want them, and what are the differences among potential user populations? How might interface agents affect the working styles, expectations, productivity, knowledge, and personal power of those who use them?

In terms of design, the meatiest problem is developing criteria that will allow us to select the appropriate set of traits for a given agent – traits that can form coherent characters, provide useful cues to users, and give rise to all of the necessary and appropriate actions in a given context. Contributions will be needed from the disciplines of dramatic theory and practice, literary criticism and storytelling, and aspects of psychology and communication arts and sciences.

In the area of implementation, much ongoing work can be appropriated. We must explore and refine existing AI techniques for understanding, inference, and computational representation of character. Techniques for constructing and enacting character can also be imported from the field of computer game design. Expert-systems techniques can be applied to such "soft" problems as learning and assimilating the user's style and preferences, developing navigational strategies, and creating alternate representations. Work on such technologies as language and speech processing, paralinguistics, story generation, image recognition, and intelligent animation can be refocused and revitalized by the agents' platform.

Finally, rapid prototyping techniques must be developed to facilitate user testing and evaluation. If we can continue to gather feedback from individual users and inspiration from popular culture as a whole, the notion of agents will evolve – as it should – in collaboration with the people from whose fantasies it arose.

REFERENCES

Brennan, S. 1984. Interface Agents. Unpublished paper.

Carbonell, J.G. 1980. Towards a Process Model of Human Personality Traits. *Artificial Intelligence* 15:49–50.

Crowston, K., and T. W. Malone. 1988. Intelligent Software Agents. *Byte* 13(13) (December):267–74.

Hayes-Roth, F., D.A. Waterman, and D.B. Lenat, eds. 1983. *Building Expert Systems.* Teknowledge Series in Knowledge Engineering, no. 1. Reading, MA: Addision-Wesley Publishing Company.

Kay, A. 1984. Computer Software. *Scientific American* 251(3):52–59.

Lakoff, G., and M. Johnson. 1980. *Metaphors We Live By.* Chicago: The University of Chicago Press.

Laurel, B. 1986. Interface as Mimesis. In *User-Centered System Design: New Perspectives on Human–Computer Interaction,* eds. D.A. Norma and S. Draper. Hillsdale, NJ: Lawrence Erlbaum Associates.

Laurel, B. 1986. Toward the Design of a Computer-Based Interactive Fantasy System. Ph.D. Dissertation. The Ohio State University.

Lebowitz, M. Creating Characters in a Story-Telling Universe. *Poetics* 13:171–194.

Meehan, J.R. 1976. The Metanovel: Writing Stories by Computer. Ph.D. Dissertation, Yale University.

Schank, R.C., and M. Lebowitz. 1979. *The Use of Stereotype Information in the Comprehension of Noun Phrases.* Alexandria, VA: Defense Technical Information Center.

Schwamberger, J. 1980. The Nature of Dramatic Character. Ph.D. Dissertation. The Ohio State University.

13

Human Agency and Responsible Computing: Implications for Computer System Design

BATYA FRIEDMAN AND PETER H. KAHN, JR.

Abstract: To understand and promote responsible computing, this chapter highlights the importance of analyses based on human agency. We first examine whether computers can be moral agents. Then we draw on research in human factors, cognitive science, and instructional technology to examine how three types of computing practices can be problematic from the perspective of human agency. The first involves anthropomorphizing a computational system, the second, delegating decision making to a computational system, and the third, delegating instruction to a computational system. Throughout this discussion, we provide alternative design goals and methods by which responsible computing can be enhanced as a shared vision and practice within the computing community.

Societal interest in responsible computing perhaps most often arises in response to harmful consequences that can result from computing. For instance, consider the frustration and economic loss incurred by individuals and businesses whose computer systems have been infected by the Internet Worm or other computer viruses. Or consider the physical suffering and death of the cancer patients who were overradiated by Therac-25, or of civilians accidentally bombed in the Persian Gulf war by "smart" missiles gone astray. Largely in reaction to events like these, we have in recent years seen a surge of interest in preventing or at least minimizing such harmful consequences. But if responsible computing is to be understood as something more than a form of damage control, how are we to understand the term? Moreover, how can responsible computing be promoted within the computing community?

In this article, we address these questions by highlighting the importance of analyses based not only on consequences of acts, but agency – on what and why some things can be held morally responsible for action. We shall first examine whether computers can be such things. While our discussion here will be largely philosophical (and somewhat condensed as each piece may well be familiar to the reader), a compelling position on whether computers can be moral agents provides an important starting point for our central task. We seek to understand how, from the moral perspective, we should conceive of the human relationship to computational systems, and to provide sketches of how to build on that conception to promote responsible computing through system design. To this end, we will examine how three types of computing practices can be problematic from the perspective of human agency. The first involves anthropomorphizing a computational system, the second, delegating decision making to a computational system, and the third, delegating instruction to a computational system.

CAN COMPUTERS BE MORAL AGENTS?

To understand the place and urgency of the question of whether computers can be moral agents, consider the issues raised by computer-based closed-loop drug administration systems. In critical care medicine, these automated systems are designed to monitor and, when necessary, adjust the administration of a variety of drugs for patients in an intensive care unit. Such computer-based systems are touted for their increased effectiveness over human-administered drug therapy, for their safety, and for their usefulness in reducing nursing demands (Bednarski et al., 1990). However, these systems, although currently recommended for use, pose ethical problems. For instance, Snapper (1991) suggests that such a computer-based system "may not be able to check as many variables as could a doctor at the bedside and so may administer the wrong drug when a doctor would administer the correct drug" (p. 289). Or such a computer-based system may not be programmed to account for a particular atypical case, and so may administer the wrong drug when an experienced doctor would administer the correct drug. In such situations, can the computer-based closed-loop drug administration system itself be held, even in part, morally responsible for the decision to administer a wrong drug? Stated more generally, can a computational system be a moral agent and thus be held morally responsible for a decision?

Toward addressing this question, consider two cases. While hiking in the mountains, Y is crushed by a falling boulder and killed. In case one, the boulder was dislodged by a slight shifting and settling of the land on which it was balanced. In case two, the same boulder was dislodged by a push from X, who desired to kill Y, believed the push would cause the boulder to fall on Y, understood that a boulder of such weight would kill Y, and freely chose to perform the act. The cases are the same in that some "thing" caused a boulder to fall, killing Y. But the cases are fundamentally different in that only in the second case was the act of dislodging the boulder the result of an intentional act. This distinction between the cases highlights a philosophical position that for a thing to be held morally responsible it must be capable of intentionality, which, at a minimum, refers to the capability of having or experiencing beliefs, desires, understandings, intentions, and volition (Scott, 1990; Searle, 1983). Given, then, that people but not land are usually considered psychologically capable of intentional states, only X (but not the land) could be held morally responsible for the death of Y. Moving now to the question at hand: If we accept that intentional states are a prerequisite for a thing to be held morally responsible, then a subset of the above question – can a computational system be a moral agent and thus be held morally responsible for a decision? – can be framed as follows: Can a computational system be considered to have intentional states?

Much of the literature in artificial intelligence would have us think so, or at least have us think it possible. One classic framing of this position can be traced to McCarthy (1979), who proposed some decades ago that machine intentionality is equivalent to human intentionality. For example, in one of his well-known analogies, McCarthy claimed that a thermostat has beliefs (of whether a room is too hot or cold) that lead to intended action (turning the heater off or on). Such intentional states, according to McCarthy, are equivalent to that of a human who can have beliefs (of whether a room is too hot or cold) that lead to intended action (taking a sweater off or putting one on).

There are two ways to understand such a position that equate machine intentionality with human intentionality. Both will frame our analyses of computer system design. In the first, whatever we may call intentionality and think we may experience in terms of feelings, beliefs, understandings, free will, or an underlying sense of self or personhood are epiphenomenal, meaning such experiences play no authentic causal role in our actions. In the second, it is claimed that machines have (or with increased technological advancements will have) psychological states similar or identical to those which comprise human intentionality (in a nonepiphenomenal sense). In other words, the first reduces humans to the status of computers, while the second raises computers to the status of humans.

Both ways of understanding are problematic. Granted, it may be that humans ultimately will never be able to prove conclusively that what we take to be intentionality is not epiphenomenal, for the position draws on a radical skepticism that calls into question every means we might have to undermine it. The argument is similar to one that charges you, the reader, are nothing but a brain in the vat (Zuboff, 1981), prodded at this very moment with electrical stimulation to induce you to think that you are reading this essay, and that you have the thoughts, feelings, and experiences that you do. Anything you might try to say to counter this position (e.g., "I think therefore I am," or less formally, "But I know deep down inside myself that that is not true,") can be counterargued with the claim that your knowledge has simply been induced by electrical stimulation.

It is a far cry, however, from not being able to prove this position conclusively false to believing, with good reason, that it is true. Phenomenologically, humans experience intentional states and believe they have beliefs, understandings, and free will. If such intentionality is epiphenomenal, it is difficult to understand biologically and psychologically why or how it ever originated within our species. Moreover, it would be virtually impossible to live in this world without taking our intentional states seriously. We would, for instance, have to abandon such beliefs that a difference exists between accidental and intended harm (since the belief in intended action is epiphenomenal), that persons can lose weight, climb hills, or read books if they so choose (since the belief in free choice is epiphenomenal), and so on for the countless intentional states that pervade our lives. Indeed, even the desire to understand how intentionality is epiphenomenal presupposes a validity to intentionality, to such psychological constructs as desire and understanding that lead to the intended action to provide an alternative explanation. The point here is that without positive evidence to the contrary, which this first position based on a radical skepticism does not provide, humans have good reason to believe that human intentionality plays an authentic causal role in our actions.

The second way of understanding the proposition that equates human intentionality with machine intentionality, that machines have states similar or identical to those which comprise human intentionality, has been substantively critiqued by Searle (1990). His Chinese room argument is well known:

> Consider a language you don't understand. In my case, I do not understand Chinese. To me Chinese writing looks like so many meaningless squiggles. Now suppose I am placed in a room containing baskets full of Chinese symbols. Suppose also that I am given a rule book in English for matching Chinese symbols with other Chinese symbols. The rules identify the symbols entirely by their shapes and do not require that I understand any of them. Imagine that people outside the room who understand Chinese hand in small bunches of symbols and that in response I manipulate the symbols according to the rule book and hand back more small bunches of symbols. Now, the rule book is the "computer program." The people who wrote it are "programmers," and I am the "computer." The baskets full of symbols are the "data base"... Now suppose that the rule book is written in such a way that my "answers" to the "questions" are indistinguishable from those of a native Chinese speaker ... All the same, I am totally ignorant of Chinese. And there is no way I could come to

understand Chinese in the system as described, since there is no way that I can learn the meanings of any of the symbols. Like a computer, I manipulate symbols, but I attach no meaning to the symbols.

In other words, because computational systems are purely formal (syntax), and because purely formal systems have no means to generate intentionality (semantics), computational systems do not have intentionality.

Searle's position has generated a great deal of debate, including twenty-six commentaries, since it appeared in 1980 (Searle, 1980) and continued more recently by Churchland and Churchland (1990). While this is not the place to review the many arguments and counterarguments in the debate, in our view and the view of others, Searle has defended his position well against his critics. This is not to say that minds and their intentional states might not someday be realized in materials or structures other than biological brains. But it is to say that computers as we can conceive of them today are not such materials or structures.

Thus we have argued, however briefly, for three propositions: (1) intentionality is a necessary condition of moral agency; (2) we can, with confidence, believe that human intentionality plays an authentic causal role in our actions; and (3) a computer system as we can conceive of it today in material and structure cannot have intentionality. From these three propositions, it follows that humans, but not computational systems, are capable of being moral agents, and that humans, but not computational systems, are capable of being morally responsible for computer-mediated actions and consequences.

DESIGN TO SUPPORT HUMAN AGENCY AND RESPONSIBLE COMPUTING

Based on this line of reasoning, we propose that responsible computing often depends on humans' clear understanding that humans are capable of being moral agents and that computational systems are not. However, as anticipated by the above discussion, this understanding can be distorted in one of two ways. In the first type of distortion, the computational system diminishes or undermines the human user's sense of his or her own moral agency. In such systems, human users are placed into largely mechanical roles, either mentally or physically, and frequently have little understanding of the larger purpose or meaning of their individual actions. To the extent that humans experience a diminished sense of agency, human dignity is eroded and individuals may consider themselves to be largely unaccountable for the consequences of their computer use. Conversely, in the second type of distortion the computational system masquerades as an agent by projecting intentions, desires, and volition. To the extent that humans inappropriately attribute agency to such systems, humans may well consider the computational systems, at least in part, to be morally responsible for the effects of computer-mediated or computer-controlled actions.

Accordingly, to support humans' responsible use of computational systems, system design should strive to minimize both types of distortion. That is, system design should seek to protect the moral agency of humans and to discourage in humans a perception of moral agency in the computational system. How might design practices achieve these goals? Given that little research exists that addresses this question directly, we seek to provide some initial sketches by examining three types of computer practices.

Anthropomorphizing the Computational System

Anthropomorphic metaphors can be found in some of the definitions and goals for interface design. For example, some interfaces are designed to "use the process of human–human communication as a model for human–computer interaction" (Eberts & Eberts, 1989 p. 86), to "interact with the user similar to the way one human would interact with another" (Eberts & Eberts, 1989, p. 87), or to be "intelligent" where intelligence is based on a model of human intelligence. When such anthropomorphic metaphors become embedded in the design of a system, the system can fall prey to the second type of distortion by projecting moral agency onto the computational system.

Moreover, even in unsophisticated designs of this type, there is some evidence that people do attribute agency to the computational system. For example, Weizenbaum (1976 p. 7) reported that some adults interacted with his computer program *Doctor* with great emotional depth and intimacy, "conversing with the computer as if it were a person." In a similar vein, some of the children Turkle (1984) interviewed about their experiences with an interactive computer game called Merlin that played tic-tac-toe attributed psychological (mental) characteristics to Merlin. For example, children sometimes accused Merlin of cheating, an accusation that includes a belief that the computer has both the intention and desire to deceive. In another example, Rumelhart and Norman (1981) attempted to teach novices to use an editing program by telling the novices that the system was like a secretary. The novices drew on this human analogy to attribute aspects of a secretary's intelligence to the editing system and assumed (incorrectly) that the system would be able to understand whether they intended a particular string of characters to count as text or as commands.

While these examples of human attribution of agency to computational systems have largely benign consequences, this may not always be the case. Consider Jenkins'(1984) human factors experiment that simulated a nuclear power plant failure. In the experiment, nuclear power plant operators had access to an expert system to aid them in responding to the plant failure. Although previously instructed on the expert system's limitations, the "operators expected that the expert system implemented in the computer 'knew' about the failures of the cooling system without being told. The system [however] was neither designed nor functioned as an automatic fault recognition system." Jenkins attributed this overestimation of the system's capabilities to the power plant operators' expectations for the expert system to know certain information, presumably the type of information that any responsible human expert would know or attempt to find out in that situation.

Because nonanthropomorphic design does not encourage people to attribute agency to the computational system, such designs can better support responsible computing. To clarify what such design looks like in practice, consider the possibilities for interface design. Without ever impersonating human agency, interface design can appropriately pursue such goals as learnability, ease and pleasure of use, clarity, and quick recovery from errors. In addition, nonanthropomorphic interface design can employ such techniques as novel pointing devices, nonanthropomorphic analogies, speech input and output, and menu selection. Or consider the characteristics of another plausible technique: direct manipulation. According to Jacob (1989 p. 166), direct manipulation refers to a user interface in which the user "seems to operate directly *on* the objects in the computer rather than carrying on a dialogue *about* them." For example, the Xerox Star desktop manager adapted for systems such as the Apple Macintosh uses images of standard office objects (e.g., files, folders, and trash cans) and tasks to represent corresponding objects and functions in the editing system (Smith et al., 1982). In this environment, disposing of a computer file is achieved by moving the image of the file onto the image of the trash can, akin to disposing of a paper file by physically placing the file in a trash can. There is no ambiguity in this direct manipulation interface as to who is doing the acting (the human user) and what the user is acting upon (objects in the computational system). The defining characteristics of direct manipulation suggest that this technique would not lead to projecting human agency onto the system. This is because direct manipulation involves physical action on an object as opposed to social interaction with another as an underlying metaphor. Additionally, direct manipulation seeks to have the human user directly manipulate computational objects, thereby virtually eliminating the possibility for the human user to perceive the computer interface as an intermediary agent.

Nonanthropomorphic design considerations fit within a larger vision for interface design that is already part of the field. For example, Shneiderman (1987) draws on Weizenbaum to advocate design that "sharpen[s] the boundaries between people and computers… [for] human–human communication is a poor model for human–computer interaction." More recently, Shneiderman (1989) writes that "when an interactive system is well designed, it almost disappears, enabling the users to concentrate on their work or pleasure" (p. 169). Winograd and Flores (1986 p. 194) similarly advocate the design of nonanthropomorphic computer tools that provide a transparent interaction between the user and the resulting action. "The transparency of interaction is of utmost importance in the design of tools, including computer systems, but it is not best achieved by attempting to mimic human faculties." When a transparent interaction is achieved, the user is freed from the details of using the tool to focus on the task at hand. The shared vision here is for the interface to "disappear," not to intercede in the guise of another "agent" between human users and the computational system.

Delegating Decision Making to Computational Systems

When delegating decision making to computational systems, both types of distortions can occur. The discussion that follows examines these distortions in the context of the APACHE system (Chang, Lee, Jacobs & Lee, 1989; Zimmerman, 1989). More generally, however, similar analyses could be applied to other computer-based models and knowledge-based systems such as MYCIN (Shortliffe, 1983) or the Authorizer's Assistant used by the American Express Corporation (Harris et al., 1989).

APACHE is a computer-based model implemented but not yet used clinically that determines when to withdraw life support systems from patients in intensive care units. Consider the nature of the human–computer relationship if APACHE, used as a closed-loop system, determines that life support systems should be withdrawn from a patient, and then turns off the life support systems. In ending the patient's life the APACHE system projects a view of itself to the medical personnel and the patient's family as a purposeful decision maker (the second type of distortion). Simultaneously, the system allows the attending physician and critical care staff to distance or numb themselves from the decision making process about when to end another human's life (the first type of distortion).

Now, in actuality, at least some of the researchers developing APACHE do not recommend its use as a closed-loop system, but as a consultation system, one that recommends a course of action to a human user who may or may not choose to follow the recommendation (Chang et al., 1989). These researchers write: "Computer predications should never dictate clinical decisions, as very often there are many factors other than physiologic data to be considered when a decision to withdraw therapy is made." Thus, used as a consultation system, APACHE functions as a tool to aid the critical care staff with making difficult decisions about the withdrawal of therapy. Framed in this manner, the consultation system approach seems to avoid the distortions of human agency described above: The consultation system does not mimic purposeful action or inappropriately distance the medical staff from making decisions about human life and death.

In practice, however, the situation can be more complicated. Most human activity, including the decision by medical personnel to withdraw life support systems, occurs in a web of human relationships. In some circumstances, because a computational system is embedded in a complex social structure, human users may experience a diminished sense of moral agency. Let us imagine, for instance, that APACHE is used as a consultation system. With increasing use and continued good performance by APACHE, it is likely that the medical personnel using APACHE will develop increased trust in APACHE's recommendations. Over time, these recommendations will carry increasingly greater authority within the medical community. Within this social context, it may become the practice for critical care staff to act on APACHE's recommendations somewhat automatically, and increasingly difficult for even an experienced physician to challenge the "authority" of APACHE's recommendation, since to challenge APACHE would be to challenge the medical community. But at this point the open-loop consultation system through the social context has become, in effect, a closed-loop system wherein computer prediction dictates clinical decisions.

Such potential effects point to the need to design computational systems with an eye toward the larger social context, including long-term effects that may not become apparent until the technology is well situated in the social environment. Participatory design methods offer one such means (Ehn, 1989; Greenbaum & Kyng, 1990). Future users, who are experienced in their respective fields, are substantively involved in the design process. As noted at a recent conference (Namioka & Schuler, 1990), Thoreson worked with hospital nurses to design a computer-based record-keeping system. In the design process, nurses helped to define on a macro level what institutional problems the technology would seek to solve, and on a micro level how such technological solutions would be implemented. From the perspective of human agency, such participatory design lays the groundwork for users to see themselves as responsible for shaping the system's design and use.

Delegating Instruction to Computational Systems

Instructional technology programs that deliver systematically designed computer-based courseware to students can suffer from the first type of distortion–computer use that erodes the human user's sense of his or her own agency. Often absent from this type of instructional technology is a meaningful notion of the student's responsibility for learning. Johnsen and Taylor (1988 p. 9) have discussed this problem in a paper aptly titled "At Cross-purpose: Instructional Technology and the Erosion of Personal Responsibility." According to Johnsen and Taylor, instructional technology "define(s) responsibility operationally in the context of means/ends rationality. The singular responsibility for a student's education becomes identified with the success of the program." They further point to the logical conclusion of this educational view of students, parents, teachers, and government: failure to educate comes to mean that the instructional technology failed to teach, not that students failed to learn.

As an example of this type of instructional technology, consider how the GREATERP intelligent tutoring system described in Kass (1989) for novice programmers in LISP handles students' errors. When GREATERP determines the student has entered "incorrect" information, the tutor interrupts the student's progress toward the student's proposed solution (viable or not) and forces the student to backtrack to the intelligent tutor's "correct" solution. Thus GREATERP assumes responsibility not only for student learning but also for preventing student errors along the way and for the process of achieving a solution. In so doing, this intelligent tutoring system – and other comparable instructional technology programs – can undermine the student's sense of his or her own agency and responsibility for the educational endeavor.

In contrast, other educational uses of computing promote students' sense of agency and active decision making. For example, just as consultation systems can to some degree place responsibility for decision making on the human user, so educational uses of computer applications software (e.g., word processors, spreadsheets, databases, microcomputer-based labs) can place responsibility for learning on the student. With computer applications students determine when the applications would be useful and for what purposes, and evaluate the results of their use. Moreover, the social organization of school computer use can contribute to students' understanding of responsible computing. As with participatory design, consider the value of student participation in creating the policies that govern their own school computer use. For example, as discussed in a recent article by Friedman (1991), students can determine the privacy policy for their own electronic mail at school. To establish such a privacy policy, "students must draw on their fundamental understandings of privacy rights to develop specific policies for this new situation. In turn, circumstances like these provide opportunities for students not only to develop morally but to make decisions about a socially and computationally powerful technology, and thus to mitigate a belief held by many people that one is controlled by rather than in control of technology." Through such experiences, students can learn that humans determine how computer technology is used and that humans bear responsibility for the results of that use.

CONCLUSION

We argued initially that humans, but not computers (as they can be conceived today in material and structure), are or could be moral agents. Based on this view, we identified two broad approaches by which computer system design can promote responsible computer use. Each approach seeks to minimize a potential distortion between human agency and computer activity. First, computational systems should be designed in ways that do not denigrate the human user to machine-like status. Second, computational systems should be designed in ways that do not impersonate human agency by attempting to mimic intentional states. Both approaches seek to promote the human user's autonomous decision making in ways that are responsive to and informed by community and culture.

What we have provided, of course, are only broad approaches and design sketches. But if we are correct that human agency is central to most endeavors that seek to understand and promote responsible computing, then increased attention should be given to how the human user perceives specific types of human–computer interactions, and how human agency is constrained, promoted, or otherwise affected by the larger social environment. In such investigations, it is likely that research methods can draw substantively on existing methods employed in the social cognitive and moral-developmental psychological fields. Methods might include: (1) semistructured hypothetical interviews with participants about centrally relevant problems (Damon, 1977; Kohlberg, 1969; Piaget, 1929; Piaget, 1932; Turiel, 1983); (2) naturalistic and structured observations (DeVries & Goncu, 1987; Friedman, 1990; Nucci & Nucci, 1982); and (3) semistructured interviews based on observations of the participant's practice (DeVries, 1986; Nucci & Turiel, 1978; Saxe, 1990). Of note, some anthropologists (Suchman, 1987) and psychologists (Allen & Pea, 1990) working in the area of human factors have with some success incorporated aspects of these methods into their design practices.

A final word needs to be said about the role of moral psychology in the field of computer system design. As increasingly sophisticated computational systems have become embedded in social lives and societal practices, increasing pressure has been placed on the computing field to go beyond purely technical considerations and to promote responsible computing. In response, there has been, understandably, a desire to know the "right" answer to ethical problems that arise, where "right" is understood to mean something like "philosophically justified or grounded." We agree that there is an important place for philosophical analyses in the field. But philosophy seldom tells us how or why problems relevant to a philosophical position involving computing occur in practice, let alone what can most effectively resolve them. Such issues require empirical data that deal substantively with the psychological reality of humans. Thus, by linking our technical pursuits with both philosophical inquiry and moral-psychological research, responsible computing can be enhanced as a shared vision and practice within the computing community.

REFERENCES

Allen, C., and R. Pea. Reciprocal Evolution of Research, Work Practices and Technology. In *Proceedings from the Conference on Participatory Design*, eds. A. Namioka and D. Schuler. 1990. Palo Alto, CA: Computer Professionals for Social Responsibility.

Bednarski, P., F. Siclari, A. Voigt, S. Demertzis, and G. Lau. 1990. Use of a Computerized Closed-loop Sodium Nitro-prusside Titration System for Antihypertensive Treatment After Open Heart Surgery. *Critical Care Medicine* 18:1061–1065.

Chang, R. W. S., B. Lee, S. Jacobs, and B. Lee. 1989. Accuracy of Decisions to Withdraw Therapy in Critically Ill Patients: Clinical Judgment Versus a Computer Model. *Critical Care Medicine* 17:1091–1097.

Churchland, P.M., and P.S. Churchland. 1990. Could a Machine Think? *Scientific American* 262:26–31.

Damon, W. 1977. *The Social World of the Child.* San Francisco: Jossey-Bass.

DeVries, R. 1986. Children's Conceptions of Shadow Phenomena. *General Social General Psychology Monographs* 112:479–530.

DeVries, R., and A. Goncu. 1987. Interpersonal Relations in Four-year Dyads from Constructivist and Montesorri Programs. *Journal of Applied Developmental Psychology* 8:481–501.

Eberts, R.E., and C.G. Eberts. 1989. Four Approaches to Human Computer Interaction. In *Intelligent Interfaces: Theory, Research and Design*, eds. P.A. Hancock and M.H. Chignell. New York: Elsevier Science Publishers.

Ehn, P. 1989. *Work-Oriented Design of Computer Artifacts.* Hillsdale, NJ: Lawrence Erlbaum Associates.

Friedman, B. 1990. Societal Issues and School Practices: An Ethnographic Investigation of the Social Context of School Computer Use. Paper presented at the Annual Meeting of the American Educational Research Association, Boston. (ERIC Document Reproduction Service NO. ED 321 740).

Friedman, B. 1991. Social and Moral Development through Computer Use: A Constructivist Approach. *Journal of Research in Computer Education* 23:560–567.

Greenbaum, J., and M. Kyng, eds. 1990. *Design at Work: Cooperative Design of Computer Systems.* Hillsdale, NJ: Lawrence Erlbaum Associates.

Harris, C.L., et al. 1989. Office Automation: Making it Pay Off. In *Computers in the Human Context: Information Technology, Productivity, and People*, ed. T. Forester. Cambridge, MA: The MIT Press.

Jacob, R.J.K. 1989. Direct Manipulation in the Intelligent Interface. In *Intelligent Interfaces: Theory, Research and Design*, eds. P.A. Hancock and M.H. Chignell. New York: Elsevier Science Publishers.

Jenkins, J. P. 1984. An Application of an Expert System to Problem Solving in Process Control Displays. In *Human-Computer Interaction*, ed. G. Salvendy. New York: Elsevier Science Publishers.

Johnsen, J.B., and W.D. Taylor. 1988. At Cross-Purpose: Instructional Technology and the Erosion of Personal Responsibility. Paper presented at the Annual Meeting of the American Educational Research Association, New Orleans.

Kass, R. 1989. Student Modeling in Intelligent Tutoring Systems – Implications for User Modeling. In *User Models in Dialog Systems*, eds. A. Kobsa and W. Wahlster. New York: Springer-Verlag.

Kohlberg, L. 1969. Stage and Sequence: The Cognitive-developmental Approach to Socialization. In *Handbook of Socialization Theory and Research*, ed. D. A. Goslin. Chicago: Rand-McNally.

McCarthy, J. 1979. Ascribing Mental Qualities to Machines. In *Philosophical Perspectives on Artificial Intelligence*, ed. M. Ringle. Needham Heights, MA: Humanities Press.

McKinley, S., J.F. Cade, R. Siganporia, O.M. Evans, D.G. Mason, and J.S. Packer. 1991. Clinical Evaluation of Closed-loop Control of Blood Pressure in Seriously Ill Patients. *Critical Care Medicine* 19:166–170.

Namioka, A., and D. Schuler, eds. 1990. *Proceedings from the Conference on Participatory Design* 1990. Palo Alto, CA: Computer Professionals for Social Responsibility.

Nucci, L.P., and E. Turiel. 1978. Social Interactions and the Development of Social Concepts in Preschool Children. *Child Development* 49:400–407.

Nucci, L.P., and M. Nucci. 1982. Children's Responses to Moral and Social Conventional Transgressions in Free-Play Settings. *Child Developement* 53:1337–1342.

Piaget, J. 1929. *The Child's Conception of the World*. London: Routledge & Kegan Paul.

Piaget, J. 1932. *The Moral Judgment of the Child*. London: Routledge & Kegan Paul.

Rumelhart, D.E., and D.A. Norman. 1981. Analogical Processes in Learning. In *Cognitive Skills and Their Acquisition*, ed. J.R. Anderson. Hillsdale, NJ: Lawrence Erlbaum Associates.

Saxe, G.B. 1990. *Culture and Cognitive Development: Studies in Mathematical Understanding*. Hillsdale, NJ: Lawrence Erlbaum Press.

Scott, G.E. 1990. *Moral Personhood: An Essay in the Philosophy of Moral Psychology*, Albany, NY: State University of New York Press.

Searle, J.R. 1980. Minds, Brains and Programs. *Behavioral Brain Science* 3:417–458.

Searle, J.R. 1983. *Intentionality*. Cambridge, UK: Cambridge University Press.

Searle, J.R. 1990. Is the Brain's Mind a Computer Program? *Scientific American* 262:26–31.

Shneidermann, B. 1987. *Designing the User Interface: Strategies for Effective Human-Computer Interaction.* Reading, MA: Addison-Wesley Publishing Company.

Shneidermann, B. 1989. Designing the User Interface. In *Computers in the Human Context: Information Technology, Productivity, and People,* ed. T. Forester. Cambridge, MA: The MIT Press.

Shortliffe, E.H. 1983. Medical Consultation Systems: Designing for Doctors. In *Designing for Human-Computer Communication,* eds. M.E. Sime and M.J. Coombs. New York: Academic Press.

Smith, D.C., C. Irby, R. Kimball, W. Verplank, and E. Marslem. Designing the User Interface. *Byte* 7:242–282.

Snapper, J.W. 1985. Responsibility for Computer-based Errors. *Metaphilosophy* 16:289–295.

Suchman, L.A. 1987. *Plans and Situated Actions: The Problem of Human-Machine Communication.* Cambridge, UK: Cambridge University Press.

Turiel, E. 1983. *The Development of Social Knowledge: Morality and Convention.* Cambridge, UK: Cambridge University Press.

Turkle, S. 1984. *The Second Self: Computers and the Human Spirit.* New York: Simon & Schuster.

Weizenbaum, J. 1976. *Computer Power and Human Reason.* NewYork: W. H. Freeman & Company.

Winograd, T., and F. Flores. 1986. *Understanding Computers and Cognition: A New Foundation for Design.* Reading, MA: Addison-Wesley Publishing Company.

Zimmerman, J.E. ed. 1989. APACHE III Study Design: Analytic Plan for Evaluation of Severity and Outcome. *Critical Care Medicine* 17 (part 2 Suppl), S169–S221.

Zuboff, A. 1981. The Story of the Brain. In D. R. Hofstadter and D.C. Dennett eds., *The Mind's I.* New York: Basic Books, Inc.

PART III

Practicing Value-Sensitive Design

14

Workplace Database Systems: Difficulties of Data Collection and Presentation

HARRY HOCHHEISER

Abstract: Software systems that track worker activity may adversely affect working environments, yet these databases may be an appropriate means of reaching legitimate institutional goals. Conflicts such as these present significant difficulties for software developers. This case study – loosely aligned with participatory design – describes the development of a medical device repair database in a large urban hospital. I first introduce the project's history and goals. Then I discuss four concerns that emerged regarding the system's potential impact on the work force and the overall success of the database: (1) comparison between employees, (2) employee perceptions, (3) inaccurate measurements, and (4) inappropriate interpretation of data. I also highlight factors affecting the developer's ability to address these concerns. Based on this case study, I offer alternative database designs which seek to balance technical requirements with human values such as protection of individual privacy and accountability.

The introduction of computer systems that track workers is likely to cause significant changes in a workplace (Agre, 1994). The nature of these changes will be determined by the types of data collected and the ways in which these data will be used. Ideally, databases provide workers and management with increased understanding of work processes. This knowledge might help to improve productivity or increase workers' control over their environment. However, these systems might also be used to scrutinize workers or provide justification for restructuring of work environments, schedules, and practices. In certain cases, these changes might decrease workers' autonomy, in a manner that can be frustrating and demoralizing (Bravo, 1993). In other cases, workplace data may be collected primarily for regulatory or bureaucratic reasons.

The practical impact of a database system is determined by a variety of factors, including organizational context, system design, and worker-management relations. Although interpersonal and political issues may be beyond the control of software developers, software design techniques may be used to encourage certain applications of the data while discouraging others. In particular, technical decisions made during system specification and development can

Many thanks to Batya Friedman, for inviting this submission and patiently reading the various revisions. Thanks to Randall Trigg, for suggesting an alternative to the "two databases" approach, and to Phil Agre, for his suggestions. Thanks to the folks at "LUH," including both management and technicians, for their feedback on this article, and for providing an environment that helped me learn about these issues firsthand. Finally, thanks to Judy.

constrain the ways in which databases will be used or abused. Consequently, concerns about the human impact of technology can complicate the difficult task of building software systems. This article discusses the development of a database system in a hospital as a case study in the organizational and technical difficulties presented by workplace data collection and presentation systems.

EQUIP: A DATABASE FOR PORTABLE MEDICAL DEVICE MAINTENANCE

Project Background

Management of portable medical equipment has historically been a problem for many hospitals. Equipment such as patient care monitors and infusion pumps must be repaired, maintained, and periodically tested for proper performance. Regulatory agencies require detailed documentation of all device repair and testing efforts. These obligations present challenges to the hospital organizations responsible for management of patient care devices. Administrators frequently use commercial and custom-built equipment databases to maintain inventory and to track device repair work.

This chapter describes an equipment management database developed at LUH (a pseudonym), a large, academic hospital in a major city in the northeastern United States. At LUH, the department of Clinical Engineering (CE) is responsible for repair and maintenance of portable medical equipment. This work is done by a team of trained, nonunionized technicians. In the past, device repair efforts were tracked through the use of MS DOS text-based databases. CE employed an individual responsible for general database upkeep, as well as one or more members of the support staff who assisted with data entry. These systems were generally difficult to use, requiring significant effort for data entry and manipulation. Furthermore, frequent crashes and inconsistent data limited the utility of these packages.

In 1990, CE decided to move to a new, more powerful system. This database – nicknamed Equip – would provide a graphical user interface based on Microsoft Windows. From the start, Equip was designed to play an important role in the device repair efforts of CE technicians. Whereas data entry personnel and department management were responsible for most of the data entry for the older databases, technicians would interact directly with Equip, using new workstations that would be located throughout the device repair shops.

Equip would also add detailed reports and purchasing facilities not found in the older databases.

After evaluating existing commercial products, CE management decided to develop a database system in-house. Microsoft Access was chosen as the development platform, and implementation of the new system began in the spring of 1993. I was the primary system developer for a significant portion of the development of Equip.

Specification, implementation, and deployment of Equip was directed by a department task force, consisting of as many as ten individuals. This group included management personnel responsible for Equipment maintenance, technical supervisors, technicians, and a software engineer (myself), responsible for system development. The task force used these meetings to discuss the system requirements and specifications. As a software developer, I was limited in my ability to influence decisions regarding basic features and capabilities of Equip. However, I had considerable influence over decisions regarding details related to system implementation. In addition to assisting with the writing of specifications, I was responsible for implementation of functionality, testing of components, and system integration.

When I began working on Equip, system design had been underway for several months. Basic requirements had been determined, several specification documents had been written, and a working prototype of the system had been implemented. Despite several problems, including an unnecessarily complicated design, this prototype was used as the starting point for further development. A completely rewritten system might have been technically preferable, but this possibility was ruled out due to deadline pressures. The working prototype also provided the basis for expectations regarding eventual system performance. These expectations limited my ability to affect significant changes to the overall system design.

The working environment at CE played a significant role in the structure of the database project. Management and workers seemed to work together fairly well, and personal interactions throughout the department were generally informal. Regular contact with the technicians and management personnel who would be using the equipment database provided me with a basic understanding of their work, and of the impact that the database would have upon equipment maintenance efforts. The casual atmosphere also proved useful for system design and testing, as I frequently asked technicians to test and critique proposed system components and interface designs.

SYSTEM GOALS

Equip was designed to be a tool for technicians. The outgoing MS DOS systems were used in a data entry model. Technicians used written forms to describe device repair and maintenance work, and these forms were submitted to support personnel for entry into the database. This process was inefficient, as it led to bottlenecks in both data entry and retrieval. The new database provides a Windows interface in a departmental network which includes shared workstations at the technicians' workbenches. These computers allow technicians to enter and retrieve data as needed, providing them with direct access to repair records. Answers to questions such as "Wasn't this pump repaired just last week?" or "What sorts of problems have other technicians found with this type of monitor?" can be used to increase the technician's ability to effectively do his job.

Equip also provides needed documentation of the work done by CE technicians. LUH, like other hospitals, is operating during a time of increased uncertainty, and the equipment database was developed to gauge and justify the level of resources allocated to the department. By documenting the amount of work done and the effectiveness with which the work was done, the equipment database serves as a defense against efforts to trim the department's budget through reductions in staff. Reports involving long-term analysis of work data are needed for the department's reengineering projects, which attempt to increase productivity through reorganization of work.

Finally, Equip is used to track data needed for regulatory and administrative purposes. The hospital accreditation organization, the Joint Committee of American Hospital Organizations, requires detailed records of preventative maintenance efforts: if devices have not been tested according to schedule, or if these efforts are not appropriately documented, problems can occur during the accreditation process. Equip also tracks information necessary for internal accounting purposes. Since CE provides services to the rest of LUH on a fee-for-service basis, device repair and maintenance records, which include records of time and supplies used in completion of a task, provide data necessary for billing in-house customers.

Database Contents

The primary function of hospital equipment databases in general, and Equip in particular, is to provide detailed records of the work done by the technicians responsible for maintenance of portable medical devices. These records are based on a comprehensive and accurate inventory, containing an entry for every device that might be serviced. The main data unit in Equip is the work order, which describes the device involved, the work done, the technician(s) who did the work, and the resources (time and components) used in performing the repair or maintenance. Data entry efforts are also recorded, through fields used to indicate the names of the individuals who initiated and completed the work order. Technicians and management can access stored work orders through searching facilities, which allow users to find work orders according to particular devices, date of work, or responsible technician.

Equip is also used to track technician efforts. Each work order has fields containing the names of the individuals who performed the repair or maintenance, along with the number of hours worked, and the dates on which those hours were worked. A separate component of Equip provides facilities for recording the time spent on activities such as training, departmental meetings, and other "overhead" activities. Equip also includes tools for inventory management and general database maintenance. A simple security system is used to discourage unauthorized data access.

Much of the work done by CE technicians involves regularly scheduled preventative maintenance (PM) of medical devices. Technicians use reports known as "PM schedules" to determine workloads and priorities. These reports are generated by comparing previous maintenance dates against required intervals, to identify devices that need to be inspected. This list can be divided according to a type of device, location in the hospital, or group of technicians responsible for the work. Once a PM schedule is generated, it becomes a worksheet for technicians.

Progress of these testing efforts can be tracked through compliance reports, which summarize the percentages of devices that have been tested within the appropriate interval. These percentages are used to measure the department's success, and Equip's reporting facilities provide users with the ability to view compliance rates across a variety of factors, such as device type or owner.

Given the evolutionary nature of the system development, the reporting facilities are neither frozen nor complete. Individuals in the department responsible for equipment maintenance generate a steady stream of requests for additional reports, aimed at providing additional perspectives on the data. These requests cannot be met as stated: the development expense would be too great. Instead, individuals needing additional reporting facilities have been provided with copies of the raw data tables underlying the database. This gives them the ability to generate their own reports, using user-friendly reporting facilities found in Microsoft Access. It was hoped that these reports would be used to document the department's successes, while identifying areas needing improvement.

SYSTEM IMPACT: OPPORTUNITIES AND CONCERNS

It was clear that this database would have a significant impact upon the department's working environment. Whereas support personnel conducted most interactions with the older databases, technicians would use new workstations to interact directly with Equip. Furthermore, Equip included time sheet data entry facilities, which would automate the previously paper-based system of tracking technicians' hours. These changes seemed likely to have a major impact upon workplace dynamics. Expectations of such changes could clearly be discerned in conversations with technicians, who spoke enthusiastically about working with the new system.

The consequences of Equip may be cause for concern. The database might be used to improve the inner workings of the department, or it might be used to justify increased demands upon technicians. These potential applications of the database may lead to problems for system design and use, because the workers' perceptions of the objectives behind the database system can determine the system's success or failure.

Opportunities

Equip was designed to provide technicians with access to information that could be used to improve device repair and maintenance efforts. In particular, the work order data stored in Equip describes all of the repairs and inspections conducted by CE technicians. Using database workstations located throughout the device repair shops, technicians can use the work order database to provide greater understanding of their work. This contextual data could lead to improvements in the efficiency and quality of device repair and maintenance.

Work orders can also be used to analyze the operations of the department as a whole. By examining records detailing the type of work done, time required to do the work, patterns in distribution of work, and other factors, technicians and management might work together to improve the operations of the department. Potential benefits from this knowledge include restructuring of work assignments, identification of inefficiencies, identification of technicians in need of increased training, and documentation in support of requests for additional resources (personnel and equipment).

Concerns and Consequences

Despite these beneficial applications, problems may arise from the use of any database. These difficulties may not be based in the technical details of the database, as the practical impact of the workplace database may be determined by organizational factors. Potential problems, and their impact upon the success of the database, can be seen in four areas of concern encountered during the development of Equip:

- Comparison between workers
- Employee perceptions
- Inaccurate measurements
- and the Influence of computers

Comparisons Between Workers: Work order and time-tracking data might be used to rate technicians relative to each other, or against some predefined performance goals (e.g., average time spent on a work order). Although these comparisons may be used for legitimate purposes, such as identifying technicians who are having difficulty with certain types of work, ratings might be used to pressure employees to work harder. Alternatively, ratings used for comparison between workers might foster competition, which might cause workplace morale to suffer considerably (Bravo, 1993).

At LUH, generally constructive relations between workers and management made abuses unlikely in the short term. However, future changes in department or hospital management might lead to increased pressure for potentially harmful interpretations of existing data. For example, the system might be used by higher-level hospital management or independent auditors hired by hospital management to provide evaluations and guidance for downsizing. Conducted properly, such applications may be entirely appropriate. However, analyses conducted by outside parties may have a greater likelihood of being inaccurate or taken out of context.

The generation and use of reports involving direct comparison between technicians provide an example of the influence of management attitudes. Since Equip was designed as a tool for technicians, reports involving comparison between individuals were not included in the original database design. However, such comparisons were generated when management was faced with concerns regarding unsatisfactory output of a particular technician. In dealing with this individual, custom reports based on data from Equip were used to provide quantitative descriptions of the problem. Management and the technician used these reports to provide a concrete basis for discussion of the problem and identification of potential solutions. In other situations, a less concerned management team might have used this data to argue for the technician's dismissal.

Employee Perceptions: Despite management's good intentions, CE technicians may have legitimate concerns about the impact that Equip would have on their working environment. The technicians are mostly enthusiastic about Equip, but worries about job security may lead to reservations. Concerns of this sort are potentially troublesome, since the technicians' perceptions of the goals of the database may have a profound effect upon the system's success or failure.

In particular, if technicians believe that the database might be used to undermine their job security or otherwise detract from their working environment, they may become inclined to report inaccurate data to insure that their efforts will be interpreted in a favorable manner. For example, the members of the Equip development team generally assumed that technicians would tend to enter a full forty hour work week into their time sheets, regardless of whether or not this was accurate. Although this was not seen as a problem for time sheet data, similar interpretations of work order data could compromise the integrity of the system. For example, inaccurate work order data could lead to problems such as decreased device performance and safety or a lack of data necessary for accreditation reviews.

Perceptions of the database system might also lead technicians to adjust their working style. Continuing emphasis on compliance percentages might motivate some individuals to focus on compliance testing at the expense of device repair. Although technicians might feel that this would cause their work to be interpreted favorably, this approach is almost certainly not desirable for the department as a whole. The use of a database does not necessarily lead to an increase of this sort of behavior, which has always been a problem at LUH.

Inaccurate Measurements: The use of the compliance percentage as a performance indicator provides an incomplete picture of the department's output. Simply counting the number of devices tested does not provide an accurate measure of the work being done, as devices have largely differing testing requirements. For example, a portable infusion pump is significantly simpler to test than a dialysis filtration unit. Furthermore, the compliance percentage does not describe the total output of the technical staff, as activities other than performance testing are not included in the compliance rate. These activities, which include device repair, training, and meetings, constitute an important component of the department's work. This potentially inaccurate metric becomes dangerous when used to evaluate the work done in the department. In particular, decisions relating to allocation of resources, structuring of responsibility, and other procedural matters may run into difficulties if they are based on incomplete models.

Despite these shortcomings, compliance percentage is likely to remain an important part of Equip. Accreditation regulations require reporting of compliance percentages, and appropriate alternative metrics are neither obvious nor straightforward. In general, any single measurement is likely to suffer from similar problems of oversimplification and potential misinterpretation. A more comprehensive, multidimensional description of the department's efforts might provide increased accuracy and reliability, but this improvement might lead to increased software development costs and complexity of interpretation. Furthermore, any alternatives would require significant changes to the management of CE's device maintenance efforts.

Influence of Computers: The potential for inappropriate data interpretation may be increased by the use of a computer database system. Equip allows the users to create attractive reports, which provide a powerful and compelling picture that may seem beyond reproach. This becomes a particular problem in environments such as LUH, where the technicians and management staff seemed to be very enthusiastic about the system. In the context of such optimism, it may be hard to question the validity of the details of data analyses, as such questions might be seen as challenging the database system as a whole.

The choices of development environment and operating system are particularly relevant for these concerns. Traditional database platforms, such as the MS-DOS-based environment used for the previous equipment databases, are often complicated and cumbersome environments that require the skills of a database professional for creation of queries and reports. Microsoft Access simplifies database development and management by providing visual querying and reporting facilities within the context of the simpler Windows interface, which provides the ability to generate additional and alternative interpretations of the data to members of support and administrative staff, who are not database experts. This increased ease of use simplifies both constructive and abusive interpretations of the work order data.

THE DEVELOPER'S ROLE IN BUILDING A SUCCESSFUL
WORKPLACE DATABASE

As the primary technical expert on a database development project, the software developer may have significant control over decisions regarding data layout, presentation, interpretation, and access. These decisions may play a role in determining the human impact of the database system. With proper understanding of the context and potential impact of a workplace database system, software developers might be able to revise specifications or system goals to account for issues such as worker perceptions, problems of interpretation, or potential system abuses. Although developers who simply implement specifications may not be able to change the design of a software system, others might have significant influence.

Explicit consideration of workplace impact concerns might have a significant impact upon the ultimate success or failure of the workplace database. However, successfully addressing these issues is not easy. Two types of efforts are required: organizational efforts to build support for consideration of human impact; and technical efforts for good system design. As with other elements of the software development process, these efforts may be iterative and more difficult than originally envisioned.

Organizational Issues

Databases such as Equip are designed to take a systematic approach towards providing desired functionality. The goals behind the system may determine the developer's ability to account for human impact concerns. For example, Equip was designed as a tool for technicians. This focus on the technicians may provide greater opportunity for including consideration of workplace impact into system design and implementation. Whenever possible, these issues should be explicitly included in discussions regarding system specification and design. Given the frequency with which software development efforts fail to meet their stated goals, it may be difficult for developers to account for human impact concerns that are not included in the software requirements (Shneiderman & Rose, 1997).

Unfortunately, it may be difficult or impossible for developers to argue convincingly for inclusion of these requirements. As is the case with Equip, potential violations of worker privacy or autonomy are not necessarily obvious. Concerned software developers might be sensitive to the differences between the intended uses and the actual uses of software systems, but customers and clients tend to think that software will be used only as originally planned. In such cases, the developer faces the challenge of presenting a compelling description of potential problems based on actual (as opposed to intended) uses of the system, along with acceptable solutions.

Developers may not be able to effectively argue in favor of system designs that require changes in the operations of an organization. In order to succeed, these arguments must overcome a variety of forces, such as institutional inertia and external requirements. At LUH, institutional practices and regulatory requirements provide strong arguments in favor of continued use of preventative maintenance compliance rates as a metric for the success of CE's technical staff, despite any potential problems or inaccuracies. Even in the absence of external factors such as regulating authorities, developers may not be able to affect changes in established organizational practice.

The developer's ability to influence system design might be further limited by power and authority concerns. Software systems are often built at the request of management, in order to meet management goals. Efforts aimed at modifying designs to suit the needs of workers might be seen as threatening to management (Greenbaum, 1993). In such cases, the system developer's personal interests may play a role, as there may be an unwillingness to challenge the authority of the managers who may wield power over the developer's continued employment and professional growth.

Finally, the cost and scheduling of software development can further complicate matters. Software development projects are notorious for being over budget and behind schedule. Design features aimed at preventing abuses of a database might add cost and delay system delivery. If these features are not directly related to the primary goal of a software system, these additional costs might be seen as inappropriate and unacceptable.

Design Issues

In providing opportunities for both constructive use and inappropriate abuse, databases such as Equip present developers with the challenge of building systems that show respect for workers without sacrificing crucial functionality. As with other tradeoffs in software development, this tension between worker's rights and legitimate management goals is not easily eliminated. A concerned developer might use creative system design to achieve a balance between these competing priorities: An example of this approach can be seen in Equip's handling of data related to individual technicians.

Individual Data

Equip contains detailed information about the activities of each individual technician. Work orders include the names of each of the technicians who participated in completion of the given task (including data entry), and time sheets categorize time spent by each technician on various tasks. Work orders also collect data regarding groups of technicians, through data entry fields indicating the group of technicians responsible for each work order.

Although individual data is collected and stored in the database, it is not always used. The two main database reports – preventative maintenance schedules and compliance reports – do not use individual names. The basic system design includes these reports for groups of technicians, but not for individuals. Other database components, such as time sheets, make more direct use of individual data.

Collection of data regarding individual performance raises some interesting challenges. Inclusion of this data opens the door for potential abuse, but total exclusion of this information eliminates useful database applications. Fortunately, there are intermediate solutions. Since individual data is not necessary for much of the core functionality, it may be possible to provide limited access to this data in a manner that would maximize system utility while minimizing the potential for harm.

Separation of Data Type from Data Presentation

Designs aimed at addressing this situation can be divided into several categories, as summarized in Table 1. These alternatives consider the data collected as separable from the data presented, allowing for a range of options that vary along several dimensions, such as functionality, usability, protection of individual privacy, accountability, and relative development cost. *Accountability* is defined as the extent to which an individual can be held responsible for his actions.

Individual Data: All data is stored in one common database, providing easy access. Information on work completed by each employee provides the basis for extensive reporting on individual workers. Since individual data is readily accessible, this solution provides no protections for individual rights and technicians are completely accountable for their actions.

Individual Data with Security: Two databases are used: one containing work order data without individual information; and a second, used to link techni-

Table 1: Possible Approaches to Storage of Individual Data

Type of Database	Functionality	Usability	Protection of Individual Privacy and Anonymity	Accountability	Relative Development Cost
Individual Data	Extensive	Easy to Use	None	Complete	Moderate
Individual Data with Security	Extensive	Somewhat Constrained	Minimal protection through access restrictions	Complete	High
Individual Data with Group Reporting	Somewhat limited: reports on groups of workers; individual data available, but not easily available	Easy to Use	Some protection through lack of reports on individual workers	Incomplete for individuals: data exists but is not readily available	Moderate
Individual Data with Equal Access	Extensive	Easy to Use	No protection but workers can use data to protect themselves	Complete	Moderate for development but higher training costs
Group Data	More limited: reports and data on individuals unavailable	Easy to Use	Significant protection through elimination of individual data	None for individual: only for group as a whole	Moderate
Aggregate Data	No individual or group reporting available	Easy to Use	Well protected: no links between workers and work done	None	Low

cians to work order and time sheet information. Core functions, such as PM scheduling and compliance tracking, can be performed entirely within the first database. The second database would provide authorized users with access to reports involving individual technicians. Security mechanisms used to restrict access to the second database might deter inappropriate or harmful uses of the data.

This approach provides all of the functionality and accountability found in the first solution, with reduced ease of use caused by the security restrictions. These restrictions provide some protection of individual rights, but this protection is not extensive. Increased development cost is a potential drawback to this approach, as development of two separate database structures, along with additional security measures, will be more expensive than a simpler one-database system. A variation of this approach might provide workers with greater protection from management by providing the workers with control of the database containing individual data.

Individual Data with Group Reporting: Individual data is collected and stored in the database, but summary reporting facilities are limited to groups of technicians. This is the alternative that is used in Equip. The lack of individual reports provides some privacy and anonymity, at the expense of somewhat constrained functionality. For example, users of Equip can identify the technician responsible for a given work order, but a tool for automatically generating summary listings of all of a technician's work orders is not provided. If necessary, such summary listings can be generated through special-purpose reports. Although these reports might constitute an invasion of a worker's privacy, they might also be used as legitimate tools for determining accountability.

Individual Data with Equal Access: Individual information is collected, and workers and management are provided with access to all of the data in the database. This variation includes an explicit commitment to providing workers with data access. This may require providing workers with training that would allow them to generate their own data reports and analyses. These alternative interpretations might be used by workers to improve their understanding of their work, or as a proactive defense against database abuses by management.

Group Data: Individual data is completely eliminated, in favor of work order and time sheet data tied to groups of individuals. This option involves reduced functionality and accountability, as reports can be generated only on groups of technicians. The elimination of individual reports leads to a significant increase in protection of individual privacy and accountability. Usability and relative development cost should be comparable to that of the "Individual Data" solution.

Aggregate Data: Work order data are collected without any indication of the individual or the group responsible for the work. Since work is not attributed to any individuals, this approach offers no accountability, but does provide extensive protection of individual privacy. However, data related to individuals or to groups are eliminated, so functionality is significantly reduced. This simpler approach should be less expensive to develop and easier to use.

Discussion

These models represent several possible designs for workplace databases containing potentially sensitive data. The model chosen for a particular database will be dependent upon a variety of factors, including the context in which it will be used, the resources available for development, and the relations between management and workers. Furthermore, it should be clear that the above approaches are not exhaustive.

   The *individual data* model, which provides complete access to data on individual technicians, can be taken as a baseline for evaluation of the other approaches. In comparison to that model, each alternative design attempts to provide greater protection of worker privacy or accountability. These designs use three mechanisms to achieve this improved protection:

- Limited data presentation tools
- Guaranteed access to data
- and Restrictions on data collected

Limited data presentation tools: Designs that limit the tools used to interpret data can constrain the uses and abuses of those data. In the *group reporting* model, data interpretation and reporting tools are limited to those which present data on groups of employees. Reports on individual technicians, or which compare workers, are not provided. This lack of support for individual reports protects workers by discouraging potentially harmful applications of the database.

   The *individual data with security* design uses security restrictions that serve as a pragmatic barrier that hinders access to sensitive data. In this instance, security restrictions act as "inefficiencies" that increase the difficulty of retrieving data, without eliminating it (Friedman, 1996). Although incomplete, these obstacles might reduce the negative impact of individual data.

Privacy in this model could be increased by placing the database containing individual data under the control of the workers. This would allow workers to limit access to any information that might be harmful or invasive. If increased worker control leads to a greater feeling of security, workers may not feel the need to manipulate data entry in order to generate a favorable description of their work. This model might be most appropriate for unionized workplaces or other environments with existing structures for relations between workers and management. However, management might find this alternative unacceptable, as it reduces management control over the data. Furthermore, development costs may be higher, due to the increased complexity of the system design.

Guaranteed Access to Data: Any system that is primarily focused on providing data access to management can be abused. The *individual data with equal access* approach attempts to address this issue by providing workers and management with equal access to the data. Workers would be provided with software tools and training necessary for generation of their own interpretations of the workplace data. These alternative viewpoints could be used by workers to defend themselves against possible abuses of the database. This ability to "keep the bosses honest" might serve as a guarantee of individual privacy and autonomy. The cost of training workers in database systems may make this alternative unattractive. However, this training may provide unexpected benefits, as workers might begin to use the database to better understand and to improve their work.

Restrictions on Data Collected: Data cannot be misinterpreted or abused if it is never collected. The *group data* and *aggregate data* models protect workers by eliminating individual data entirely. In these models, work orders and time sheet entries would be either linked to group membership, or totally anonymous. Without individual data, individual workers, or groups of workers (in the aggregate model), cannot be compared.

These models also limit potentially constructive applications of the database. Improvements based on individual data will not be possible when using a database based on group or aggregate data. For organizations that need some form of individual data, group or aggregate data will not be sufficient. Similarly, group data may not be appropriate for workplaces that do not have preexisting groupings of workers.

As long as individual data is collected, restrictions on data use may be incomplete. Security measures or a lack of reporting tools are unlikely to deter persistent management from accessing data. Motivated management personnel may use monetary resources or organizational pressure to overcome these barriers. In extreme cases, the mere existence of the database may present a problem, as higher-level management or independent auditors might demand access to individual data (Rule, McAdam, Stearns & Uglow, 1980).

Of course, protection of individual interests might not be a goal shared by management personnel working on a given project. For example, managers interested in increased control over workers might try to build databases that would provide detailed accountability information (Clement & Gotlieb, 1988). In such cases, developers may be unable to argue for collection of group or aggregate data.

The choice of model used in a database is a complicated tradeoff involving several competing factors. Designs that increase complexity or cost require justification; in the absence of concrete risk, these alternatives may seem unnecessarily complicated. Developers faced with these decisions must strike a balance between the human values issues described above and the design requirements of the software development project.

RESOLUTIONS

Equip was built using the "individual data, group reporting" model. Rudimentary security measures limit access to certain components of the database, and reporting facilities are limited to groups of workers. Information regarding individual technicians is available, but harder to access. Due to time constraints, to development schedule pressures, and to expectations based upon existing database systems, alternative designs were not discussed in any detail. Given the seemingly low risk of inappropriate uses of the database, this design seemed appropriate. A wider range of alternatives might have been discussed if issues of human impact had been raised earlier in the specification and development process.

The timing of my involvement with the development Equip limited my ability to influence the system design. Ideally, human impact concerns should be considered throughout the development of system goals and specifications. However, system development was well underway when I began working on the database in the fall of 1993. At that point in time, specifications had been written, and a working prototype had been implemented. These established products of the development process, along with deadline pressures for installation of the system, precluded any major revisions to the existing specifications.

Management attitudes towards Equip minimized the need for significant revisions to the system design. The management of CE was well aware of the difficulties of accurate data interpretation and the potential dangers of workplace databases. This awareness seemed to decrease the danger of inappropriate uses of the work order data.

Both technicians and management at LUH anticipated that Equip would improve the understanding of device repair within the department. Given this optimism, any arguments for revising the design in order to protect workers' dignity would have required convincing the involved parties of the existence of potential dangers. This might have been accomplished through group discussions based on extreme situations. For example, technicians might examine the impact of Equip in the presence of department management personnel concerned only with cutting costs and reducing payroll. Alternatively, management might consider the impact of malicious or dishonest workers who might embellish data input to meet their own agenda. Such discussions might have provided both technicians and workers with a better understanding of the impact of Equip.

Ironically, the generally positive relationship between technicians and management at LUH may have increased the difficulties of addressing potential adverse impacts of Equip. In a contentious environment, workers and management might be more worried about the possibility of abuse or manipulation of the database. Developers might use this increased concern as an argument for design modifications aimed at addressing these problems. In these situations, hostile relations between management and workers may provide greater opportunities for designing systems that protect workers' rights and dignity.

CONCLUSIONS

In addressing design questions regarding the types of data collected and the facilities used to interpret those data, software developers play an important role in determining the human consequences of workplace database systems. Developers interested in minimizing any harmful repercussions of their work are faced with the challenge of identifying difficulties involved with planned and potential uses of their software and with effectively communicating these issues to the clients and customers driving system development.

Much of this challenge is related to educating customers, clients, and users about the fluid nature of software and data. Software developers are familiar with the ease with which data can be shaped and manipulated to meet a wide variety of ends, and how these interpretations may vary over the lifetime of a software system. By educating customers and users about the evolving nature of software and data, developers might be able to build support for system designs that attempt to protect affected workers. These efforts may not be comprehensive, but workers and management will benefit from a greater understanding of the impact of these database systems.

The development of the equipment database at LUH provides an example of the difficulties involved with addressing these issues once the basic system requirements have been determined. To avoid these obstacles, developers should stress the importance of raising questions of human values early in the course of system specification and design. Subsequent development, testing, and support efforts should return to these questions, in order to account for changes in system design or broader organizational context.

Examination of workplace dynamics, system goals, and potential uses and abuses of worker activity data requires investigation and inquiry that extend far beyond the traditional limits of software development work. This combination of intangible factors presents a daunting task for the software developer. However, examination of these issues is not without rewards: a careful understanding of the environment within which a database will be used, and the ways in which it will be used, will provide the developer with the perspective necessary for the development of software that will meet appropriate goals while respecting the needs of both management and workers.

REFERENCES

Agre, P. 1994. Surveillance and Capture: Two Models of Privacy, *The Information Society*. 10:2, 101.

Bravo, E. 1993. The Hazards of Leaving Out the Users. In *Participatory Design: Principles and Practices*, eds. Doug Schuler and Aki Namioka. Hillsdale, NJ: Lawrence Erlbaum Associates.

Clement, A., and C.C. Gotlieb. 1988. Evolution of an Organizational Interface: The New Business Department at a Large Insurance Firm. In *Computer-Supported Cooperative Work: A Book of Readings*, ed. Irene Grief. San Mateo, CA: Morgan Kaufman Publishers, Inc.

Friedman, B. 1996. Accounting for Human Values in System Design: An Exemplary Case Study. Unpublished manuscript.

Greeenbaum, J. 1993. A Design of One's Own: Towards Participatory Design in the United States. In *Participatory Design: Principles and Practices*, eds. D. Schuler and A. Namioka. Hillsdale, NJ: Lawrence Erlbaum Associates.

Rule, J.B., D. McAdam, L. Stearns, and D. Uglow. 1980. Preserving Individual Autonomy in an Information-Oriented Society. In *Computer Privacy in the Next Decade*, ed. Lance Hoffman. New York: Academic Press.

Shneiderman, B., and A. Rose. 1997. Social Impact Statements: Engaging Public Participation in Information Technology Design. In *Human Values and the Design of Computer Technology*, ed. Batya Friedman. Stanford, CA: CSLI Publications.

15

Eliminating a Hardware Switch: Weighing Economics and Values in a Design Decision

JOHN C. TANG

Abstract: This case study begins with the seemingly straightforward decision to eliminate an on/off switch from a microphone that is bundled with a computer workstation. However, using a microphone attached to a computer in an office setting raises issues about the privacy of conversations held within range of the microphone. How should the "costs" of dealing with the projected suspicion of end users toward a microphone that cannot be turned off be weighed against the cost savings of eliminating the on/off switch? What other "costs" associated with this change should be considered in the design decision and how should such often intangible costs made visible? The questions raised in this case study point toward the need to develop design processes that can account for users' values – in this case privacy and security – along with the cost of production.

This case study chronicles a decision revolving around the elimination of a hardware on/off switch on the microphone for a computer workstation. On the surface, the decision seemed to be a simple attempt to reduce cost, and ultimately, that rationale was the deciding factor in eliminating the switch from the microphone. I was involved in attempting to raise some other salient issues that bear on the decision. How would eliminating the switch affect the end users who use the microphone and workstation attached to it? Would users who relied on the microphone switch to guarantee their audio privacy now feel more vulnerable? How would the lack of a switch affect the people who design software that uses the microphone? Would developers who relied on the switch to protect users' privacy now have to change their software to provide that protection? These are questions that should be considered in the design (or redesign) of artifacts, but are too often overshadowed by economics and more traditionally valued metrics.

SETTING THE STAGE

Some of the dynamics of this case study are the result of the different perspectives of the groups involved, so it is important to set the stage. The setting for this case study is a medium-sized computer workstation company. The company had recently begun including microphones as part of their desktop computer workstations. These microphones enabled users to take advantage of the audio input (and output) capabilities that were built-in to the workstations. At the time, most people thought that the microphone might be used for recording voice attachments to e-mail messages or creating other audio files.

My perspective came from being part of an advanced development group in the company that developed proof-of-concept prototypes of new systems to demonstrate how people might use our technology. Our group developed systems that used audio–video connections over the network to support remote collaboration, such as desktop video conferencing systems. Thus, our group developed systems that could take advantage of the microphone to enable interactive communication among workstation users. After our group built a prototype and gained some experience with the prototype in real use, we passed on our technology and experiences to a business unit within the company to turn it into a product.

Our group became aware of a proposal to change the design of the microphone. This proposal was discussed by the product development team responsible for contracting with an outside vendor that produced the microphone. This product development team was responsible for contracting all the workstation peripherals (e.g., keyboard, mouse), and was largely driven by reducing the cost of providing these peripherals.

An important difference between the two groups is that the product development team was more closely related to bottom line profitability of the company. Since their decisions had a direct effect on the production costs, their perspective was shaped largely by the issues, people, and politics concerned with reducing those costs. As with many companies, increasing profitability by reducing production costs was a major driving concern. On the other hand, as an advanced development group, we were greatly removed from those cost issues. Our group's charter was to explore how people would use future products built on our company's technology. It was difficult to trace our group's immediate contribution to the company's bottom line (although we certainly thought our contribution was valuable to the company in many ways). These differences explain much of the contrast in perspectives between the two groups, as well as the relative influence of the two groups on the final decision.

SHOULD THE MICROPHONE HAVE AN ON/OFF SWITCH?

The first version of the microphone bundled with the desktop workstations had a hardware on/off switch on it. The proposed change of the microphone design eliminated the power switch. It should be noted that the main reason for the switch on the original microphone was because it was battery powered. Users were expected to turn the microphone on when using it, and turn it off when they were finished to conserve battery life. In practice, users often forgot to turn off their microphones and ran their batteries dead, leaving their microphone inoperable the next time they wanted to use it. Although this was mainly a human memory issue, the switch was also not easy to operate. Furthermore, it was not easy to visually determine whether the microphone was turned on or off. Without a prominent visual reminder, it was hard for users to remember that the microphone needed to be turned off or on.

One of the major changes in the revised microphone was that it would draw power from the computer, eliminating the need for a battery. This design change was driven largely by the previously noted problem of users unintentionally draining their microphone batteries. In this sense, the revised design responded to a problem that users had in keeping their microphones sufficiently powered. A logical implication of this design change was that an on/off switch on the microphone was no longer necessary.

This seemed like a rather straightforward decision, especially from the perspective of designing for users who were using the microphone to record voice messages or sound files. However, I concluded that it would have some adverse effects on our projected use of the microphone in the future. Our group was using the microphone as part of desktop conferencing prototypes that allowed people to make audio–video connections to other people through their networked computer desktops. A major concern that users have of these systems is privacy – making sure that they are not seen or heard when they do not want to be. Although we promised that our software would not allow any unwanted eavesdropping connections, many people were not satisfied with that assurance. Users had more trust in a hardware switch that disabled the camera and microphone than they did in our software mechanisms for effectively disconnecting the camera and microphone when not in use.

From our perspective of making sure to protect people's privacy in desktop conferencing applications, we reasoned that removing the switch would be problematic for certain uses of the microphone. We were concerned that the product development team for the microphone might not be aware of how their decision to delete the switch might affect other efforts to develop future applications that used it. Designing a microphone to record voice messages or sound files (which was the design center at the time) was less sensitive to users' privacy concerns than the interactive communication applications that we were expecting in the near future.

OPENING A DESIGN DISCUSSION

Our group composed a message outlining our concerns and sent it to an appropriate e-mail distribution list. This distribution list not only included members of the product development team responsible for providing the microphone, but also included people from groups throughout the company that had an interest in audio issues (e.g., marketing, software engineering, sales). A discussion of such a design issue over an e-mail distribution list was a fairly common practice within the company.

In the message, we pointed out that we expected that the microphone would soon be used to support interactive communication among workstation users. For such applications, we felt that an accessible on/off switch that controls the microphone is important to give users a sense of control over their audio privacy. Furthermore, an obvious visual indicator should inform the users whether the microphone is on or not. We also thought a package that integrated the microphone with a video camera (for desktop video conferencing) should be considered, although that was not a major part of the ensuing discussion.

A somewhat lively discussion over e-mail and face-to-face meetings followed. A major part of the response from the product development group was that eliminating the switch would save a quarter in the cost of producing the microphone. "It would save 25% of the manufacturing cost?" we asked, somewhat curiously. "No, twenty-five cents," was the response.

One thread of the discussion argued whether saving twenty-five cents might cost us thousands of dollars in customer purchases by those who were concerned about the loss of privacy with an unswitched microphone. Some evidence cited to support this argument was a U.S. government guideline (CERT Advisory CA-93:15, 21 October 1993) that could be interpreted to prevent government customers from purchasing computer equipment that did not provide appropriate safeguards for protecting audio privacy. A microphone without an on/off switch could be construed as being vulnerable to being tapped into.

A suggested alternative for those with concerns about audio privacy was to simply unplug the microphone from the workstation. Although unplugging the microphone would certainly protect privacy, it would be highly unlikely that users would do this regularly. The microphone plugged into the back of the workstation, and it would be highly inconvenient to access the jack for repeated plugging and unplugging.

Some developers of other audio applications (e.g., connecting the computer to the telephone) also contributed their support for our concerns of how their applications might be affected by the elimination of the switch. Some marketing people also observed that removing the switch might be perceived as evidence that the company was not attuned to the needs of users in the multimedia market. At a time when some competitors were aggressively seeking to capture the multimedia market, it could be damaging to produce a product that appeared to take a step backward from protecting users' privacy.

The gist of the discussion focused on the need to reduce the cost of the microphone, and thus the need to demonstrate that eliminating the switch would somehow cost the company more than the manufacturing costs saved. In one sense, it became an argument of hard, cost-saving numbers against issues of projected future use, privacy, and usability. We were not in a position to provide such cost estimates (especially under the time constraints). The impact of the issues we were raising was hard to measure, both because it was somewhat speculative and long-term in nature, and because it was hard to quantify (especially in terms of cost).

This interaction could have generated an interesting design discussion that embraced the consideration of both the economics of production and the use of the technology. Instead, the conversation was dominated by the production costs, largely because they are well known and quantifiable. However, the real economic question that needs to be answered is "Will a product make money?" Many factors, including "Is it usable?" and "Does it respect users' privacy?" ultimately go into deciding whether people will use and buy a product. This case prompted me to reflect on how to pay attention to values such as usability and privacy, especially when they come up against economic values which have been historically so dominant.

OUTCOMES OF THE DISCUSSION

In the end, the on/off switch was eliminated from the redesigned microphone. Although we had generated a valuable discussion about the issue, we were not able to influence the final decision for a variety of reasons. Our group had no organizational or political influence on the product development group who had the fnal say. Furthermore, a prominent and influential leader in the company had gone on record in favor of eliminating the switch for cost-saving reasons. This statement was made before we had started any dialog on the matter, and was not reconsidered in light of the issues we were raising. Finally, we had gotten involved in the process at a very late stage. Our group was not in the loop of these kind of decisions; we had heard about it in passing while discussing a separate issue with a member of the product development group. By the time we had heard about it, the decision had already achieved significant momentum, and would have required very compelling reasons to reverse.

We heard some additional reasons in defense of the decision beyond the cost-reduction argument. One claim was that regular users of the microphone for interactive communication are probably not concerned about privacy. This statement is misguided. Although most of us have live microphones in our offices in the form of a telephone handset, we are all still very concerned with privacy, and rely on the assurance that the microphone is disconnected when the phone handset is "hung up." Would we feel comfortable using the phone if there was no hang-up switch and we relied on the phone companies' assurance that their switching software disconnects the phone when not in use?

Another claim was that none of the microphones that other companies were bundling with their computer products included an on/off switch. We countered that this difference could be seen as a competitive advantage. We could position ourselves as looking beyond the current uses of the microphone (recording sound files) to the need to support future interactive uses of the microphone. For interactive communication, privacy assurances are a major concern, and a switch is the most straightforward way to guarantee security.

The one encouraging outcome was that the product development group began to consider offering a variety of microphones with the workstation, in part due to their recognition that there are many different uses for such a product. One proposed option is to offer a higher-quality microphone on a longer stand that would be more appropriate for desktop conferencing use. For that microphone, they contemplated adding an on/off hardware switch in light of the issues we raised.

One implication of the decision to eliminate the switch is that more responsibility was shifted onto the software designers to assure that the software control of the microphone input was secure. There was a known vulnerability in the software that could allow others to tap into the microphone. This problem was not considered serious because the hardware switch on the microphone would turn off the microphone when not in use. Removing the switch brought the need to address the software security of the microphone to the forefront. In addition to engineering a software solution, these mechanisms would have to be documented and customers would have to be alerted to using them, all of which had real costs associated with them. Such a change in system software also had potential implications on any application software that used the microphone. Although this software issue needed to be addressed regardless of the elimination of the switch, it is interesting to trace the ripple effects of this hardware decision throughout the market.

Alternatively, users could purchase a different microphone that did have a hardware switch that was easy to use. For our desktop video conferencing prototypes, our group opted to use a device that contained both a video camera and microphone that had a very visible and easy to reach power switch (that controlled both the camera and microphone), and a light to indicate whether the unit was on.

When we deployed our desktop videoconferencing prototype with a group of users, several expressed concerns about the impact of our prototype on their privacy. We pointed out the various mechanisms that we had included to help ensure their privacy, including the switch that turned off the camera and microphone. Most users did take note of the switch, and felt comfortable enough with the privacy safeguards that they were willing to try using our prototype. However, in our observations of their use of the prototype, they did not make extensive use of these privacy mechanisms (averaging approximately one use per person per week) (Tang et al., 1994). Although we could not log the number of times people used the switch to turn off the camera/microphone unit, responses to a questionnaire indicated that only a few users ever used the switch, and even then only rarely. As users gained experience with using our desktop conferencing prototype, they were able to see that, beyond our software mechanisms for preventing unwanted eavesdropping, social mechanisms were effective and natural for protecting privacy.

We concluded that while the users did not actually use the switch, without it, users might not have been willing to even try the prototype and discover that the switch was not needed to ensure privacy. Others who have studied desktop video conferencing systems in use have also found users' privacy fears subside once they start using the system without actually using the features included to help protect privacy (Fish et al., 1993). However, even though these features are not frequently used, it does not mean that they should be removed from the design. Although not used per se, these features may play a key role in how users perceive the overall system, influencing whether they are willing to accept and use the system at all. Especially when introducing a new technology, including these features that provide a sense of protecting privacy may be important in helping users accept using them.

It has been a couple of years since this decision was made, and there is no way to attribute any fluctuation of sales in desktop workstations to the new microphone design without the switch. We are not aware of any customers who stopped buying the workstation because of the revised microphone design. On the other hand, audio applications that use the microphone have not become popular on our desktop workstation products. There are many reasons why audio applications have not flourished, but I would argue that a significant reason is that the design of the technology has not facilitated the use of the audio capabilities of the workstation. For example, we have heard that in some workplaces where privacy and security are very important, users are not allowed to plug in our bundled microphone because of its privacy vulnerability (without an on/off switch). In order to use the audio capabilities of our workstations, these users would have to buy a microphone that did have a hardware switch. It is this kind of added obstacle that can prevent the widespread adoption and use of a technology.

Curiously, soon after the microphone on/off switch discussion, the company introduced a video camera that could be purchased for use with our desktop workstations. The video camera was intended to be used for desktop video conferencing systems that were becoming available on our platform. The production of this camera was overseen by the same product development group that worked on the microphone. Without any input from our group, the camera was produced with a shutter that could be slid over the camera lens to block its view. This shutter was promoted as a privacy safeguard to ensure users that visual eavesdropping could be prevented.

It is interesting that the video camera inherently brought the issue of privacy to the forefront, whereas the microphone did not. Perhaps this was because other cameras on the market had shutters of some kind. Or, maybe they were driven by the misconception that being seen is more dangerous than being heard. Experience in desktop video conferencing to date demonstrates that being heard is typically of more concern than being seen (Bly et al., 1993; Fish et al., 1993). Of course, since the video camera was an option to purchase and not bundled with the workstation, it was less sensitive to production cost, because that could be passed on to the customer rather than absorbed in the overall production cost. In retrospect, it would have been interesting to understand what rationale was used to justify the expense of including a shutter for the camera.

WHAT CAN WE LEARN FROM THIS CASE STUDY?

The purpose of telling this story is not to question the decision that was ultimately made. To this day, we cannot definitively evaluate the impact of this decision. On the one hand, eliminating the switch saved the company money on a component that apparently does not have a major effect on the overall usability (or at least sale-ability) of the system. On the other hand, use of the microphone has not grown, in part because its design does not lend itself to secure use. One might ask that if we cannot even understand the impact of the decision in retrospect, how can we possibly predict its impact beforehand at design time? This case study raises this question without answering it, but we have learned some useful lessons along the way.

Even if the microphone switch design was only a minor reason why audio technology has not flourished on our platform, it reflects a development process that did not shape the design of the technology in relation to how it would be used. Paying attention to the use of technology enables us to consider values such as usability and privacy in addition to the traditional values of providing functionality at the lowest cost. What can we learn from this case study to help us incorporate some of these noneconomic concerns into the design process?

Perhaps the most obvious lesson is to include a use-oriented perspective early and throughout future design processes. One of the reasons we were not able to adequately discuss the design of the switch is that we were not involved until very late in the process. At that point, we were unable to overcome the momentum that the decision had gained. While eliminating the switch might have seemed like a straightforward decision that did not require much design debate, it turned out to have implications beyond the hardware design to software design and end user work practices. This case is a good example of how many design decisions, no matter how small, can have a potential impact on the end user, and should be considered in that light.

There is a growing field investigating a more use-oriented perspective on design including participatory design (Muller & Kuhn, 1993), applying anthropological studies of work practice to guide design (Suchman & Trigg, 1990; Blomberg et al., 1993), and contextual design (Wixon et al., 1990). By working together with social scientists, usability experts, and the users themselves, designers can better understand how their products will be used and what values must be considered for the products to gain user acceptance. The qualitative issues (e.g., usability and privacy) are often more influential in determining user acceptance than simply how much they cost.

This case also demonstrates that we should attempt to include design values that are hard to measure, such as ease of use and protecting user privacy. To some extent, this means acknowledging that it is not always possible to compare factors representing different design values according to a quantifiable metric. In this case study, the product team's goals of reducing cost were very narrowly specified and easily measurable. By contrast, our group's concerns about ease of use and privacy were more broad and qualitative. While it may be easier to justify a decision based on narrowly defined, quantifiable metrics, the important issues that may ultimately determine user acceptance and purchase may not exhibit those characteristics. Especially in competitive markets where differences in functionality and cost may be relatively small, addressing nonmonetary values (such as ease of use or privacy) in design can be an important differentiating feature. When introducing a new technology or feature, it seems especially important to consider these issues as they often help shape prospective users' response to a product. In the case of privacy, if users rule out even trying a product because it does not *appear* to respect privacy issues, then they will never discover that their privacy concerns may be managed adequately.

On the other hand, one way to include these values into a design discussion is to construct monetary figures for the indirect costs that are often associated with these values. For example, complicated systems often generate more work for the customer service organization, as they must often explain how to use the system to confused users. The costs of fixing usability problems in products are just beginning to appear in the literature (Coutaz, 1995). The cost to service or repair usability problems could be used to justify the added expense of designing out usability problems in the first place. Alternatively, estimates of how many users might decide not to buy a product because of a poor privacy model could be made and the associated costs calculated (e.g., the lost revenue of 2% of potential buyers cancelling their orders). While such estimates are likely to be inaccurate, they will at least provide a concrete representation for the issue within the economic frame of reference. It is currently very difficult to predict the financial impact of compromising a design's ease of use or predict how the marketplace will reward attention to privacy issues. However, we should attempt to document case studies of how these values can translate into cost savings in the long run.

Overly relying on economic arguments to the exclusion of issues of usability and privacy is not an effective design process. These issues need to be raised early in the process, especially since their impact and implications are not as easily quantified, and may take more effort to understand. We need to encourage design groups (especially those closer to making products and generating profit from them) to explore design methods that incorporate these use-oriented values in their design process.

REFERENCES

Blomberg, J., J. Giacomi, A. Mosher, and P. Wenton-Wall. 1993. Ethnographic Field Methods and Their Relation to Design. In *Participatory Design: Principles and Practices*, eds. D. Schuler and A. Namioka, 123–156. Hillsdale, NJ: Lawrence Erlbaum.

Bly, S.A., S.R. Harrison, and S. Irwin. 1993. Media Spaces: Bringing People Together in a Video, Audio, and Computing Environment. *Communications of the ACM* 36 (1), 28–47.

Coutaz, J. 1995. Evaluation Techniques: Exploring the Intersection of HCI and Software Engineering. In *Software Engineering and Human-Computer Interaction*, eds. R. Taylor and J. Coutaz, 35–48. Berlin: Springer-Verlag.

Fish, R.S., R.E. Kraut, R.W. Root, and R.W. Rice. 1993. Video as a Technology for Informal Communication. *Communications of the ACM* 36 (1), 48–61.

Muller, M. J., and S. Kuhn, eds. 1993. Special Issue on Participatory Design. *Communications of the ACM* 36 (4).

Suchman, L.A., and R.H. Trigg. 1990. Understanding Practice: Video as a Medium for Reflection and Design. In *Design at Work: Approaches to Collaborative Design*, eds. J. Greenbaum and M. Kyng, 65–89. Hillsdale, NJ: Lawrence Erlbaum.

Tang, J.C., E.A. Isaacs, and M. Rua. 1994. Supporting Distributed Groups with a Montage of Lightweight Interactions. In *Proceedings of the Conference on Computer-Supported Cooperative Work (CSCW)'94*, 23–34. New York: ACM Press.

Wixon, D., K. Holtzblatt, and S. Knox. 1990. Contextual Design: An Emergent View of System Design. In *Proceedings of the Conference on Computer Human Interaction (CHI)'90*, 329–336. New York: ACM Press.

16

Steps toward Universal Access within a Communications Company

JOHN C. THOMAS

Abstract: In this chapter I discuss four thrusts within NYNEX to make communication systems more accessible: (1) methods currently employed by NYNEX to help increase access; (2) R & D efforts at our Science and Technology laboratories that push the envelope of new technologies like machine vision and speech recognition; (3) efforts to leverage "access" in our successful bid to become ISO 9001 compliant – here we have sought to develop and document procedures that require developers to consider access from the beginning when it is easiest to address; and (4), an experimental effort to develop and popularize audio access to the internet. Together, these endeavors work to provide internet access for people who for visual, literacy, or economic reasons might otherwise be barred from participation.

> *Mighty oaks from tiny acorns grow.*
>
> —*Anonymous*

Possibly no invention since the printing press has had such a profound influence on life as the telephone. How did all this start? Originally, Alexander Graham Bell was working on a scheme to provide the deaf community with greater access to information. The first vision of the telephone was for a few point to point connections but soon the vision evolved to provide telephone access to all residences and businesses. Early on, it was realized that a communication system is valuable only if it is pervasive. Today, we are seeing a similar phenomenon in the explosive growth of the internet. As more and more people gain access to "the net," it becomes more valuable – therefore, attracting more people to get on the net.

Providing access for people with special needs is not just for "them" – it's for everyone. Providing access as universally as possible provides three benefits for a communications company: (1) By increasing the diversity of the community, it increases its value for everyone; (2) By increasing access, it allows for an increased market size; 3) By having to deal with special needs, it forces technologists, developers, marketers, and executives to think "out of the box" – to ques-

---

I would like to thank Sara Basson, Elizabeth Macken, and Batya Friedman for comments on earlier drafts of this chapter, and Sara Basson and Jim Kondziela for helping to develop the ideas for audio access to the internet.

tion assumptions, to reexamine what Peter Drucker (1995) calls the "Theory of the Business." Once, such a rethinking led to the development of the telephone itself and thereby eventually to a whole different world. It could happen again. It is precisely in the dialectic between technological possibilities and people's needs that inventive design is created (Thomas & Carroll, 1978). While scientists and engineers often focus on trying to introduce novelty through new technology, innovation can be equally present by focusing on a new set of needs.

At the time of this writing, NYNEX is the Regional Bell Operating Company (RBOC) for most of the northeastern United States. There are plans to merge with another RBOC – Bell Atlantic – and the name of the new company will be Bell Atlantic. NYNEX Science and Technology, Inc. is a wholly owned subsidiary of NYNEX. We do applied research in technologies of long-term interest to the parent corporation, provide technical advice, and develop innovative systems (both for increasing internal efficiency and for providing new customer services). About 15% of our funding is currently shareholder sponsored exploratory work and about 85% is specifically funded by internal client groups. My own current role is diverse but includes managing speech technology, human–computer interaction, and many new service concepts.

In this chapter, I will discuss four ways in which NYNEX is dealing with making its services more accessible. First, I will quickly review some of our company's recent and long-standing attempts to make service more universal. Second, I will look at some technologies that our laboratories are developing. Technologies such as machine vision, speech recognition, and speech synthesis provide ever greater promise for increased access for those with special needs. Third, I will describe how our effort to improve and systematize our internal development processes at Science and Technology provides an opportunity to help our organization consciously move in the direction of greater access. Fourth, I will discuss a specific project, "Audio Access to the Internet" whose aim is to greatly increase access to the internet. I hope that readers of this chapter may gain new perspectives on ways to avoid bias and strive for more universal access within their own contexts.

MAXIMIZING ACCESS

Relay Chat

One of the oldest services offered by the Bell System (including NYNEX) is to have human operators "translate" from teletype to voice. This is typically used when someone with a speech or hearing disability wants to communicate over the phone with a hearing person. This service is offered throughout the NYN-EX region, though the exact service description is done on a state by state basis. For instance, the service in New York is described as follows:

New York Relay Center greatly improves telecommunications for anyone who is deaf or has a hearing or speech disability.

For a TTY user to communicate with someone using an ordinary phone, the user makes a call to the New York Relay Center. Special operators – called communications assistants – place the call, read the messages and orally relay the conversation confidentially to the desired party. Oral responses are then typed back to the TTY user.

Talk as long as you like. There are no additional charges for using the Relay Center beyond what the call would normally cost if dialed direct. This is available twenty-four hours a day, seven days a week.

Special Services for the Visually Impaired

Bills in both Braille and large print are available for those who request them. In addition, special adjuncts to phone dials are available with raised numbers/letters, larger holes for rotary dials, and a specially marked operator key for easy access.

Special Needs Product Demos

NYNEX has recently entered into a partnership with the New York State Office of Advocate for the Disabled, Technology Related Assistance for Individuals with Disabilities (TRIAD) Project to provide special needs phone devices to TRIAD's seven statewide regional centers. These centers offer seniors, people with disabilities, family members and employers an opportunity to test certain assistive phone devices before they buy them. Each center is staffed with knowledgeable employees and open daily for walk in customers.

Languages

NYNEX currently offers both Spanish yellow pages and Spanish speaking directory assistance operators. The plan is to promote and support NYNEX products and services in three other languages: Cantonese, Mandarin, and Korean. Limited market trials are under consideration for additional languages as well.

We test prototypes of services before deployment by bringing in people representative of potential users, and thereby identify possible problems with the interface including the wording of prompts. For example, NYNEX has a product called "Voice Dialing" (service mark) which allows users to dial a number simply by saying the name of the person they want to call. For example, you can associate the name "mom" with the phone number of your mother and then pick up the phone and say "mom." The number will be dialed automatically. Obviously, this is advantageous for people with certain physical handicaps, (see the following section on speech recognition), but it is also a technology that is partially "language independent." Although we haven't provided prompts in every possible language, (only English and Spanish) the user may speak English with any accent or speak another language.

Some language problems are associated with subtleties of meaning and reference. These can vary considerably among cultural groups even if they all "speak the same language" such as English (Thomas, Kellogg, Grudin & Ishii, 1993). For instance, a prompt in an early prototype of Voice Dialing said, "Please dial the phone number for <name>. Then, if you have a touch-tone phone, press the pound sign." It turned out that many people do not know what the "pound sign" is, and some would make mistakes (e.g., hitting the star key, which sent them off the system) when they heard that prompt. In one case, a subject during the posttest interview explained that, although he knew he had somehow made a mistake, the prompt had said distinctly to press the "pound sign" but there was none on the telephone. When the experimenter asked the subject what a "pound sign" looked like, he said, "You know, the pound sign!" and drew the British pound sign. (It turned out that though living now in the New York area, he had recently moved from a British Caribbean country).

NYNEX, as part of the activities related to the Telecommunications Act of 1996 is committed to implementing the Universal Design Principles. A Universal Design Team has been established with representatives across the company. The purpose is to: (1) ensure current and future NYNEX products and services, as well as communications with our internal and external customers, are accessible to individuals with disabilities; and (2) work with thirty-five other industry and private sector leaders in developing recommendations for federal guidelines promoting accessible telecommunications products and services. Not only are these actions in response to the Telecommunications Act of 1996; they may be wise marketing moves as well. When SUNY-Buffalo recently gave a sample of elderly individuals with disabilities various telecommunications assistive devices, their usage of the NYNEX network doubled. Pacific Bell finds that people who are blind, have vision impairments, are deaf or have mobility disabilities, generate significantly higher revenues than the average customer.

TECHNOLOGIES FOR INCREASED ACCESS

Speech Recognition

Speech recognition technology basically translates human speech into data, commands, or text. Everyone may occasionally find themselves in situations where they are temporarily unable to use their eyes and/or hands to interact with machinery. For example, someone may be fixing dinner in the kitchen and simultaneously using speech recognition to control a computer or phone. In such cases, stopping the ongoing activity of dinner making, washing and drying hands, and then using a keyboard or touch tone keypad on the phone is highly inconvenient.

For special populations, however, speech recognition provides more than a convenience; it opens up a whole new world. For instance, a quadriplegic programmer may use speech recognition for interacting with a computer, including entering text. The technology allows them to practice their trade as well as to control various phone features.

Using speech recognition over the phone introduces some problems, however. For one thing, many phones do not contain high quality microphones; for another, the phone system "cuts off" the very high and very low frequencies (because they do not propagate well). Finally, there is little control over background noise.

Speech recognition was first deployed in a real network based application by NYNEX in 1989 (Thomas, 1995) in a so-called intercept application. In this application, a customer dials a number which has been changed or disconnected. In electro-mechanical switches, the dialed number was not stored as data but used directly to actuate switches. When the call failed to terminate, the customer was prompted to say the number dialed, and the system would recognize the digits and inform the customer of the new number.

Since the network had no information about who was placing the call, the recognition system had to be speaker independent; that is, it needed to handle whoever called (regardless of accent) under whatever conditions (e.g., background noise). This is a far different situation than testing a speech recognition device under known conditions of noise, microphone, and accent. Because of the difficulty of doing speaker-independent continuous digit recognition over the network, we also gave customers an option to use their keypad or talk with a human operator. This system was successfully deployed in the field for five years (Yashchin & Ortel, 1991).

A much more extensive application of speech recognition over the network is called Voice Dialing. In this application, the customer "trains" the recognizer to their own voice with two training trials. After thus associating a phone number and an utterance, the customer can now "dial" a number by voice alone. This is handy for most people but especially valuable for people with limitations in eyesight, memory, or manual dexterity. (This includes people with temporary limitations due to multi-tasking such as driving a car). We have also developed an extension of this technology for controlling network functions such as turning call forwarding on or off. This is called "Voice Activated Network Control" or VANC. Such voice controls are not only more convenient but can also be made more intuitive than a sequence of button presses. Thus, "Cancel Call Forwarding" is easier to remember than the keystroke "*68." Again, while such a capability is a convenience to the majority of customers, for some with special needs it can be crucial.

Speech Synthesis

Probably the most famous example of speech synthesis as an aid to people with special needs is the use of synthetic speech for Stephen Hawking, a brilliant physicist at Oxford University who has Lou Gerhig's disease, or amyotrophic lateral sclerosis (ALS), and consequently is unable to talk. Yet, through the use of a speech synthesizer, he continues to give brilliant lectures. He not only is one of the premier physicists in the world, but has a special talent for explaining complex ideas in nontechnical ways with humor and insight. In this case, it becomes obvious that the term access has a double meaning. Often we think of "giving" the handicapped access to resources. In this case, it becomes obvious that the access technology provides the "gift" of Steven Hawking's mind to the rest of us. Listening to him "talk" through the synthesizer feels much closer than reading the printed page (cf. Thomas, 1983).

"Universal access" is a two way street. It is not only giving access to people with special needs. It is giving everyone else the benefit of as much perspective and productivity as possible. By virtue of having special needs, individuals oftentimes have a different and therefore an especially valuable perspective.

Speech synthesis is a technology that translates text (such as ASCII stored in a computer) into spoken speech. Speech synthesis technology has reached the point where it is nearly as intelligible as human speech. However, it is not so natural or pleasing sounding as natural human speech. Generally, speech synthesizers have difficulties on three grounds: proper name pronunciation, voice timbre, and prosody (how we say what we say).

In our laboratory, we generally try to work on technical problems with a long-term vision and shorter-term results. So, for instance, the long-term vision of improved prosody for speech synthesis could be to have a computer speak with the same expression as a Shakespearean actor. Since any level of context can impact how an actor would say a line, this is essentially equivalent to the general artificial intelligence (AI) problem – certainly, a long-term challenge! Along the path of this ambitious, long-term vision, we try to choose projects that provide some more immediate benefit to NYNEX by solving part of the problem. In the case of speech synthesis, we focused on providing "reverse directory" information. In such a service, the customer dials a phone number and hears the associated name and address. One application for such a service is for credit verification. Another application helps customers who question their bills. Customers often see a phone number they don't recognize. But, if they are given the name and address, they generally do recognize that the call was indeed placed.

Current synthesizers make many odd prosody judgments about names and addresses. For example, an address might be on the north part of State Road in Plainfield, New Jersey or it could be on State Road in North Plainfield, New Jersey. As human readers, we make a distinction between saying, "State Road North (pause; change in pitch), Plainfield, New Jersey" and "State Road (pause; change of pitch), North Plainfield, New Jersey." Our synthesis algorithms helped address such problems and thereby greatly improved the comprehension of listeners. (Yashchin, Basson, Kalyanswamy & Silverman, 1992).

Machine Vision

Another technology of tremendous potential for everyone, but especially for people with visual difficulties, is machine vision. A particular application called Optical Character Recognition is already a part of the Kurzweil reading machines for the blind which read printed characters into a speech synthesizer for audio output. Presently such machines tend to be limited to words printed in specified fonts. However, we worked in our laboratory for several years to improve technology so that hand printed characters could also be read fairly accurately. Such technology has application for government agencies such as the IRS, the Census Bureau, and the Post Office as well as for blind people. It would also allow the possibility of turning noncoded information, such as faxes, into ASCII so that they could be stored and manipulated more easily.

In addition, investigators in the general area of machine vision are looking into automatic collision avoidance systems, security systems, and automatically finding video and still images from large collections. To the extent that descriptions could be automatically generated from scenes, these descriptions could be presented auditorily to blind individuals.

In addition, a form of machine vision could be used to help blind or visually impaired people navigate and avoid obstacles. Perhaps auditory warnings could also be helpful for people with parietal lobe damage who might otherwise disregard potential obstacles on one side of the world. There are more subtle kinds of visual enhancements that could be realized via computer as well. Lens systems can help overcome myopia, or astigmatism for instance. But an intelligent vision system could help "fill in the gaps" for someone with a partial field blindness. Currently, our own machine vision work focuses on "reading" diagrams of telephone facilities (Chhabra, Chandran & Kasturi, 1993).

Wireless Access

Another technology that we have worked on in our labs is wireless phone access (sometimes referred to as Mobile Phone or Personal Network Service). Wireless access technologies, by allowing someone to have access to the public switched network from virtually anywhere, could be valuable to someone with limited mobility and/or emergency needs for access. For example, a person with heart disease or diabetes could carry a wireless device everywhere. With a single button push, the user could simultaneously place a phone call to go to an emergency service operator who would be apprised of the user's location and background information. If the user were conscious, they could also be connected via a voice call.

Virtual Reality

Virtual reality is, by its very nature, essentially a technology to increase access. It allows people to "go" places virtually that are too expensive, limited, or dangerous to go to in reality (Stuart & Thomas, 1991). It is finding use today in tele-operations, medicine, entertainment, and training.

Our own work in virtual reality has focused on the provision of three dimensional sound. One application would allow a user to "move into" a three-dimensional organization chart. The user would hear, for instance, the head of an organization explaining its mission but hear in the background, various department heads softly describing their missions. By navigating, the user could home in on one of these department heads and hear their description clearly but hear the various supervisors in the background softly describing their projects as well. By clearly separating the apparent location of the sound sources (and by their being in different voices), the user may use what is called the "cocktail party effect" to focus in on the audio of interest to them. A small version of such a system was prototyped for the artificial intelligence lab. While such a system would give blind users a way to "navigate" an organization chart, it was also felt that it was useful for ordinary users. The audio descriptions themselves are fairly easy to obtain and hearing the person talk about themselves and their roles seems to provide the listener with a more in-depth understanding than merely looking at an organization chart. This year, we hope to complete a more extensive prototype and do more systematic testing.

Another application involves using audio virtual reality in conjunction with wireless technology to help blind users navigate in a complex environment (like New York City). The idea is to place various landmarks in a virtual auditory space. As the user traveled in the real environment, some of these landmarks would get closer and some would get farther away, thus helping to orient the user. Since blind users obviously use auditory cues for other purposes as well, it might be useful to be able to easily turn this feature on and off. Unfortunately, we have not yet been able to build and test the proposed system.

PROCESS IMPROVEMENT[1]

Background

The optimum time to address special needs is in the very earliest stages of design (Paciello, 1996). When Caller ID was first introduced, customers who wished to use the service but could not read the ID box had to pay $40.00 to have a voice chip installed. Today, manufacturers incorporate the chip in the design and it is sold in the same price range as the visual-only box. Moreover, sighted customers also find the voice chip a great convenience. The question is, how can we get designers to consider universal access from the beginning?

One possible answer comes from utilizing a strong current trend in industry to become ISO 9001 compliant. ISO is the International Standards Organi-

---

[1]NYNEX Science and Technology was audited on December 10–13, 1996 and, based on that successful audit, has been recommended for ISO 9001 registration. In addition, NYNEX is currently developing training packages that illustrate how to incorporate principles of universal access into work practices for NYNEX developers, marketing people, and service representatives. NYNEX has also become actively involved in the Telecommunications Access Advisory Committee in Washington, D.C. Insight into the Committee's work can be seen at http://www.trace.wisc.edu/taac.

zation and a set of standards originally conceived for manufacturing is now being applied to all systems, including software. The standard itself basically requires that a company document its processes, that it follows those processes and can prove it does so. Therefore, if those written processes include an up-front consideration of universal access, and if a company wants to get or keep its ISO 9001 registration, universal access must be considered up front. I am currently engaged in an attempt to incorporate such considerations in the written development processes of NYNEX Science and Technology. In order to understand the dynamics of this process, a little more background will be useful to the reader.

NYNEX Science and Technology grew quickly during the late 80s and early 90s. It evolved primarily as eight separate laboratories finding their own customers, defining their own projects, and then developing, delivering and servicing them. While each of the labs was successful, there was little knowledge sharing about what worked in terms of product development. In the spring of 1994, it became apparent that we needed to take a careful look at our processes and find a way to document them.

In some earlier cases, development processes and selection of vendor products reflected a concern for providing wide access. For example, Science and Technology was involved in the design of a new workstation for operators and the numeric keypad was designed so that it could be attached either left or right to accommodate left- and right-handed operators. We also ensured that color was used as a redundant coding device (not a single differentiator) even though the vast majority of the operators are currently female and hence the proportion of color blind operators is very small. However, in another case, equipment was designed that would make it inconvenient for left-handed operators.

Attention to making access as wide as practical was thus dealt with on an ad hoc basis. It depended entirely on the particular sensitivities of the people on the project. We wanted a more systematic approach.

Opportunity

In the spring of 1995, I attended the Computer Human Interaction (CHI) workshop on avoiding bias in computer systems organized by Batya Friedman. (Friedman, Brok, Roth & Thomas, 1996). Coming back to NYNEX, it occurred to me that our being in the middle of defining, documenting, and refining our processes provided a wonderful opportunity for further ensuring that we make services that are as accessible (nonbiased) as possible.

ISO 9001 Registration

In the late fall of 1995, it was decided to focus our process improvement efforts first on gaining ISO 9001 registration. ISO 9001 is structured into a series of twenty clauses and some of these are particularly relevant to ensuring wide access to our systems (ANSI, 1994; Schmauch, 1995).

For example, Element 4.10, Inspection and Testing, may include procedures that help ensure that a wide representation of possible users make up any test group. Element 4.4, Design Control includes the Clause 4.4.45, Design output and seems an obvious place to include considerations for people with special needs. However, there is a caveat. In order to achieve ISO 9001 registration, you must have written procedures and a way to prove that you follow your own procedures. Therefore, documentation of procedures must be done carefully so that an unrealistic burden is not imposed on the developers. For example, if we said that, "every product design is looked at from the perspective of every conceivable special need" then we would be in noncompliance with the standard unless we literally did that. In some cases, the research necessary to even determine what the implications of a design for every possible special need would cost more than the lifetime revenue of a product. Therefore, quality standards need to be written in a way that ensures a reasonable level of effort.

My involvement has been both proactive and reactive. I have contacted the process owners who are dealing with the various clauses of interest and brought up my concerns. In addition, each section of the quality manual is sent out for review. This gives an additional opportunity for input. Rather than positioning broad access as an extra step for developers to take, I am positioning it as a normal part of participative design and a way to avoid later problems (cf. Thomas & Kellogg, 1989).

Challenges

Defining processes that the entire organization can live with is a daunting task that requires input from and negotiation among many stakeholders. As mentioned previously, the organization needs to avoid putting more restrictions on its flexibility than it can live with; at the same time, there is a genuine effort to improve how we do things and one way to do that is to provide a set of rules to be followed. It is too early to note precisely how these trade-offs will be instantiated, but it is clear that the attempt itself has increased people's awareness of the issues. Given the extreme time pressure of our schedule to achieve registration in the current year, implementing further restrictions may be more feasible as a part of our ongoing process improvement efforts in the next few years.

A broader frontal action also suggests itself, however. Imagine that the ISO 9000 standard itself, in its next release, requires companies to explicitly consider whether products and services will be accessible to a wide audience or will be biased in some way. This would put all producers on a level playing field and force developers to pay attention to access early in the design process.

AUDIO ACCESS TO THE INTERNET

Background

In thinking about providing wider access for people, one idea that arose in a brainstorming session is audio access to the internet. This would provide wider access in several respects. First of all, blind users would be able to access the internet more easily. Second, people could access the internet from mobile phones. Third, a huge group of people who cannot afford a computer could get (limited) access over their phone. Finally, people who cannot read and write could get access to the internet. Three of us meet periodically to carry forward the idea. During the course of this, we have found other people have considered the idea of using audio as an adjunct to screen-based internet access (Hemphill, 1996; Novick, House, Fanty & Cole, 1996).

Concept Development

The growth of the internet is phenomenal (Krol, 1994). Yet, some people are not on the internet and not likely to have access in the near future. The proportion of people with computers at home has grown steadily in the past two decades, except in the poorest quartile of the United States population where the percentage has stayed relatively constant for the past two decades at just under 10%. Besides the obvious economic barriers to buying a computer with a modem, there may be other barriers such as a lack of peer support, fear of technology, and in some cases, lack of requisite reading and writing skills. Yet, over 95% of United States homes have access to telephone service. Although all the graphics and photos that are now popular on the internet could obviously not be presented on a "plain old telephone" system, many of the textual messages could be played via speech synthesis.

Current Scenarios

Audio Net provides audio access to the internet over an ordinary telephone line. Users include four groups: (1) mobile phone users; (2) the economically disadvantaged; (3) blind users, or persons otherwise unable to use an ordinary computer interface; and (4) people with the money to buy a computer and web access but who are unwilling to spend that much money without seeing how it could benefit them. The services and interfaces for these four groups will probably turn out to be different. The marketing strategy (advertising, pricing, channels, etc.) certainly will be. In all cases, however, users will call a number from any ordinary phone (both touch tone and automatic speech recognition (ASR) input should be available). After identifying themselves; e.g., by keying in or saying their home phone number and a password, they will be connected to a central computer bank. This computer will download the individual's profile which will include: speech templates, billing information, interface preferences, on-line service list, home phone information, and personal computer phone line information (if any). The central computer will also have speech recognition and speech synthesis cards in it. The computer will be able to access a variety of internet services. To examine how some of these might work from the user's perspective, let's look at each of the four groups in turn:

1) The mobile phone user would dial a number and speak his or her own password. They would be in an audio gateway which will begin speaking menu choices. The user might "scroll" forward and backward through an audio menu à la a patented phone interface method called the radio analogue. In this interface, the user could essentially have the illusion of voice control over a radio. He or she might say "scan," "next," "previous," etc. Alternatively, at any time, the user may say any one of several commonly used keywords to go directly to one of the associated services. (Obviously, various alternatives would be carefully designed and tested before a final service were offered). The user may "listen" to e-mail read by synthesis. The user may listen to news items picked by keywords stored in their profile. The user may listen to stock quotes listed in their profile. The user may "log in" to a paid service such as Compuserve, Prodigy, or America Online (AOL). At this point, the NYNEX Central Computer would serve as a protocol converter between the ASCII and voice. The user might also may also use Netscape. Hopefully, major players such as those named above will provide a stripped down access version without graphics. Otherwise, the graphic images could be stripped out by the NYNEX Central Computer.

The user might surf the internet, control the sending of files, or add to a bookmark list for later perusal. With the cooperation of AOL, e.g., the user might wish to engage in audio chat rooms. In later years, chat rooms could be *both* audio and visual via our converters.

2) The economically disadvantaged user will be unable to pay a few thousand dollars for a computer and therefore also be unable to subscribe to a service like (the current) AOL. Yet, they may have occasion to use the internet for special purposes. For instance, Value Added Surfers/Providers might offer to let people know where the best buys are. People might have a trading post, be able to search for jobs, listen to the positions of political candidates on various issues, query about social programs, find out about local and federal governmental services, and access community networks. This could all be done via audio.

3) Blind users could use the audio interface as a way to let them surf and use the internet. Just as movies and television programs with additional annotated channels for the deaf are becoming more common, one can imagine that volunteers may begin orally annotating commonly visited web sites.

Again, it is important to remember that we would not only be providing blind users access to the internet, but allowing everyone else on the internet, access to blind users and their ideas. Indeed, this is a special case of increased value through wider access.

4) Users who are considering getting computer access to the internet could call our number and "try out" the internet by audio. Of course, it would not be as quick in many cases as using a visual interface, but they could uncover the kind of information that is out there. We might encourage such users to train a speaker-dependent keyword vocabulary to help speed up their navigation.

If such a service were to become at all widespread, we might imagine some information providers would take the opportunity to cater to the audio interface. For example, politicians might wish to put subject-selectable speeches on the internet. One could use audio keyword access to hear Bob Dole, Pat Buchanan, Forbes or Clinton talk about flat tax, foreign policy, etc.

The Tower Records people could play musical selections, and one could order records. One could practice French, or perhaps, despite the bad microphones, people might have weekly "Karioke contests." Users could have a "name those sounds" contest with ten free AOL hours to the first person who correctly identifies: the chirp of a cricket, the sound of a home run being hit, a basketball dribble, the roar of an elephant, the sound of Niagara Falls, car brakes whose lining is gone, the sound of a football being kicked off, and the first five notes of the second movement of Beethoven's Seventh Symphony. A similar game could be played with lines from movies, or voices of famous people saying unfamous things. In addition, you might expect a station like WNYC public radio to be willing to record all its programs (it does anyway and makes them available by tape) and put the programs on disk so that they would be accessible by keyword match to content. Thus, a person interested in NYNEX might scan through the last two weeks of news programs for any mention of NYNEX and play the segments around it.

Such possibilities may become reality fairly soon. A recent workshop sponsored by the National Research Council and the National Science Foundation entitled, "Toward an Every Citizen's Interface to the National Information Infrastructure" recognized that the gap between information "haves" and "have-nots" may grow unless steps are taken to increase universal access. Much discussion focused on audio access to the internet. Web sites with a heavy audio component to them already include: http://www.addict.com and http://www.guitar.net. After searching many bookstores and failing to find any Welsh spoken language texts, I found an on-line course with audio at http://www.cs.brown.edu:80/fun/welsh. The National Center for Accessible Media (http://www.boston.com/wgbh/ncam) is pushing for closed-captioning of movie clips available on the web and "descriptive video services." Commercial ventures may also find increased access profitable. A Netscape spinoff, Navio (http://www.navio.com) is trying to make the internet available on all kinds of non-PC devices.

Clearly, audio access to the internet is only one avenue of increasing accessibility; ISO 9001 registration provides another possibility as does the new NYNEX committee on universal access. Hopefully, readers of this chapter may see ways to increase access through their own actions, perhaps in some of the ways described here, and perhaps in other ways – perhaps small, perhaps subtle. Who knows what oaks may grow?

REFERENCES

ANSI/ISO/ASQC 9001.1994. American National Standard. *Quality Systems – Model for Quality Assurance in Design, Development, Production, Installation, and Servicing* Milwaukee: ASQC Quality Press.

Chhabra, A.K., S.A. Chandran, and R. Katsuri. 1993. Table Structure Interpretation and Neural Network Based Text Recognition for Conversion of Telephone Company Tabular Drawings. In *Applications of Neural Networks to Telecommunications* eds. J. Alspector, R. Goodman, and T. Brown. Hillsdale, N.J.: Earlbaum.

Drucker, P.F. 1995. *Managing in a Time of Great Change.* New York: Truman Talley Books.

Friedman, B., E. Brok. S.K. Roth, and J. Thomas. 1996. Minimizing Bias in Computer Systems. *SIGCHI Bulletin* 28(1): 48–51.

Hemphill, C. 1996. Voice Navigation of the Internet: Completing the Multimedia Experience. *ASAT*: 211–214.

Krol, E. 1994. *The Whole Internet.* Sebastopol, CA: O'Rielly Associates.

Novick, D., D. House, M. Fanty, and R. Cole. 1995. *A Multimodal Browser for the World-Wide Web.* Technical Report CSE-95-18, Department of Computer Science and Engineering, Oregon Graduate Institute of Science & Technology.

Paciello, M.G. 1996. Designing for People with Disabilities. *Interactions* 3(1): 15–16.

Schmauch, C.H. 1995. *ISO 9000 for Software Developers.* Milwaukee, WI: ASQC Quality Press.

Stuart, R., and J.C. Thomas. 1991. Virtual Reality in Education. *Multimedia Review,* 2 (2): 17–27.

Thomas, J.C., and J. Carroll. 1978. The Psychology Study of Design. *Design Studies* 1 (1): 5–11.

Thomas, J.C. 1996. The Long Term Social Implications of New Information Technology. In *New Infotainment Technologies in the Home: Demand Side Perspectives,* eds. R. Dholakia, N. Mundorf, and N. Dholakia. Hillsdale, NJ: Erlbaum.

Thomas, J.C. Usability Engineering in 2020. 1995. In *Advances in Human–Computer Interaction,* ed. J. Nielsen. Norwood, NJ: Ablex, 1995.

Thomas, J.C. 1995. Human Factors in Lifecycle Development. In *Human Factors in Speech Technology,* eds. R. Bennett and J. Greenberg. Boca Raton: CRC Press.

Thomas, J.C., W.A. Kellogg, J. Grudin, and H. Ishii. 1992. *Cross-cultural Issues in Human Computer Interaction.* CHI 92 Workshop, Monterey, CA.

Thomas, J.C. 1991. The Human Factors of Voice Interfaces. *Journal of the Washington Academy of Sciences* 80(3): 138–151.

Thomas, J.C., and W.A. Kellogg. 1989. Minimizing Ecological Gaps in Interface Design, *IEEE Software* (January), 78–86.

Thomas, J.C. 1983. Studies in Office Systems I: The Effect of Communication Medium on Person Perception. IBM Research Report. *Office Systems Research Journal* 1(2): 75–88.

Yashchin, D., and B. Ortel. 1991. Experience with Speech Recognition in Automating Telephone Operator Functions. *Proceedings of the 2nd European Conference on Speech Communications and Technology.* Genova, Italy: Instituto Internationale della Communicazioni.

Yashchin, D., S. Basson, A. Kalyanswamy, and K. Silverman. 1992. *Results from Automating a Name and Address Service with Speech Synthesis.* American Voice Input Output Society, 1992.

Social Choice About Privacy: Intelligent Vehicle-Highway Systems in the United States

PHILIP E. AGRE AND CHRISTINE A. MAILLOUX

Abstract: Broad coalitions of companies, governments, and research institutions in several countries are currently designing massive electronic infrastructures for their roadways. Known collectively as Intelligent Vehicle-Highway Systems (IVHS), these technologies are intended to ease toll collection and commercial vehicle regulation, provide drivers with route and traffic information, improve safety, and ultimately support fully automated vehicles. Although many aspects of IVHS are uncertain, some proposed designs require the system to collect vast amounts of data on individuals' travel patterns, thus raising the potential for severe invasions of privacy. To make social choices about IVHS, it is necessary to reason about potentials for authoritarian uses of an IVHS infrastructure in the hypothetical future. Yet such reasoning is difficult, often veering toward utopian or dystopian extremes. To help anchor the privacy debate, this article places IVHS privacy concerns in an institutional context, offering conceptual frameworks to discuss the potential interactions between IVHS technologies and the computer design profession, standards-setting bodies, marketing organizations, and government administrative agencies.

Intelligent Vehicle-Highway Systems (IVHS) is the name given to a range of technologies, currently being designed or already deployed, for improving the efficiency of road-based transportation systems through the massive use of computer and networking technologies. IVHS systems are being planned in several countries (Jurgen, 1991). IVHS development in the United States is being coordinated and funded largely by the Department of Transportation (DOT) through the Intermodal Surface Transportation Efficiency Act of 1991 (ISTEA), together with numerous state Departments of Transportation (e.g., Roper & Endo, 1991; Smith, 1993).

Aside from general considerations of industrial policy, the high degree of government involvement in IVHS development is necessitated by state control of most roadways and by the nature of IVHS, whose market viability may depend upon technical compatibility among a wide range of products offered

This chapter originated in discussions at the Santa Clara Symposium on Privacy and Intelligent Vehicle-Highway Systems, organized at the Santa Clara University School of Law in July 1994 by Professor Dorothy Glancy and the members of the Santa Clara Privacy-IVHS Research Project. The opinions we express are nonetheless our own responsibility. We wish to thank Jonathan Allen, Roger Clarke, Chris Hibbert, Lee Tien, and Lauren Wiener for their helpful comments. We also wish to thank Sheri Alpert and Jim Gentner for their assistance in obtaining IVHS documents. Although the issues have evolved somewhat since we wrote the article upon which this chapter is based (see Branscomb & Keller, 1996), we have not tried to bring our analysis up to date.

by a large number of companies. The necessary architectural framework is being developed by a large-scale government-industry collaboration, in which the prospective producers of commercial IVHS systems are represented by a nonprofit organization known as the Intelligent Vehicle-Highway Society of America (abbreviated as IVHS America).[1]

The IVHS project raises numerous social issues. Transportation is a major part of the fabric of daily life, and social choices about transportation systems inevitably reflect and reinforce values about family, community, nationality, work, autonomy, and liberty. Although the debate behind the IVHS initiative certainly does not reflect a thorough rethinking of these matters, the ISTEA bill nonetheless required the DOT, as part of the process of establishing a national IVHS architecture, to investigate a wide range of 'nontechnical' issues that might affect the acceptance and implications of IVHS systems.

Among these nontechnical issues is privacy. IVHS systems may require the collection of vast amounts of digitized information about roads and traffic, thus creating the potential for abuse of this information by private companies or government agencies. It is a straightforward matter to spin worrisome scenarios of the physical tracking of dissidents, the harassment of people found driving on the wrong side of town, the fashioning of sales pitches aimed at people who pull into the competition's parking lot, and the oppressive monitoring of drivers of commercial vehicles (Gillmor, 1993). To take just one relatively benign and wholly plausible scenario, consider a marketing project recently undertaken by the State of Kentucky on behalf of its tourism industry (McDowell, 1994), "Kentucky's database showed that only 350,000 of the 2.5 million Canadians who drove through the state last year stayed overnight" (p.18). Says the State Commissioner of Travel Development, "Our research showed that 83% of them come from January to June, headed for Florida, South Carolina and the beaches of Alabama and Mississippi" (p. 18).

Based on this information, the state government instituted a publicity campaign in Toronto and began using direct mail advertisements to persuade Canadian tourists to stop in Kentucky. The use of commercial marketing techniques by public agencies on behalf of private business interests has become a common practice (Kotler, Haider & Rein, 1993). Since it is explicitly framed in terms of a geographical space, namely the governmental jurisdiction, this

---

[1]The proceedings of the IVHS America conferences (e.g., IVHS America 1993) are the best source of information on IVHS systems in the United States. Since we wrote the article on which this chapter is based, IVHS America has changed its name to the Intelligent Transportation Society of America (ITS America).

kind of marketing will benefit in a straightforward way from systems such as IVHS that capture extensive locational and travel information. Although IVHS may not originally be designed with market research applications in mind, the existence of large-scale databases of travel information will surely lead to pressures to put these databases to remunerative use.

Such worries become even more acute if we find it probable that participation in IVHS will someday be mandatory, whether as a matter of law or one of practicality. Since many of these worries are easily explained within the traditional public discourse on privacy issues, it seems likely that they will attract public attention and controversy. Public resistance to IVHS may therefore affect its commercial success. Borins (1988), for example, describes the failure of a proposed road-pricing system in Hong Kong based on Automatic Vehicle Identification (AVI), which was attributed to privacy concerns and resentment of new taxes. Despite government promises of data confidentiality, the project was rejected by numerous advisory boards and professional associations. An unusual opportunity may therefore exist to conduct a public debate about the privacy issues raised by IVHS systems and perhaps to adjust the design of these systems to mitigate some of the dangers before they have become widely established.

We wish to draw attention to some of the institutional dimensions of debate over IVHS. Like all important technologies, IVHS will interact heavily with the social institutions of markets, engineering, and public administration, and with the underlying culture. These anticipated interactions are sufficiently profound that it can be difficult to draw boundaries between the technology itself and the institutions that surround it. Predicting the social character of these interactions can be even more difficult. We propose to trace the outlines of these problems, offering some concepts that might be helpful in the substantive prognostications that will necessarily dominate the debate. We pursue this project under three headings:

1) We will discuss the limitations of prevailing cultural understandings of threats to privacy. A crucial difficulty is widespread lack of detailed knowledge about the technical and institutional machinery of data collection. We will suggest that increasing the visibility of this machinery may make the prospect of privacy invasion more concrete in nonexperts' daily experience, thereby supplying one prerequisite of genuine social choice about IVHS.

2) We will explore the technical practices underlying the design of computer systems such as those employed in IVHS. We will argue that privacy violations are not accidental consequences of computer design, but are inherent in deep-

ly rooted design practices. More socially acceptable methods will probably not be employed unless persuasive arguments and technical alternatives are made known to the designers.

3) We will suggest that potential solutions to the privacy problems posed by IVHS systems may lie in the social dynamics of technical standards. Embedding some relatively straightforward design principles into the IVHS design standards may provide some protection against future diversions of IVHS-collected personal information to improper purposes. The critical technical decisions will emerge through a combination of public and private mechanisms. Although broad public participation in these decisions is desirable in principle, it is unlikely in practice. Unless the inherent tension between expert decision making and public participation can be alleviated, we suggest, the controversy will inevitably shift toward elite manipulation of public opinion.

REASONING ABOUT IVHS

To debate about technology is to argue about the future. This is particularly true in the context of IVHS because of its far-reaching implications. What is uncertain is not precisely the technology, but the unfolding interaction between the technology, narrowly speaking, and the evolving social structures that condition its deployment, use, and future development. This section explores some of the preconditions of rational social choice about such matters. Although broad public awareness of privacy issues is certainly one of these preconditions, this awareness must be formulated in terms that are concrete enough to translate into action. Genuine consent to technological innovations requires a concrete awareness of privacy issues as they are manifested in daily life.

Perhaps the most common form of objection to IVHS, already alluded to in the introduction, is its potential for contributing to a Big Brother form of society in which mechanized surveillance becomes a routine and pervasive part of life. Despite its powerful hold over both scholarly and popular discussions of computers and privacy, Big Brother imagery should be understood as a cultural phenomenon. Concerns about surveillance have their roots in historical experiences of the secret police and their practices of routine observation of innocent people. These concerns took a particularly compact and potent literary form in Orwell's dystopian allegory in 1984.

As the next section will explain in more detail, this 'surveillance model' (Agre, 1994) is only one possible way of conceiving the potential dangers of IVHS. It has several distinguishing elements. One of them is the use of visual metaphors: Big Brother is specifically "watching," and in doing so is not understood to intervene in what he watches. (Of course, Big Brother might decide to intervene later on; the point is that the surveillance itself is not disruptive.) Another is the idea that Big Brother stands in for a centrally coordinated bureaucracy, as opposed to a heterogeneous collection of local power relationships. Together, these ideas structure thinking about privacy concerns in specific ways. The paradigm is the state and its powers, and the dangers are political in character. Of course, specifically political values may well be in danger. The point is that the Big Brother metaphor also carries this state-centered model into other realms, such as the use of monitoring technologies in the workplace. Every metaphor has limits, and it will be important to explore these in the context of particular proposals.[2]

An analysis by Reiman (1995) bears reflection in this regard. Building on the visual metaphors of the Panopticon (Foucault, 1977), with its capacity to maintain its inmates under constant and anonymous observation, he argues that the prevalence of surveillance technologies would not simply provide the means for an exogenous oppression of individuals, but that it might also lead to internal psychosocial changes through its chilling effect. Shorn of the ability to enter into relationships of responsibility and trust, individuals will tend to gravitate toward a safe average, suppressing their individuality and creativity in favor of a thoroughgoing orientation to the demands of an omniscient observer.

This argument depends, among other things, on the proposition that people know they are being watched, or at least that they will become aware of this pervasive surveillance in the future. Yet people generally are not aware of the details of the threats to their privacy. For example, although the public expresses a high level of concern about privacy issues (Privacy and American Business, 1993, p. 9), it nonetheless has a low level of awareness of the machinery of the personal information industry: how it gets its information, where the information goes, what is done with it, and so forth (Privacy Rights Clearinghouse, 1993, p. 11–13; Smith, 1994, p. 146–150). The awareness of privacy concerns is abstract, on the level of "they know everything about us."

Unless it takes on paranoid proportions, this abstract conception of surveillance does express a genuine truth about the place of information technology

---

[2]For further evaluations of the prophesy of 1984, see Howe (1983) and Laudon (1991, p. 492).

in society. Yet, with its nonspecific "they" and "everything", the abstract conception is a cause for concern in itself, for several reasons:

- It contributes to a corrosive atmosphere of distrust in society.

- It discourages participation in democratic processes by making it impossible to identify specific villains or imagine specific remedies.

- It permits interested parties to oversimplify the issues by emphasizing the role of government to the exclusion of industry, or vice versa.

- It promotes fatalism by suggesting that our privacy is already wholly lost.

- It precludes an understanding of the social forces that lead to an extension of surveillance to new realms of life, and indeed makes it difficult to recognize that such as yet uncolonized realms even exist.

- Finally, it leaves meaningless the thousands of everyday interactions in which the machinery of information-collection could otherwise be seen in operation – at work, in commerce, in medical care, and so forth.

In light of these concerns, one useful goal might be to facilitate a more concrete awareness of the machinery of information collection by rendering it more visible.[3] Such an arrangement would make visible not only the mechanisms of data collection, but the practical arrangements (such as lines of sight, markings, physical barriers, and so forth) that make information collection possible. If certain kinds of information are collected to provide certain services or guard against certain hazards, and if the full range of psychosocial effects of such data collection have been honestly reckoned to weigh less than the benefits, then the administrative procedures and the technology itself might be designed to open their social and technical workings to public view. The resulting reflection and debate may then lead to alternative social choices.

If the visibility of information collection permits a concrete awareness of privacy issues as they arise in daily life, it will become possible to speak meaningfully of 'consent' as it relates to social choice about novel technical arrangements (Flaherty, 1989, p. 380). In what sense can someone be said to consent to IVHS and the information collection that attends it? When a sensor is installed by a roadside to count the passing cars, the resulting information is aggregated and anonymous and thus generally regarded as unlikely to significantly affect any individual's interests. Technologies associated with law enforcement might identify individuals, for example by taking pictures of the license plates of speeders. But the installation of such systems is consented to or

---

[3]Visibility is more frequently called 'transparency', a term we find overly ambiguous.

refused at the level of the whole society, at least nominally, through the procedures of democracy.

Nonetheless, a fully developed IVHS system will have a large number of features that are, or at least ought to be, matters of individualized consent. Consent, however, normally implies a clear understanding of the proposition and the ability to give consent freely, and neither of these conditions is provided for automatically by all potential IVHS designs. The collection of personal information in IVHS may not be readily apparent to individual drivers, and the uses of that information will certainly occur at a great distance, with consequences that are difficult to discover and even more difficult to weigh. Moreover, individuals faced with choosing or forgoing particular elements of IVHS technology will not necessarily have any genuine choice, inasmuch as the use of IVHS might become a practical necessity for living a certain kind of life (much as credit cards have become for most professionals), a condition of affordable insurance (itself often mandated by the state), or a necessity of avoiding extreme crowding at tollbooths and other ill-maintained remnants of the unautomated world. Thus to say that IVHS technology is 'voluntary' is not nearly good enough.

The complexities of consent are particularly apparent when personal information is collected through market transactions (Gandy, 1993, p. 205–209). Widespread ignorance about the nature and scope of the personal information industry may reflect a major category of market failure. Although an individual might experience indignation in learning about the circulation of his or her personal information among marketing organizations, for example, that state of affairs arose largely through that individual's own actions in entering into large numbers of freely chosen private contracts. In the terms of classical market economics, such people, lacking important information, have not been able to estimate the actual costs of the contracts they have entered into.

The inability to make rational market judgments due to a shortage of information is, of course, a common phenomenon. Meyerson (1990) considers the general problem of form contracts, which are standardized contracts presented by firms such as banks, insurance companies, and car rental agencies, on a take it or leave it ('adherence') basis. These, of course, constitute the vast majority of contracts entered into by most people, and they routinely incorporate clauses which most people do not know about or do not understand. This imperfection creates a perverse economic incentive for firms to fashion contract language that shifts more costs and risks onto customers than they would accept if they had a full rational understanding of the consequences of what they are signing (Braucher, 1988). When the unknown or misunderstood clauses pertain to secondary uses of transactional information, the covertly shifted costs could be considerable, inasmuch as customers can lose control over highly personal details of their lives. Since computer technology allows information to be copied, forwarded, and recombined without limit at low cost, the effects of this propagation can wildly exceed the estimates that the individual tacitly made in agreeing to each successive contract.

The complexities of consent are not limited to the sphere of market exchange. Given that infrastructure and information tend to last for long periods, it can be equally difficult for a democratic society to make informed social choices about the future consequences of technologies. In their most extreme form, such uncertainties are expressed in such terms as, "even supposing that IVHS will be used only for civilized purposes in the near term, it is unacceptably dangerous given that a future authoritarian government could easily convert it to repressive purposes." What follows from such arguments? Should they be regarded as inherently antitechnological in nature? Although their vagueness, speculative character, and appeal to extreme situations may invite dismissal, political repression is nonetheless a massive historical reality, and it is important to take such arguments seriously by refining them to more tractable forms.

What patterns can we discern in the evolution of institutional uses of technologies, and how can these provide precedents for making rational choices about IVHS? Current experience with the accumulation of personal information certainly provides plenty of relevant material (Smith, 1994). For example, people who administer databases of personal information frequently say that once information is stored, the imagination works overtime to come up with additional uses for it. In the context of government, this process is frequently mediated by the definition of particular stigmatized classes of people, whether gang members (Le, 1993) or immigrants (Pear, 1994) or sex offenders (Kiernan, 1993) or 'deadbeat dads' (Hopfensperger, 1994). This type of inference can bring debates about IVHS down to earth, grounding them in fairly well established logics of institutional dynamics and technical practices.

COMPUTER SYSTEMS DESIGN AND PRIVACY

The term IVHS refers to a wide range of potential technologies. The architecture specification process currently being undertaken by DOT and IVHS America envisions twenty-eight separate 'user services' falling into six general areas: Travel and Traffic Management, Public Transportation Management, Electronic Payment, Commercial Vehicle Operations, Emergency Management, and Advanced Vehicle Safety Systems. In practice, these categories are largely an effort to place some conceptual order on a vast number of partially separable systems supplied by hundreds of separate vendors. It is only in a limited sense, then, that DOT and IVHS America are 'designing a system,' as opposed to attempting the delicate and deeply political coordination of numerous developments, many of which could conceivably proceed independently.

Although each element of this maze should ideally be analyzed in its own terms, in the fullness of its particular technical and political context, it is nonetheless possible to reason usefully about the politics of privacy in IVHS design on the level of computer design in general. Agre (1994) has distinguished two sets of metaphors for understanding privacy. We have already mentioned one of these, the 'surveillance model,' with its reliance upon visual metaphors. Computers, though, do not work by looking at things. Despite limited advances in research on computerized vision, computers fundamentally operate on languages – mathematical languages to be sure, but languages that at least share the formal grammatical structures of natural human languages. When applied to tasks involving interaction with human activities, the vast majority of computer systems operate according to a different logic, the 'capture model.' The capture model derives from the conventional notion of computer functionality: A computer cannot support an activity unless it can represent the salient features of that activity within some suitable representation scheme, and it cannot represent anything that it cannot 'capture' through digital inputs from keyboards and other devices in the physical and social world.

The capture model focuses attention on something that the surveillance model does not, namely the practical arrangements by which human activities are 'captured.' Computers cannot simply watch things; to the contrary, the activities that computers track must be organized in ways that facilitate automated representation. More specifically, in order to be represented in the terms provided by some formal language, a human activity must have a precise type of structure imposed upon it so that a computer can, so to speak, 'parse' the activity in the terms it can represent. Participants in the activity, moreover, must collaborate with this process. The synthesis and imposition of these 'grammars of action' (Agre, 1994 p. 107) has been central to applied computing practice from the technology's earliest days. Grammars of action are found, for example, in early systems analysis techniques (Couger, 1973), and they persist in such recent developments as workflow analysis (Medina-Mora et al., 1992) and business practice reengineering (Hammer & Champy 1993).

As a general rule, computer system development and implementation go much more smoothly when grammars of action have already been imposed upon the activities in question for other reasons, such as work discipline, regulatory auditing, or process standardization. In the case of traffic management, indeed, many of the necessary grammars of action were imposed before the computer age for purposes of efficiency, safety, and manual toll collection. One of these grammars is the discrete space of possible travel routes permitted by limited access highways. Other elements of existing road travel grammars include the division of roads into discrete lanes, between which drivers are legally obliged to make discrete lane changes, and the specification of intersections, with a substantial body of legal constraints on their use.

Grammars of action also govern the operation of individual vehicles, inasmuch as the vehicle's controls define a discrete space of operations such as turning the ignition on and off, locking and unlocking doors, shifting gears, operating the lights and other such devices, and so forth. Many recent passenger cars enforce complex constraints upon the use of these controls, for example preventing the ignition from being turned on unless the automatic transmission is in 'park,' preventing the transmission from being put into gear unless the brake pedal is depressed, automatically locking the doors when the transmission is first put into gear, automatically unlocking the doors when the ignition is turned off, and so forth.[4]

The grammars of action employed by IVHS systems will build on these preexisting grammars, perhaps adding additional elements such as the specification of particular lanes in which specific advanced equipment might be used for automated driving or toll collection. In fact, several vendors currently provide systems for commercial trucks that capture much of the truck's internal state while it is operating, as well as locational information from the Global Positioning System (GPS) and other measurements (e.g., Qualcomm, n.d.).

Central to the creation of a grammar of action is the elaboration of an 'ontology' – a set of ideas about what the world is made of, and how these basic units and relationships might be reflected in computerized representations. As business systems have captured large numbers of transactions, a fairly standardized database technology has arisen to impose a uniform order upon the resulting computerized records, and to make those records available to a wide

---

[4]We owe this observation about the grammars of automobile operation to a correspondent whose name we have unfortunately lost.

range of standardized operations (ordering, searching, comparing, etc). These are the databases that are at issue when concerns about informational privacy are raised.

The relevant point for present purposes is that these design practices make it natural to record information in individualized form. Since the whole purpose of this type of design is to 'capture' states of affairs in the world, producing structures in a computer that mirror the structures of the world outside, the natural endpoint of this process is an explicit record of which specific people, cars, and other entities were involved in each specific transaction. This is one reason why it is so common for managers of computer systems to equate 'privacy' (a social and moral concept) with 'security' (a technical concept) – the canons of design are maintained, and steps are taken to ensure that the resulting databases of personal information are only used for those purposes that the organization owning them has designated through its policies. If it is proposed to protect privacy by, for example, making all transactions anonymous, then this will require innovation that diverges from, and goes beyond, the conventionally taught and learned practices of design. It is therefore particularly important that privacy issues be considered at the beginning of the design process, while basic architectural commitments are being made, and not restricted to (perfectly legitimate) concerns with data security.

The collection of individualized information strikes to the heart of concerns with personal privacy. The assignment of a unique identifier to every person and/or car is the key to the assembly of a dossier that combines information from multiple sources in a coherent, lasting form that invites a wide variety of uses. It therefore matters precisely which of the many services envisioned by the IVHS planning process actually requires the capture of individualized information. Some services, such as the measurement of traffic flows, may seem wholly indifferent to the identities of individual drivers and cars, but even in such cases there exist plausible schemes (for example, counting cars by automatically scanning their license plates from video cameras as they go by) that generate aggregate information indirectly through the gathering of more individualized forms of information.

Large technological systems like IVHS are not created out of thin air or produced by organizations with no prior commitments or interests. Inspection of the *IVHS Architecture Development Program Interim Status Report* (US Department of Transportation and IVHS America 1994), dated April 1994, makes this evident. This report presents twelve-page "architecture concepts" by the four "architecture development teams," each consisting of a single lead firm and a group of smaller firms, university research groups, and state government agencies. Each architecture is to be evaluated by "stakeholders" (public sector infrastructure providers, private sector "product and service providers," "users and fleet operators," and "national interests") through a formal comment process involving ten "implication areas" (deployment, equity, financing, institutions, market, operations and maintenance, policy and regulation, privacy, safety, and standards).

The status report summarizes the questions pertaining to the privacy area as follows:

> This area describes the effect of the architectures on the privacy of individuals and organizations. Factors to consider include: Will the architectures require some level of mandatory participation? Will there be information security safeguards? Will there be the opportunity for the marketplace to use gathered information and will the architectures accommodate law enforcement capabilities? (page 22)

This passage leaves many issues unaddressed. The notion of privacy is not defined, either for individuals or organizations. The relationship between privacy and security is not articulated. And no guidance is offered on how privacy interests are to be weighed against market and law enforcement interests. In practice, it is nearly impossible to evaluate most of the 'architecture concepts' against these criteria. The individual proposals are worth considering individually because they are nearly incommensurable in their modes of presentation, their framing of the issues, their degree of detail, and their attention to social factors.

The first proposal, by a team led by Hughes Aircraft, provides a detailed account of the use of a specific technology involving 'tags' on cars that communicate wirelessly with roadside 'beacons' that interact over a computer network with regional Transportation Management Centers (TMCs). The proposal evinces considerable reflection upon privacy issues and its discussion of the matter is worth quoting in full:

> The Architecture does not require anyone to give up their privacy. The tag-beacon approach uses 'blind' IDs. A vehicle owner stores a unique randomly chosen ID into the tag when it is purchased. No one other than that person needs to know the ID.
>
> There are four exceptions to this rule and they are accepted by the owner/driver involved. Two of them, Commercial Vehicle Operations and transit transactions require that individual vehicles be identified.
>
> The other two are transactions in which the vehicle owner wants the ID to be known temporarily. Stolen vehicle recovery is based upon beacons monitoring for the owner's vehicle ID. The fourth exception is toll collection where the vehicle owner prefers a credit card rather than a cash card form of payment. (Note that the pri-

vacy risk associated with credit card use is something which most people accept.)
(page 33)

The second proposal, by a team led by Loral and IBM, is entirely different. Without mentioning specific technologies, it is organized around highly centralized information collection by regional TMCs. Its discussion of privacy has a different character:

> There is no mandatory participation required of any citizen with respect to his or her privacy. IVHS should be viewed as a "subscription" rather than a "participation" service. Our Architecture will provide for safeguarding of any personal or private information within the System, including locations and records of commercial vehicles, and financial transaction information associated with electronic payment of tolls, fees and fares. These safeguards will be implemented using advanced, secure, encryption and authentication techniques (page 46).

The emphasis, in other words, is on maintaining the security of personal information rather than minimizing its role in the operation of the system.

The third proposal, by a team led by Rockwell International, is by far the best thought out proposal on a systems level. Its emphasis is on maximizing generality through a rational process of system decomposition and definition of generic interfaces, taking into account the widest possible range of services and managerial issues. No explicit attention is given to privacy issues, and little is said about the precise content of the 'information' and 'data' that circulate through the system. A number of illustrations make clear, though, that individuals pay for their use of the system by means of a 'transaction card' which is depicted as listing "Your Name," "Your Bank," and "Account No." and is thus presumably not anonymous.

The fourth proposal, by a team led by Westinghouse Electric, contains by far the most detailed account of how a future transportation infrastructure would be organized. Whereas the other three proposals refer to transportation services in a generic way, or else rely on existing and familiar categories of services, this proposal provides a detailed account of the participating agencies and their exchanges of both passengers and information. In particular, it is the only proposal with a significant emphasis on public transportation. Its only discussion of privacy appears in a table (page 72) of the "Westinghouse Team's Approach" to each of the implication areas; under the heading of "privacy" the entry reads, in its entirety: "Providing safeguards to protect organizational and personal privacy."

It is clear, then, that the four working proposals in the DOT interim report take wildly different approaches to privacy, and in particular that their outlooks on privacy are integral parts of their larger philosophies. These philosophies, in turn, are closely related to each lead company's specific strength. The Hughes proposal is built around a specific Hughes technology, the tag-and-beacon scheme (which, however, is similar to technologies provided by a number of other companies). The Loral/IBM proposal is clearly built around a mainframe philosophy, which is clearly tied to IBM's historical strength. The Rockwell proposal is not organized around a specific technology, but rather places great emphasis on the systems integration skills that are Rockwell's particular strength. And the Westinghouse proposal envisions a wide range of custom transportation vehicles and systems, corresponding once again to that company's strength. Each lead firm, in other words, has prepared a proposal that, if accepted, would place its own strengths at the center of future IVHS development.

IVHS development is thus plainly, among other things, a matter of attempted agenda setting by the largest interests involved in the development process. Each proposal makes clear that a technology such as IVHS is not designed from scratch as a response to an abstract list of desiderata such as privacy. Rather, each competing organization must present its own capabilities as responsive to the demands of the technical tasks and the formal decision procedures. Those organizations which have coherent selling points to offer on the issue of privacy have presented them, while others have emphasized other points. As a practical matter, then, decisions about privacy will always be made as part of a much larger institutional calculus.

PRIVACY, STANDARDS, AND DECISION MAKING

IVHS envisions a massive extension to the infrastructure of transportation. But IVHS is not a single machine or a single project. It is, rather, a framework for the development and deployment of a wide range of technologies that must work together. Furthermore, it is a system that must support vehicles that move throughout the extent of any given continent (Kayton, 1991). Additionally, American firms feel they must move quickly to establish standards in order to head off competition from foreign competitors (Berardinis, 1992). These are the motivations for the formal architecture development project being undertaken at public expense by DOT and IVHS America. Although this particular process is not aimed at the creation of a formal set of standards for the operation and interoperation of IVHS technologies, it will surely inform the work of the standard-setting bodies, and the resulting sets of standards will, in any event, play a crucial role in defining the marketplace for IVHS products and services. Consideration of IVHS standards holds some promise for alleviating some of the system's potential dangers regarding privacy.

Standards serve many purposes, but in the present context their salient purpose is allowing artifacts purchased from different suppliers to operate together. A paradigm example might be pipe threads: When a pipe and an elbow conform to the same standard, they can be fastened together regardless of who made them. As this example illustrates, standards frequently become entrenched in the marketplace, whereupon they take on a life of their own without anybody necessarily having to enforce a codified version of them. Manufacturers of new pipes employ nonstandard threads at their peril, since customers may wish to install the new pipes in existing plumbing systems that use the existing standards.

Standards may become entrenched for other reasons as well. One familiar example is the QWERTY keyboard, which has never been displaced by optimized keyboards because of individual typists' great investment in their skills for using it (David, 1985). New typists, moreover, anticipate a world in which the vast majority of keyboards use the QWERTY layout, making it reasonable to learn to use those keyboards rather than the alternatives. Keyboard manufacturers, likewise, anticipate a market in which the vast majority of typists are accustomed to the QWERTY layout and little demand exists for keyboards that can only be used by people who have learned to use the alternative layout.

Given the decentralized nature of the IVHS industry and its customers, it is likely that a wide variety of standards will become entrenched there as well. IVHS differs from many parts of the computer industry, though, in the degree of conscious forethought and design that is being invested in the definition of an all-embracing architecture. The IVHS picture thus contrasts somewhat with the evolutionary metaphor proposed by authors such as Nelson and Winter (1982) and Basalla (1988), who emphasize the role of circumstance in determining which technologies are taken up within the marketplace and then, having become established, proceed to supply part of the environment conditioning the selection of future technologies.

This state of affairs is intriguing from a political perspective. As Winner (1988) has argued, artifacts can embody political stances in the ways in which they structure relationships among people. He provides the example of a set of bridges in New York whose clearances are low enough to block access to buses, thus effectively excluding people who do not own cars from visiting Jones Beach. Standards may thus be used to enforce organizational and social divisions. Yet standards may help in protecting privacy. If standards for the collection and use of information during IVHS operations are defined without the need for individualized information, then these standards might become entrenched as well. To the extent that future revisions or additions to the currently envisioned IVHS system must interconnect with a massive installed base of existing machinery and software, they will need to exchange data in the recognized formats and protocols. In order to divert IVHS data to new purposes, such an institution would have to swim against the tide of entrenched standards in order to collect data that can be tied to individuals at all. It is not entirely clear at the moment to what extent this proposal is feasible, but now is the time to explore the possibility, while the standards are still being settled.

Other scenarios are certainly possible. IVHS-type systems are currently most advanced for commercial vehicles. This is not surprising, given the powerful competitive pressures in the trucking industry, as well as the pressures upon state regulatory agencies to improve the efficiency of their interactions with commercial freight haulers. For example, the HELP (Heavy Vehicle Electronic License Plate) System is being developed in ten western states to automatically identify, classify, and weigh passing trucks, collecting fees electronically and flagging to roadside inspection stations only those vehicles for which more detailed manual checks are necessary. The HELP System captures the Vehicle Identification Number (VIN) of each truck as a matter of course through wireless data exchange, since this information is the basis of the regulatory agencies' record-keeping. Since this type of system, which is already in operation in several states, has a head start over systems intended for the use of private citizens, the danger arises of its protocols extending to become standards for all vehicles. The point is that the social dynamics of standard-setting can follow a variety of disparate paths, depending on the sociology of standardization and the economics of entrenchment.

Decisions about IVHS will be made in a variety of forums, each with its powers, limitations, arguments, and degrees and kinds of participation. Since IVHS will probably have substantial effects upon the lives of virtually everyone, and particularly since the government is funding many aspects of the most fateful early stages of development, it would be desirable to see broad public participation in the processes of social choice that are defining IVHS systems. The problems with this idea are precisely the classical problems of expert decision making in a democracy. For example, as Horwitz (1994) has argued, regulatory decision making within the US government has been shaped by a tension between an emphasis on expertise, whose constraining criterion as defined through the process of judicial review is a minimal level of substantive rationality, and an emphasis on public participation, whose constraining criteria are procedural. In the case of IVHS, the government-sponsored technical decision making is being organized by a complex amalgam of government agencies and alliances of private interests, with most of the formal standard setting (as opposed to broad sketching of architectures) occurring in wholly private forums.

Decision making around IVHS, as with many emerging technologies, suffers an inherent imbalance of power. Although the DOT/IVHS America *Interim Status Report* (1994) includes individual travelers and public interest groups among the identified categories of IVHS architecture stakeholders, these latter groups are not well organized. Only a small proportion of the eventual users of IVHS technologies are even aware of these technologies' existence, and consequently the portion of the population with active concerns about potential hazards from IVHS cannot support public interest organizations that might aspire to represent their interests. Individual drivers who might be faced with a choice between submitting to automatic detailed tracking of their movements and forgoing the benefits of IVHS systems will have essentially no capacity to bargain over the architecture of the system once it has been specified and fielded. It may be argued that this situation can be averted through market mechanisms if the private firms seeking to establish businesses based on IVHS technology decide that substantial numbers of potential drivers will actually forego IVHS technology altogether out of concern at its privacy implications. Yet such a scenario makes several assumptions: that these firms can accurately anticipate future customers' fears, that customers will know enough about the potential privacy hazards to make rational purchasing decisions, that the disadvantages of foregoing IVHS are not themselves unreasonably severe, that the services will not therefore become *de facto* (or even *de jure*) obligatory, and that the business advantages of privacy-invasive systems do not outweigh the loss in potential sales.

Legislative solutions, the traditional channel for public participation, may be limited in their ability to protect privacy in IVHS. One category of possible legislation could prevent individualized information from being used for non-IVHS purposes or surrendered to the government without a subpoena. But such legislation cannot in itself prevent the erosion of these protections later on. Another category of legislation could seek to influence the architecture of IVHS systems. This approach would probably not be effective once the architecture development process become well advanced, and it would require great care to devise suitable legislative language, given the highly technical nature of the issues. A prohibition on the capture of personal information, though, could be formulated with relative ease, provided that a broad public consensus were to develop in the near term behind such a proposal.

If no mechanisms arise for ensuring informed and effective public participation in IVHS development, contests over IVHS will move to the ground of symbolic manipulation in the public sphere. Concern on this count is raised by the framing of privacy issues in a US Department of Transportation report to Congress, mandated by ISTEA, entitled *Nontechnical Constraints and Barriers to Implementation of Intelligent Vehicle-Highway Systems* (US Department of Transportation, 1994). Within this language of "constraints and barriers," protection of privacy is not defined as one of the functionalities of IVHS; rather, fears about privacy are defined as an obstacle to its implementation. User's perceptions of a system's hazards are treated as a sort of failure mode of the larger sociotechnical system of which machine and user are part (Agre, 1995). For example, the report states that: "... DOT has concluded that IVHS technologies are less likely to be constrained because of concerns about the improper invasion of privacy when:

- The benefits of these technologies are clearly understood.
- The benefits are perceived as outweighing any adverse effects on privacy.
- It is perceived that the information will be properly protected; and
- Basic principles are followed to safeguard privacy. (page 8-3)

Although the DOT report asserts that "[t]he DOT will ... insist upon appropriate conduct in the handling of personal information" (page 8-8), the "basic principles" and "appropriate conduct" are not further specified beyond two sentences on the use of anonymous radio 'tags' in some existing automatic toll collection systems (page 8-4). The danger is that organizations seeking to implement IVHS systems designed without true architectural support for privacy protection will resort to symbolic manipulations to change public perceptions rather than changing the architecture itself.

Privacy activists may succumb to their own temptations to manipulation. We have already argued that the rhetoric of Big Brother employed by the surveillance model may not accurately describe the phenomena involved in computerized tracking of human activities. Lacking broad public understanding of the issues, privacy activists must make a pragmatic decision. Considerable passions can be raised through appeal to the powerful cultural symbols mobilized by the surveillance model. And these passions may indeed result in the short term in stronger and more genuine privacy protection than would reasoned explanations of the true shape of the issues. Without an effective organization, individual activists may discover that early proposals (like the *Interim Status Report*) will be too vague to critique and that later, specific proposals will embed unfortunate commitments too deeply to be overhauled from scratch.

CONCLUSION

In this paper we have explored various contexts of social reasoning about IVHS, relating it to the institutional structures of markets, engineering, standard setting mechanisms, and democratic processes. Our aim has not been to offer detailed accounts of these systems or detailed proposals for design, policy, or activism. Instead we have argued that, because of their potentially pervasive nature, IVHS technologies pose significant social challenges in relation to each of these institutions. Debate about IVHS is thus largely a debate about the future development of a larger social order, and particularly about the interactions between technological systems and social structures.

In renegotiating the technologies and institutions of transportation, we as a society are necessarily renegotiating the very nature of social individuality, inasmuch as social identity in American society is tied up with the ubiquity of the automobile. Since privacy is a crucial aspect of moral individuality, privacy issues in IVHS are thus central to the deeper social meaning of the technology. Moreover, these privacy issues are sufficiently profound to require reforms in the ways in which the institutions of engineering conceptualize human beings and their activities. Public participation in this reform process brings significant challenges of its own, but the price of failure is even greater: an increase in the rational administration of daily life.

REFERENCES

Agre, P.E. 1994. Surveillance and Capture: Two Models of Privacy. *The Information Society* 10(2):101–127.

Agre, P.E. 1995. Conceptions of the User in Computer System Design. In *Social and Interactional Dimensions of Human-Computer Interfaces*, ed. P. Thomas. Cambridge, UK:Cambridge University Press.

Alpert, S. 1995. Privacy on Intelligent Highway: Finding the Right of Way. *Santa Clara Computer and High Technology Law Journal* 11(1):97–118.

Basalla, G. 1988. *The Evolution of Technology.* Cambridge, UK: Cambridge University Press.

Berardinis, L.A. 1992. Smart Highways Get the Green Light. *Machine Design* 64(16): 66–70.

Borins, S.F. 1988. Electronic Road Pricing: An Idea Whose Time May Never Come. *Transportation Research* A 22A(1):37–44.

Couger, J.D. 1973. Evolution of Business System Development Techniques. *Computing Surveys* 5(3):167–198.

David, P.A. 1985. Clio and the Economics of QWERTY. *American Economic Review* 72(2):332–337.

Foucault, M. 1977. *Discipline and Punish: The Birth of the Prison.* Translated from the French by A. Sheridan. New York: Pantheon.

Garfinkel, S., D. Weise, and S. Strassman. 1994. *UNIX HATERS.* San Mateo, CA:IDG Books.

Gillmor, D. 1993. On the Road to Nosiness? The Same Gear that Would Smooth Out Traffic Jams Could Be Used to Snoop on You. *Detroit Free Press.* (October 18) page A1.

Hammer, M., and J. Champy. 1993. *Reengineering the Corporation: A Manifesto for Business Revolution.* New York:Harper.

Hopfensperger, J. 1994. Child Support Deadbeats Get Reprieve from Ridicule. *Minneapolis Star Tribune* (August 8) page 1A.

Horwitz, R.B. 1994. Judicial Review of Regulatory Decisions. *Political Science Quarterly* 109(1):133–169.

Howe, I., ed. 1983. *1984 Revisited: Totalitarianism in Our Century.* New York:Harper and Row.

IVHS America. 1993. *Proceedings of the 1993 Annual Meeting of IVHS America: Surface Transportation: Mobility, Technology, and Society,* 14-17 April, Washington, DC, Washington, DC:IVHS America.

Jurgen, R.K. 1991. Smart Cars and Highways Go Global. *IEEE Spectrum* 28(5):26–36.

Kayton, M. 1991. Standardization of Intelligent Vehicles and Highways. *Proceedings of the Institution of Mechanical Engineers, Part D (Journal of Automobile Engineering)* 205(D3):193–197.

Kiernan, L.A. 1993. New Law Tough on Offenders: Those with Sex Convictions Must Register with State. *Boston Globe.* (August 15) page 37.

Kotler, P., Haider, D.H., and Rein, I. 1993. *Marketing Places: Attracting Investment, Industry, and Tourism to Cities, States, and Nations.* New York:Free Press.

Latour, B. 1988. The Prince for Machines as Well as for Machinations. In *Technology and Social Change*, ed. B. Elliot. Edinburgh:Edinburgh University Press.

Laudon, K.C. 1991. Comment on *Preserving Individual Autonomy in an Information-oriented Society.* In *Computerization and Controversy: Value Conflicts and Social Choices.* Boston, eds. C. Dunlop and R. Kling. San Diego, CA:Academic Press.

Le, T. 1993. Police Group Unveils Anti-Gang Strategy. *Los Angeles Times* (February 5) page B4.

McDowell, E. 1994. The Scrambling Is on for Off-Season Tourism. *New York Times* (September 5) pp. 17–18.

Medina-Mora, R., T. Winograd, R. Flores, and F. Flores. 1992. The Action Workflow Approach to Workflow Management Technology. In *Proceedings of CSCW-92*, 281–288, Toronto, Ontario.

Meyerson, M.I. 1990. The Efficient Consumer Form Contract: Law and Economics Meets the Real World. *Georgia Law Review* 24(3):583–627.

Nelson, R.R., and S.G. Winter. 1982. *An Evolutionary Theory of Economic Change*, Cambridge, MA:Harvard University Press.

Pear, R. 1994. Federal Panel Proposes Register to Curb Hiring of Illegal Aliens. *New York Times.* (August 4) page A1.

Privacy and American Business. 1993. *Louis Harris Survey on Consumer Privacy Concerns.* Hackensack, NJ:P & AB Information Service.

Privacy Rights Clearinghouse. 1993. *First Annual Report of the Privacy Rights Clearinghouse.* Center for Public Interest Law, University of San Diego.

Qualcomm. c. 1994. Omnitracs Two-Way Satellite-Based Mobile Communications [brochure].

Reiman, J. 1995. Driving to the Panopticon: A Philosophical Exploration of the Risks to Privacy Posed by the Highway Technology of the Future. *Santa Clara Computer and High Technology Law Journal* 11(1):27–44.

Roper, D.H., and G. Endo. 1991. Advanced Traffic Management in California. *IEEE Transactions on Vehicular Technology* 40(1):152–158.

Smith, B.L. 1993. The Virginia Department of Transportation's Strategic Plan for an Intelligent Vehicle-Highway Systems Program. In *The Proceedings of the 1993*

310   Philip E. Agre and Christine A. Mailloux

Annual Meeting of IVHS America: Surface Transportation: Mobility, Technology, and Society, 376–380. 14–17 April. Washington, DC: IVHS America.

Smith, H.J. 1994. *Managing Privacy: Information Technology and Corporate America.* Chapel Hill, NC:University of North Carolina Press.

US Department of Transportation and IVHS America. 1994. *IVHS Architecture Development Program Interim Status Report.* (April).

US Department of Transportation. 1994. *Nontechnical Constraints and Barriers to Implementation of Intelligent Vehicle-Highway Systems: A Report to Congress* (June).

Winner, L. 1988. Do Artifacts Have Politics? In M.E. Kraft and N.J. Vig, eds., *Technology and Politics.* Durham, NC: Duke University Press.

Name Index

A

Adler 5, 6
Agre xi, 9, 12, 14, 15, 91, 94, 99, 239, 289–
        310, 293, 297, 306
Allen 232, 289
Alpert 289
Amundson 67, 69, 82
Appadurai 2
Aristotle 211
Austin 93, 94

B

Backstrom 185
Badhorn 166
Baecker 7
Bailar 167
Bailey 167
Baker 165
Bannon 91, 97, 101
Barley 137
Basalla 303
Basson 271, 277
Battle 118
Bednarski 222
Bee 150
Beell 155
Bell 271
Bennett 101
Berardinis 302
Berlins 34
Berscheid 147, 165
Binnick 163
Blackmon 194
Blankenship 143
Blascovich 175
Blomberg 6, 267
Bly 266

Bodker 6
Bogen 94
Bond 165
Borg 139
Borins 291
Borning 42
Bowers 92, 93, 95
Bradburn 166
Branscomb 289
Braucher 295
Bravo 239, 245
Breimhorst 65
Brennan 211, 215
Britell 78
Brok 280
Brose 201
Broverman 150
Brown 7, 143, 147
Bullen 101
Buss 174, 176
Buxton 7
Byrne 143, 147

C

Carbonell 217
Carli 143
Carney 142, 143
Carroll 272
Champy 298
Chandran 278
Chang 139, 228
Chen 185
Chhabra 278
Chin 131
Churcher 92, 93
Churchill 165

Subject Index

A

accomplishment space 71–74, 86
AIDS 27, 36, 126
airline reservation system (see Apollo, Sabre)
algorithm 7, 14, 21, 22, 25, 26, 28–33
Americans with Disabilities Act (ADA) 65, 67, 71, 81–87
anthropomorphism 9–10, 14, 137, 196–197, 198, 207, 210–211, 221, 226–228
APACHE 55, 228, 229
Apollo 21, 22, 25
Apple Computer 56, 57, 164
Archimedes Project 75–81
audio access 282
Authorizer's Assistant 228

B

Bell Atlantic 272
British Nationality Act of 1981   33, 34
British Nationality Act Program (BNAP) 33, 34
Brooklyn Bridge 52, 53

C

Caller ID 279
categorization 7, 8, 91–105, 107–109, 115–116
Challenger 52, 53, 59
communication 11, 73, 107, 109, 112, 115, 211
    electronic 2, 14, 92–93
communicative action 92–93
complexity 7, 22, 47, 48, 126, 212
computer agent (see computer persona)

computer error 10, 24, 48, 51–54, 126, 203–204
computer ethics 6, 222
computer persona 9–10, 14, 205, 207–209
    accessibility 207, 215–216
    cartoon 194–195
    competence 207, 214–215
    cooperation 10, 191, 192–196
    dramatic character 11, 195, 207, 208, 210–211, 216–218
    faces 10, 163–190, 193, 194
    flattery 10, 137, 147–150, 198
    gender stereotypes 137, 150–155
    personality traits 10, 137, 143–146, 163–167, 177, 182, 197, 208
    politeness 10, 137, 139–143
    responsiveness 207, 213–214
    trust 10, 191, 196
computer-supported cooperative work (CSCW) 6, 91–94, 115–116, 192
CTSS 32

D

database 2, 14, 26, 121–131, 239–258, 289–310
delegation of decision making to computer systems 10, 201–202, 221, 228–230
Desert Survival Task 145
design practice 12, 36–39, 58, 75–81, 101–102, 112, 116, 120–130, 138, 142–143, 147, 149–150, 154–155, 164, 198, 204–205, 214, 225–232, 248–256, 292
design process 257, 281
deskilling 124–125